MW00777681

ESSAYS ON REVELATION

ESSAYS ON REVELATION

Appropriating Yesterday's Apocalypse in Today's World

EDITED BY

GERALD L. STEVENS

PICKWICK *Publications* · Eugene, Oregon

ESSAYS ON REVELATION
Appropriating Yesterday's Apocalypse in Today's World

Copyright © 2010 Wipf and Stock Publishers. All rights reserved. Except for brief quotations in critical publications or reviews, no part of this book may be reproduced in any manner without prior written permission from the publisher. Write: Permissions, Wipf and Stock Publishers, 199 W. 8th Ave., Suite 3, Eugene, OR 97401.

Cover image: "Adoration of the Beast," Scene 40, Third Panel, Apocalypse Tapestry of Angers in the Apocalypse Gallery, Château d'Angers, France. Photograph by Gerald L. Stevens.

Pickwick Publications
An Imprint of Wipf and Stock Publishers
199 W. 8th Ave., Suite 3
Eugene, OR 97401

www.wipfandstock.com

ISBN 13: 978-1-60608-879-1

Cataloging-in-Publication data

    Essays on Revelation : appropriating yesterday's apocalypse in today's world / edited by Gerald L. Stevens.

    xxii + 218 p. ; 23 cm. — Includes bibliographical references and indexes.

    ISBN 13: 978-1-60608-879-1

    1. Bible. N. T. Revelation—Criticism, interpretation, etc. 2. Bible. N. T. Revelation—Hermeneutics. I. Stevens, Gerald L. II. Title.

BS2825.2 E7 2010

Manufactured in the U.S.A.

Dedicated to our students, past, present, and future

Credits and Permissions

Ms 180 (Douce Apokalypse) Illumination of Rev 5 Copyright © *Akademische Druck-u. Verlagsanstalt,* Austria (ADEVA), Uersperggasse12, A-8010 Graz. Used by permission. All rights reserved.

Fragment of $\mathfrak{P}^{115}$ Copyright © Egypt Exploration Society, 3 Doughty Mews, London WC1N 2PG. Used by permission. All rights reserved.

Photographs by Richard Warren Johnson Copyright © 2010 Richard Warren Johnson, 4415 Jeff Davis Street, Marshall, Texas. Used by permission. All rights reserved.

Photographs by Gerald L. Stevens Copyright © 2010 Gerald L. Stevens, 3777 Mimosa Ct. New Orleans, Louisiana. Used by permission. All rights reserved.

Diagrams by Sylvie T. Raquel Copyright © 2010 Sylvie T. Raquel, 614 Silbury Ct. McHenry, Illinois. Used by permission. All rights reserved.

Unless otherwise noted, Scripture quotations are taken from the *New Revised Standard Version* (NRSV) Copyright © 1989 by the Division of Christian Education of the National Council of the Churches of Christ in the USA.

Scripture quotations marked (NASB) are from the *New American Standard Bible* Copyright © 1960, 1962, 1963, 1968, 1971, 1972, 1973, 1975, 1977, 1995 by The Lockman Foundation.

Scripture quotations marked (NIV) are taken from the Holy Bible, New International Version®, NIV®. Copyright © 1973, 1978, 1984 by Biblica, Inc.™ Used by permission of Zondervan. All rights reserved worldwide. www.zondervan.com

Contents

Contributors

James Jeffrey Cate, PhD
Professor of Christian Studies
California Baptist University
Riverside, California

Renate Viveen Hood, PhD
Assoc. Prof. of Christian Studies, New Testament
University of Mary Hardin-Baylor
Belton, Texas

Stephen N. Horn, PhD
Pastor
First Baptist Church
Lafayette, Louisiana

Richard Warren Johnson, PhD
Professor of Religion
East Texas Baptist University
Marshall, Texas

Sylvie T. Raquel, PhD
Assist. Prof. of New Testament and Greek
Trinity International University
Deerfield, Illinois

Gerald L. Stevens, PhD
Professor of New Testament and Greek
New Orleans Baptist Theological Seminary
New Orleans, Louisiana

Figures

Preface

GOOGLE THE SEARCH STRING "book of Revelation" and the hits are all over the map of what the human mind possibly can conceive. Many websites and the books they promote boldly brandish a purely futurist approach to the book's imagery. The inquiring mind is left without even a hint that other legitimate interpretive options exist. Mercifully, the wait is not too long for some of these outlandish futurist predictions to be proven patently false. The "demise of the United States in the coming year," referring to the year 2009, proclaimed on one website in 2008 already has been added to a huge junkyard of falsified predictions.[1] The problem is, once falsified, these obviously delusional interpretations leave the inquiring mind with a strong sense that the book of Revelation is nothing but a complete joke safely to be ignored and without a semblance of relevance to contemporary issues.

Is such an impression accurate? This collection of essays is an attempt to suggest what may be a more productive way of approaching this piece of the New Testament canon. The contributors are academy and pastor scholars trained in modern interpretive methodologies. They also are committed to bringing the book of Revelation down to earth for their collegiate audiences—as well as for the sharp and inquiring mind

1. Accessed Aug. 10, 2009 at http://the-end.com/2008GodsFinalWitness/?gclid=CP 3FhoH6mZwCFVlM5QodRkcJeg. The economic meltdown of United States financial institutions in the fall of 2008 was interpreted as the first warning blast of Revelation's seven trumpets. This reference to the demise of the United States in 2009 has now been removed from the webpage at least as of April 2010. Websites are a pretty convenient tool these days for false prophets. One simple stroke of an HTML editor's delete key, and, Poof! Like Harry Potter magic the false prophecy disappears without a trace. The whole interpretive series of this false prophecy is based on a prediction of the end by May 27, 2012. As the time approaches, we can be confident that date too will disappear like magic.

in the pew. They desire to demonstrate the validity of the book's incisive, prophetic critique of contemporary culture and society, politics and religion without the false props of sensationalized headlines ripped from today's online news feeds, blogs, and Twitter streams.

The interpretive assumptions that inform the hermeneutical approach to this effort in general are those of the traditional historical-critical method but informed by evangelical presuppositions, including the reliability of the text and the authority of its inspiration. That is, Revelation first is to be understood from within its own historical context facilitated by reasoned argument but guided by evangelical presuppositions. To this general effort are added additional literary approaches such as close reading of the narrative itself and contributions from the social sciences.

The essay topics were not dictated by the editor, a predetermined theme, or the publisher. Contributors were allowed to choose topics according to their own interests, special training, and vocational pursuits. The common denominator among all of the contributors is the desire to re-canonize the book of Revelation after the book has been eviscerated of its biblical authority and contemporary relevance in countless false prophecies and egregious violations of hermeneutical principles that would not be allowed for a second if dealing with the four Gospels, for example. The contributors inherited this desire from their teacher, who agreed to edit this volume at their suggestion and on their behalf.

Essay topics range over various fields of inquiry asking sundry questions. Some approaches apply a close reading of the text in its literary and historical context. Others wrestle with considered discussions in theology and ethics applied to the complex issues of politics and society. Most essays conclude with "Questions for Reflection." This brief list of questions has pragmatic and pedagogical purpose. The hope is to stimulate classroom discussion and small group Bible studies, often attempting to draw out contemporary implications of topics or issues developed in the essays. The overarching desire is that this collection of essays would be both academically stimulating in the collegiate classroom but also pragmatically useful in the local church.

The blockbuster movie *Avatar* (2009) broke several box office records on the way to becoming the highest grossing movie of all time worldwide, surpassing the mark dominated for twelve years by the director James Cameron's other mega-hit, *Titanic* (1997). Work on the present book of essays on Revelation was in full swing as *Avatar* was mesmerizing millions with its computer-generated graphics bringing to life the surreal world of Pandora and her indigenous population of Na'vi humanoids in tune with their environment and respectful of the forces that supported life on their planet. The story weaves a number of common themes in literature and film—personal self-discovery, crossing cultural boundaries, avarice, commercialism, imperialism, ecology, and more.

What struck me the most about the movie *Avatar* were two connections I perceived with the book of Revelation: (1) a fantasia story told with incredibly astonishing images; but (2) really a story of our own society's present predicament of conflicted loyalties and demoralizing, dehumanizing values that make us less human than humanoids and less moral than a species not even from this planet. The prophet John wrote his own script of mesmerizing images to astonish the mind and arrest the thoughts. As the images of one series of judgments pass into another, somewhere along the way John's audience probably began to perceive that the real story was not "out there" on the mental screen but "right here" where they lived in Asia Minor struggling with Rome's own form of imperialism, conflicted loyalties, and demoralizing, dehumanizing values.

Our quest in reading Revelation is not to gain a wild-eyed astonishment at the images projected, where so much focus on reading Revelation seems to be in the popular press. Our quest is to hear in fresh, vital, and challenging ways John's critique of any claim from culture or society that attempts to dethrone the Ruler of earth's kings or assails the sovereignty of the One who sits on heaven's throne. If we leave Revelation's auditorium simply exclaiming about the stupendous special effects, completely absorbed with asking no more than "How did they do *that*?" we probably have aborted the actual conversation the director was trying to engage in the first place in making the movie. The declaration, "and they have conquered him through the blood of the Lamb and through the word of their testimony, for they loved not their lives even to death" (Rev 12:11), at a minimum communicates that infinitely more is at stake with this movie than its special effects.

Gerald L. Stevens
New Orleans, Louisiana
Easter 2010

Acknowledgments

My own quest to understand Revelation began as a teenager enraptured (pun intended) with the study notes of his *Scofield Reference Bible*. Radio was the Internet of my teenage years, and I remember so vividly going out to sit in the car to catch that thirty-minute program every Sunday night after church (we had church on Sunday nights in those days) of that dispensationalist preacher from Texas carefully dissecting the eschatological nuance of every news item of the past week. As I listened, I was amazed that the Bible could be so current, so detailed, so accurate. I also was on the edge of my seat, heart pounding, that the Antichrist already was on the stage ready to reveal himself to the world any minute. The problem for that Texas preacher was that this avid radio listener also was a studious nerd who kept copious notes of his own. After a few months, the self-contradictory statements and interpretive misfires began to pile up noticeably. Eventually, the allure of "signs of the times" reading of the headlines every week began to show a fool's gold shine. The quest began to find a better way for interpreting Revelation.[2]

I am still on that quest. I do not consider myself to have arrived. I simply know that I do not have to do as much interpretive backtracking today with things that I say as I did forty years ago. I have been down many paths in my journey. Early seminary days turned me in an amillennial direction. Early ministry days turned me back to my earliest premillennial roots, even before my dispensational boot camp days. Today, I tell my students that, as far as interpreting Revelation is concerned, I am just a yard dog. I bark at anything that comes in the yard. Even if after

---

2. A helpful rundown of options with their strengths and weaknesses is given by Stanley J. Grenz, *The Millennial Maze*.

a good sniffing inspection I let you in the yard to join me in a nap on the sunny porch, I still keep one eye on you while I'm sleeping.

In this journey I cannot begin to thank all those who so patiently bore my impatient (sometimes, perhaps, impertinent) questions. To pastors, Sunday School teachers, youth leaders (God bless you), church members, seminary professors, fellow ministers, fellow teachers, and my own students I owe a deep sense of gratitude and appreciation for helping me along in my journey by your answers, your questions, and your extended conversations. I could not love the book of Revelation as I do today without your contributions to the discussion and your investment in my life and thought. Someone at some point will hear an echo of these contributions on almost every page I write.

I especially want to thank my former students who now are teaching and preaching colleagues who engaged this project brainstorming the concept at an annual SBL meeting. You know those conversations. They are wild rides of fantasy that are fun to enjoy for the moment while waiting in the hotel lobby for the rest of the group to rendezvous for the dinner outing, but never seriously entertained as an actual proposal that will take on a life of its own. Au contraire! So here we are, book of essays in hand. So, gang, we have all assembled here together in our literary entourage. Time to go teach the book of Revelation!

Finally, thank you to my wife, Jean, who, as always, bore the isolation this project induced with the sweetest of spirits and the most supportive of hearts. She has never flagged in her enthusiasm for my writing as an integral part of my teaching career. May she ever derive the greatest sense of satisfaction and the richest sense of blessing in knowing she fulfilled her call so completely to support one who heard a call so deeply.

Abbreviations

BNTC	Black's New Testament Commentaries
ESV	English Standard Version
GNT4	*Greek New Testament*, 4th Edition
HCSB	Holman Christian Standard Bible
IDB	*Interpreter's Dictionary of the Bible*
INTF	Institute for New Testament Textual Research
IVPN	InterVarsity Press New Testament
JSNTSup	Journal for the Study of the New Testament: Supplement Series
KJV	King James Version
LCL	Loeb Classical Library
NASB	New American Standard Bible
NCBC	New Century Bible Commentary
NET	New English Translation
NICNT	New International Commentary on the New Testament
NIV	New International Version
NJB	New Jerusalem Bible
NKJV	New King James Version
NLT	New Living Translation
NRSV	New Revised Standard Version
NTL	New Testament Library
SBLSymS	Society of Biblical Literature Symposium Series
SHBC	Smyth & Helwys Bible Commentary
SNTSMS	Society for New Testament Studies Monograph Series
WBC	Word Biblical Commentary

SCRIPTURE

OLD TESTAMENT

Gen	Genesis

Exod	Exodus
Lev	Leviticus
Num	Numbers
Deut	Deuteronomy
Josh	Joshua
Judg	Judges
1–2 Sam	1–2 Samuel
1–2 Kgs	1–2 Kings
1–2 Chr	1–2 Chronicles
Neh	Nehemiah
Esth	Esther
Ps (Pss)	Psalm (Psalms)
Prov	Proverbs
Eccl	Ecclesiastes
Song	Song of Solomon
Isa	Isaiah
Jer	Jeremiah
Lam	Lamentations
Ezek	Ezekiel
Dan	Daniel
Hos	Hosea
Obad	Obadiah
Mic	Micah
Nah	Nahum
Hab	Habbakuk
Zeph	Zephaniah
Hag	Haggai
Zech	Zechariah
Mal	Malachi

New Testament

Matt	Matthew
Rom	Romans
1–2 Cor	1–2 Corinthians
Gal	Galatians
Eph	Ephesians
Phil	Philippians
Col	Colossians
1–2 Thess	1–2 Thessalonians
1–2 Tim	1–2 Timothy
Phlm	Philemon

Heb	Hebrews
Jas	James
1–2 Pet	1–2 Peter
Rev	Revelation

APOCRYPHA

2 Esd	2 Esdras

PSEUDEPIGRAPHA

2 Bar.	*2 Baruch*
1 En.	*1 Enoch*
Jub.	*Jubilees*

OTHER ANCIENT SOURCES

APOSTOLIC FATHERS

1–2 Clem.	*1–2 Clement*

EUSEBIUS

H.E.	*Historia Ecclesiastica (Church History)*

JOSEPHUS

Ant.	*Jewish Antiquities*
J. W.	*The Jewish War*

PLINY THE YOUNGER

Ep. Tra.	*Epistulae ad Trajanum*

PLUTARCH

Quaest. Graec.	*Quaestiones Graecae (The Greek Questions)*

SUETONIUS

Dom.	*Domitianus*

1

A Vision in the Night

Setting the Interpretive Stage for John's Apocalypse

GERALD L. STEVENS

SETTING THE SCENE

THE TWILIGHT OF EVENING always stirred the old man. As if beckoned by the shimmering stars, he would rise up to the small window cut into the rock face of his cell to gaze intently into the dark night, the iron bars pressing out the wrinkles on the tired old face. Sometimes, he would sink back with tears in his weary eyes. What could he possibly hope to see with such feeble eyes? His island of exile put too many miles of misty sea between him and the shores of his homeland.

He never had news of loved ones left behind. Was he staring into the night wondering what had become of them? Perhaps he worried if they had been beaten, robbed, or imprisoned, as he and others had been. Once, news did arrive with a fresh detachment of prisoners, but only to sadden him greatly. A prisoner from Pergamum told how Antipas, a close friend of the old man's, had been brutally murdered by a violent mob. They had seized Antipas from his own house and killed him in front of his wife and two daughters. Were the occasional tears for Antipas? Did he fear his own family's fate?

Indeed, he looked quite out of place surrounded by the destitute solitude of his lonely cell. Why was he a prisoner? Surely he looked innocent enough! He just did not look the part of a criminal, nor hardly

1

equal to the grave charges laid against him. Yet he had been condemned to this forlorn penal colony . . . Patmos! The name struck terror in even hardened criminals. How he feared coming to this place! Working the rock quarries was hard enough for young prisoners in the strength of youth, but for a weak and wizened old man! His surely was the sentence of death. The unstable mines were a constant danger. His fragile life was jeopardized by accidental cave-in or even the cruelty of the guards. And the quarry dust! Always suspended in the stale air, the dust starved off the lungs. Prisoners coughed incessantly, the fine dust filling and burning their lungs. Their eyes never escaped the scratching of the sharp grit.

The old man's wrinkles filled with white trails of perspiration. The chalky rivulets meandered aimlessly, fighting to evaporate in the oppressive humidity. The clammy air was uncooperative, already loaded with the salty sea.

Surely he knew his end was near. But though timeworn in appearance, he never tired of his evening vigil. His mind was still keen, still filled with mystery, still thinking on a higher plane. His heart was still strong, still filled with courage, still beating with a higher hope. But each labored day further eroded his strength. He sensed the ebb tide of his life. And the more he felt his aged body ebbing away, the more agitated he grew in spirit. While sure he himself would have faith to the end, he yet worried for the others: fellow partakers in the tribulation, the kingdom, the perseverance. How would they fare after his soon departure? Who would lead them on to victory?

Oh, for one last assurance that all was secure! That the kingdom would prevail. Some fresh word from on high to leave as a final testament of faith. One last message of courage and of hope for those faithful believers he would leave behind. Who but knew this could be his last Lord's Day to worship? He prayed earnestly as never before, pouring out his heart. Reaching into the depths of this soul, he reached out into the depths of the night. Deep spoke unto deep until his arms finally sank in exhaustion, and he slumped to the cell floor. Yet, he never quit praying—as if even his last, salty breath would be a prayer.

The rambunctious sea breakers that usually frothed in fury against the steep cliffs of the island shoreline had retired for the night. But the stars continued their sentinel on the late night sky. Distant but intense, the tiny flares flickered against the black velvet curtain. Their silent shimmering was broken only by the siren voice of the night wind echoing through the rocky cliffs.

Suddenly, stillness swept the night sky and silenced the wind. The moment was pregnant with purpose. Adrenalin shot into the old man's ancient veins. An awesome Presence invaded his cell with a frightening reality. His pulse pounded in his ears. His breath grew short. He listened.

The old man was startled by a dramatic voice that resounded out of heaven and shook the sky with authority. The clarion trumpet became a deafening roar cascading down the cosmos. Like the giant sea breakers, the voice crashed against the island cliffs. The heavenly voice spoke to the old man, and John, the Prophet, was given the vision for which he had prayed so diligently in the humble confines of his Patmos cell—John's marvelous Vision in the Night. The Ruler of the kings of the earth, Jesus Christ, the Son of Man, gloriously appeared to his faithful servant.

John's vision has been passed down through generations of believers for all to hear once again to renew their faith and assure their hope. Listen now once more to the words of John of Patmos, the Seer of Revelation:

> I, John, your brother who shares with you in the tribulation and kingdom and perseverance in Jesus, was on the island called Patmos, because of God's word and my testimony about Jesus. I was in the Spirit on the Lord's day, and I heard behind me a loud sound like a trumpet, which said, "Compose what you observe in a scroll commissioned to the seven churches, that is, to Ephesus, Smyrna, Pergamum, Thyatira, Sardis, Philadelphia, and Laodicea."

> I turned in order to apprehend the voice speaking to me, but upon turning, I saw seven golden lampstands. In the middle of the lampstands was one like a Son of Man, clothed in a foot-length robe, and wrapped around the chest with a golden belt. His head and hair were white as white wool, like snow. His eyes were like flaming fire; and his feet were like fine bronze fired in a furnace. His voice was like the sound of many waters, and in his right hand he had seven stars. Out of his mouth proceeded a sharp, two-edged sword, and his face was like the sun blazing in its noontime brilliance.

> Now, when I beheld his visage, I fell lifeless at his feet. And he set his right hand upon me and said, "Stop fearing! I am the First and the Last, even the Living One. I was dead, but behold, I am alive forever; indeed, I possess the keys of death and of Hades." (Rev 1:9–20)[1]

1. All translations in this chapter are the author's own from the standard edited Greek text.

CATCHING THE SPIRIT

The scene above was an imaginative beginning to a sermon series on the book of Revelation by a young pastor. He wanted to set the book's context historically. He chose to picture a first-century prophet of Asia Minor named John in prison on the island of Patmos and seven churches to which he was related. This pastor, however, felt like a salmon swimming upstream. He was fighting the strong currents of sensationalized publications on Revelation that crowded the Barnes and Noble shelves at the mall. Church members regularly reminded him how thoroughly these books informed their thoughts. Such publications, however, he knew made a mockery of sound interpretive principles. The minister felt a great homiletic burden to awaken his church members to a better understanding of the book, to catch the true spirit of John's vision.[2]

FIGURE 1. Mosaic over Traditional Patmos Cave Entrance. The traditional site of John's vision on the island of Patmos was a cave, where, according to church tradition, John's scribe taking down his dictation during the visionary experience was Pacorus (photograph by Gerald L. Stevens).

So how do we catch the spirit of John's vision? Do we have to "see" what he "saw"? What, exactly, did he "see"? Did he see some physical phenomenon while he was perfectly lucid and awake? Or, did images

2. The young pastor was the present writer. Cf. Longenecker's engaging historical fiction, *The Lost Letters of Pergamum*, involving the evangelist Luke and Antipas of Pergamum.

come to him in a dream? More cynically, did John have a hallucinogenic experience that resulted from a strange diet on the island or was induced in some other way? Or, did he simply think deep thoughts while in a state of meditation and randomly imagined bizarre pictures to encapsulate their meaning?

The bottom line is, we really do not have a clue to answer such questions. While John did indicate that he was "in the Spirit" when he auditioned the voice that spoke like a trumpet, parsing out what John's own experience might have been might very well prove impossible.[3] Fortunately, however, the reader of Revelation actually does not have to dissect John's own personal experience to understand John's meaning. John was commissioned to write in order to communicate his vision. Thus, while John saw, we read—and our reading is how we catch a vision of John's vision without going through the same experience that John had or even understanding exactly what happened to John on the island of Patmos. John's experience was personal, but ours is literary. Our understanding is not based on what we see but how we read ("blessed is the one who reads," Rev 1:4).

READING JOHN'S VISION

So how do we read John's vision as a *literary* production? Several options are open to us.[4] The option chosen by contributors to this volume is a reasoned approach based on historical research and modern methods of interpretation. The overarching commitment is evangelical, and the effort is grounded in the assumption of authorial purpose.[5] While the basic exegetical meaning of the text may be past, the application always is imminent. The contributors are convinced that regardless where one lands on the question of Revelation as prophecy—preterist, historical, futurist, idealist, or some ingenious Baskin-Robbins combination—the visions can be given dynamic voice, because they: (1) continually beg

3. Notice the wiggle room Smalley acknowledges in allowing that "saw" can be translated as "perceived," *The Revelation to John*, 30.

4. The purpose for this volume is not to survey the options and argue pros and cons. The general field in play is hermeneutics. Two books can assist the reader in grappling with these options. One is the short and easy to read paperback by Fee and Stuart, *How To Read the Bible for All Its Worth*. The other book by Klein, Blomberg, and Hubbard, *Biblical Interpretation*, is distinguished by more depth and theory.

5. That the author had a purpose for writing, that this authorial intent is discernable by the reader, and that this purpose serves as the reader's exegetical compass.

for application in real terms in real time, even right now, (2) insistently challenge the reader to revisit decisions about life's ultimate loyalties, and (3) inevitably demand a response. This call for application, challenge to commitment, and demand for response is Revelation's trumpet sound we should hear and to which these essays attempt to give voice.

Sign Language for the Persecuted

John's first word is *Apokalypsis* (Ἀποκάλυψις). We get our word "apocalypse" from this root, which means "uncovering," "unveiling," or "revelation." In other words, Revelation's first word immediately identifies the book as a specific type of literature. The apocalyptic style was well known in the time John wrote. One of its premier features was a high degree of symbolism.

We need to be careful using the word "symbolic." Saying something is symbolic is not saying unreal. A skull and crossbones symbolizes death. We see this symbol on a bottle of insect poison. That a symbol is used to evoke the idea of death for this poison product does not mean the product really cannot cause death. The symbols themselves are not the reality, but they point beyond themselves to a reality. Dismissing a religious truth because that truth is presented symbolically is as naïve as dismissing the real danger of a bottle's content when seeing a skull and crossbones on the product label. The reader should not jump to the false conclusion that use of the term *symbol* or *symbolic* in this volume is trying to say what is being discussed is unreal.[6]

John indicated that God "made known" the revelation to him. The verb John used is *sēmainō* (σημαίνω), which means "sign" or "signify."[7] God "signed" or "signified" the truth of the vision through his angel sent to John. Like an interpreter for the deaf signing a pastor's sermon, an angel signed the realities of heaven from God to John, and John himself

---

6. A good technical discussion of the issues involved in understanding the concept of symbol is covered in Beale's commentary, *The Book of Revelation*, 50–69. A helpful table comparing major millennial perspectives on Revelation on what images are thought to symbolize is found in *The Holman Illustrated Study Bible*, 1874–77.

7. Part of a large group of words with a similar range of meaning of non-verbal communication. You might recall the story of Zechariah, the father of John the Baptist, who was made dumb by disbelieving the word of the angel Gabriel; as a result, Zechariah had to communicate with gestures to the crowd, and the crowd later had to do the same to Zechariah (Luke 1:22, 69). Today we have entire systems of "sign language" for those who cannot speak.

then became his own interpreter for persecuted believers in Asia Minor. For this sign language, John was able to capitalize on a genre of literature whose very essence was the power of symbols. In so doing, he wrote in ways that made the truths speak even louder than prosaic words.

Revelation of Jesus Christ (1:9–20)

Most readers of Revelation realize that the book is highly symbolic. However, what most do not realize is that *John does not reveal what we do not already know*. John himself makes the nature of his revelation clear by the qualifier he puts on his first word. John wrote that the "revelation" was "of Jesus Christ." The preposition "of" could mean either that Revelation was *from* Jesus (like "of van Gogh" could be a painting by van Gogh) or that Revelation was *about* Jesus (like "of van Gogh" could be a painting of van Gogh himself). That Revelation is *from* Jesus seems to be the whole point of verse 1. However, after the opening introduction in 1:1–8, the entire last part of the first chapter is a vision whose central figure, "Son of Man," universally is recognized to be Jesus Christ. So, in a very real way, even if we say from v. 1 that Revelation is *from* Jesus, we also can say from vv. 9–20 that Revelation is *about* Jesus.

More importantly, this "Son of Man" vision in 1:9–20 is the opening vision of the book. The opening vision of any apocalypse is the most important one, because that vision becomes the key to interpreting all others. That the central figure in this key opening vision is Jesus is crucial to the entire interpretive enterprise of Revelation. Since we already know Jesus well from the Gospels, then we know well this central figure of Revelation. The first vision tells the reader clearly that John's Revelation more reveals truths about Jesus than teasers about the future. If Revelation will find its true stance as a canonical book, then the reader will not have anything in the book of Revelation that is not in perfect concord with the meaning and message of all four Gospels. Concord means that any picture of Jesus drawn from the pages of Revelation must square up with the picture drawn from the Gospels.

A Preview of Coming Attractions (1:5–7)

John gears up the reader for this opening Son of Man vision in 1:9–20 with a preview in 1:5–7. This preview presents truths about Jesus to be unpacked in more detail in the opening vision. The rest of Revelation then unpacks the opening vision itself.

In the preview in 1:5–7, John conveyed to the seven churches a benediction of grace and peace. The benediction has a triune origin: God, the Spirit,[8] and Jesus. About Jesus, John wrote:

> from Jesus Christ, the faithful witness, the firstborn of the dead, and the ruler of the kings of the earth. To the one who loves us and freed us from our sins by his blood; he made us a kingdom, priests unto his God and Father; to him be eternal glory and might. Amen.
>
> > Look! He is coming enshrined in the clouds;
> >   every eye will see him,
> >   even those who pierced him;
> >   and all earth's clans will wail on his account.
> > Indeed, amen!

Three main truths surface here: (1) truths about Jesus—that is, the gospel; (2) truths about believers—that is, salvation; and (3) truths about judgment—that is, the second coming. These truths are the traffic controllers guiding all the visions of Revelation as they come in for a landing on the reader's imagination. Attention turns to the precise wording in which John conveyed these truths.

Truths about Jesus—the Gospel

The first spiritual truth embedded in Rev 1:5–7 is about Jesus himself. Jesus' own story *is* the gospel, which concisely can be stated as the endpoint of that biography: (1) Jesus crucified, (2) Jesus raised, and (3) Jesus glorified. One clearly can see these three foundational Christian dictums in a statement of the gospel in Paul's classic summary in 1 Cor 15:5–8. John phrased all three dictums in 1:5–7 as titles of Jesus.

The first dictum, Jesus crucified, is encapsulated in the title, "faithful witness" (Rev 1:5). Notice that John has customized the dictum for his persecution context: Jesus crucified becomes a paradigm of the believer's existence. Being faithful to Jesus means you will be putting yourself out there for inevitable trouble. Jesus' own faithfulness meant his death. He prayed in the Garden of Gethsemane, "not what I will, but what you will" (Mark 14:36). He went all the way to the cross, and *that* is why he became Savior. He called disciples to a similar path (Mark 8:34).

---

8. Signified as "the seven Spirits before his throne," evoking the manifold and complete operations of the Holy Spirit.

FIGURE 2. Panorama of Island of Patmos. This view of the island of Patmos is near the top of the island close to the traditional cave entrance traditionally understood as where John had his vision (photograph by Gerald L. Stevens).

The problem for disciples is the real potential for abandoning the Savior in the time of crisis. Abandonment is a key part of the Gethsemane story (Mark 14:27). By describing the crucified Jesus as the "faithful witness," John called persecuted believers of Asia Minor not to abandon their premier duty in life—faithful witness. John himself had been faithful in his own witness, which landed him on Patmos (Rev 1:9). How could following a crucified Savior take any other path in faithful witness and be true to that Savior? Surprisingly, John faced a huge problem on this very point. He encountered blatant compromise of the gospel in the setting of the seven churches of Asia Minor. To his dismay, influential church leaders were abandoning this call to faithful witness, apparently without any compunction or at least minimal awareness that the heart of the gospel message was being destroyed in the process.[9]

The second foundational gospel dictum, Jesus raised, John also framed as a title, "firstborn of the dead." This phrasing was very savvy on John's part. He thereby immediately turned attention away from the resurrection of Jesus himself to implications of the resurrection for Jesus' own disciples. While the disciple's call is to faithful witness, even to the point of death, death never is the end to any disciple's story. Resurrection—the heart of the gospel—means that God did not abandon Jesus on the cross. The early church proclaimed that God himself raised Jesus from the dead.[10] What God did for Jesus, Jesus guaranteed for his followers (John 11:25). So, for persecuted believers, the obligation of faithful witness, whatever the cost, is not without the promise of ultimate vindication.

9. Rev 2:14, 15, 20.

10. Acts 2:24; 10:40; 13:30; cf. Rom 10:9.

The third foundational gospel dictum, Jesus glorified, John framed as another title, "ruler of the kings of the earth." Early Christians proclaimed that Jesus ascended to his Father in glory and eventually would share the fullness of that glory with believers.[11] In this third, carefully crafted title, John has brought that heavenly glory back down to earth. He reminds readers of the vulnerability of every earthly dominion to the forces of death and Hades that Jesus alone controls (Rev 1:18). Though rulers presently may be particularly unaware, surrounded in the delusory trappings of human glory and might, all powers and principalities of this life fall under the indomitable dominion of Jesus. No matter how powerful from an earthly perspective, every ruler falls, and all kings die. For persecuted believers under the austere and seemingly invincible dominion of Rome, this gospel dictum is a stark warning not to be seduced in life's loyalties by those who do not hold the keys of death and Hades. Politically, John's title is a shot across the bow of the Roman Empire's ship of state.

Truths about Believers—Salvation

While the first spiritual truth embedded in Rev 1:5–7 is about Jesus, the second truth is about believers. Believers have access to the realities of salvation offered by Jesus. In describing this salvation, John focused the reader's attention on God's initiative, the human predicament, Jesus' solution, and the believer's destiny.

God's initiative in salvation is seen in the description, "to the One who loves us" (Rev 1:5). Jesus loved the lost with God's prevenient love. This love has implications of God's covenant love for Israel, picked up later in Revelation in the imagery of the 144,000 from the twelve tribes of Israel (Rev 7). The human predicament is seen in the expression "freed us from our sins." Talk of freedom infers a problem of bondage. A human slave could seek manumission and sometimes become a freed-person in this life. However, human slavery to sin had no manumission except by God's power. The next phrase, "by his blood," means Jesus is God's powerful solution to the human predicament of bondage. John did not use the more explicit "by his death on the cross" because he already has begun to merge two thoughts that for him were inseparable: faithful witness and shed blood. Implications for the believer will abound in Revelation (cf. Rev 12:11).

11. Luke 24:51; Acts 1:9; 3:13; 7:55; Rom 8:17; 2 Cor 4:4; Col 3:4; 1 Thess 2:12; 1 Tim 3:16; Titus 2:13; Heb 1:3; 2:9; 1 Pet 1:11, 21; 4:13; 5:1, 10.

Finally, John wrote about believers' destiny in that Jesus "made us a kingdom, priests" (Rev 1:6). In the first-century world, as you will see in the essays to follow, kingdom language was an integral part of political discourse. In Rome's world, no king ruled unless he was a client king at the pleasure of the emperor. This client-king relationship, for example, controlled Herod the Great's rule over Judea, and that of his sons and grandsons after him.[12] Rome seemed to be the destiny maker. Yet, in Jesus, a kingdom was established right under Rome's nose for which Rome had no say and no ultimate control. The reason Rome had no real dominion over this kingdom was precisely because this kingdom was priestly. The destiny for those in this kingdom was determined by the world's only real superpower, God the Almighty.[13] John emphasized that this kingdom must be understood as a spiritual service to God, even as the call to Israel of old (Exod 19:6). That service probably should be understood in terms of John's witness theme throughout Revelation.[14]

Truths about Judgment—the Second Coming

Today's rampant confusion of convoluted end-time scenarios constantly falsified by actual historical developments is our own Tower of Babel. What often is obscured in the din of this theological noise is the dire need for an adequate doctrine of judgment. To displace all of divine judgment to the end of history only makes a mockery of God's present sovereignty. God's coming in judgment at the end of history has no justification if he already has not been expressing his judgment in some way throughout history.[15] Thus, in as much as we attempt to indulge an incorrigible voyeurism to know the future, especially in attempting to divine some end-time plot, we deny ourselves the power to understand the present. John's

12. Herod the Great (37–4 B.C.E.); sons: Archelaus (Judea, 4 B.C.E.–6 C.E.); Antipas (Galilee and Perea, 4 B.C.E.–34 C.E.); Philip (Transjordan, 4 B.C.E.–37 C.E.); grandson, Herod Agrippa I (Judea, 40–44 C.E.); great grandson, Herod Agrippa II (regional districts, 54–66 C.E.).

13. For whom alone John reserved the title *pantokratōr*, παντοκράτωρ, often translated as "Almighty" (cf. Rev 1:8; 4:8; 11:17; 15:3; 16:7, 14; 19:6, 15; 21:22).

14. Rather than some Camelot Court Jesus will set up in downtown Jerusalem in which Paul Lancelot and the other apostles bring rebellious nations into humiliating submission with superior military forces. I never have understood why if Jesus refused to use the power of the sword in the first coming (Matt 26:51–52) he should draw one in the second coming.

15. Cf. Beale, *The Book of Revelation*, 185, though he does not make the systematic point being emphasized above.

use of second coming truth, in other words, is a way to impress upon his readers the significance of decisions made right now.

One of John's most prominent literary strategies throughout the book of Revelation is that of baptizing Old Testament themes and imagery unto Christ. That is, to gain biblical focus on God's work of salvation from beginning to end, from Genesis to Jesus, John used the interpretive lens of the gospel—the realities of Jesus. This strategy is especially true in his ingenious allusion to two Old Testament texts in Rev 1:7. One text is Dan 7:13 and the other is Zech 12:10–14. The Daniel text is about the Son of Man's enthronement over all nations after God's judgment of evil empires—quite appropriate for the gospel context of the exaltation of Jesus despite the power of the Roman Empire. The Zechariah text is about God's redemption of Israel in the face of being overwhelmed by enemy nations once she has repented of her rejection of God in rejecting God's messenger—again, appropriate in the light of John's theme of extending promises for Israel to repentant followers of Jesus.[16]

To say that God is coming in judgment is not to say that he has not come in judgment already. Whatever reality awaits a final judgment "out there" to be executed in a future coming already will have been taking shape "right here" in a present coming in judgment. When a thirsty person begs for water, God is judging our response right now. The final judgment will validate that present judgment, but also throw out any justification for appeal as if one still had time to make amends.[17] One cannot speak of a second coming of Jesus if he has not come already in judgment on our actions here and now. Without a present judgment, any supposed second coming judgment has no *modus operandi*.[18]

Characteristically, John took these Old Testament texts about Israel and gave them christological focus. He also brought home the weight

16. Interestingly, Jesus combined these same two texts in his famous "eschatological discourse" to his disciples in Matt 24:30.

17. One can note the above is simply a restatement of Jesus' parable of the sheep and goats, Matt 25:31–46.

18. Present judgment is why John 3:36 evokes the eschatological language of divine wrath, which sounds like a reality restricted to the end time, yet puts the verb related to that very wrath in *present tense* ("abides"). The traditional theological terminology for this apparent appropriation of end-time features into present experience in certain New Testament texts is "realized eschatology." John's nuance in Revelation, however, is a little more complex than saying he has a realized eschatology, even less that he has an exclusive "futurist" eschatology.

of their significance in terms of personal accountability and culpability. These features surface in the words "every eye will see him." The "every eye" is John's addition to the Zechariah text. The original text's application is broadened from Israel to all persons in this new age inaugurated by Jesus who behave like Israel had in the past by rejecting God's messenger. Jesus himself lamented this rejection penchant of Israel while overlooking the city of Jerusalem (Matt 23:37), and Stephen brought home the point in his response to the Sanhedrin by recounting Israelite rejection of Moses (Acts 7:27). John also broadened the original application by adding the words, "of the earth" to the description of which tribes mourn; no longer just tribes of Israel mourn.

These special additions by John of necessity transform the meaning of "even those who pierced him." In John's deliberately broadened context, such an expression no longer can be restricted solely to the Roman soldiers attending the crucifixion. Anyone who rejects Jesus suddenly becomes liable to the action of piercing him, a participant in his death, by becoming a willing accomplice to the crime. Just as John brought the reality of final judgment back from the future into the present, he also brought the reality of the cross forward from the past into the present. Suddenly, in Jesus, the meaning of all of time collapses into the one reality of the present. Every individual is called to decision about Jesus now, and that decision simultaneously is constrained by events that either already have transpired (the cross) or inevitably will (the second coming).

REALIZING JOHN'S BLESSING

In Rev 1:3 John pronounced a blessing on the reading and hearing of the words he had written. He then affirmed that the time was "near." That affirmation should not be falsified by end-time speculations that silence the book's capacity to speak to any generation and betrays the very essence of faithful witness and call to decision now.[19] Our sneak peak into specific elements of John's introduction reveals the integrity of his bless-

19. This charge should not be read as promotion of an "idealist" approach to the prophetic component of John's message. Still, we would point out that the spirit of prophecy in the New Testament undeniably was suffused with a strong sense of imminence, which generated its regular appearance in worship assemblies and anticipated speaking a relevant word to its own audience, even as Paul acknowledged in 1 Cor 12 and 14. We are asserting this spirit of imminence in New Testament prophecy in general is the most probable context for understanding John's claim of "near" in particular in Rev 1:3.

ing. In the opening words of Revelation John signaled clearly his task of reimaging gospel truths about Jesus, believers, and judgment. He did so in ways that intimate his book will not reveal any truth about Jesus we do not already know through the Gospels. The essays in this volume attempt in their own sundry ways to contribute to this effort:

- of revealing the true character of Jesus in full concord with the four Gospels

- of faithful witness to Jesus' claims of ultimate loyalty in life

- of a call to decision now

QUESTIONS FOR REFLECTION

- "While John saw, we read . . ." In what ways is our appropriation of the book of Revelation impacted by the fundamental difference between John's experience as personal and ours, of necessity, as only literary?

- Can you give further examples how saying something is "symbolic" is not saying "unreal"?

- If John does not reveal what we do not already know about Jesus, why does the Jesus pictured in so many books about Revelation seem to appear so different than the Jesus of the Gospel accounts?

- Do a search on the Internet for "persecution of Christians." Be ready to share what you discover and your reactions to what you encounter. Consider the paradigm of Jesus as the "faithful witness" as conceptualized by John. How would such a concept "fit" into an end-time picture of the "coming of the kingdom"?

- The Internet is abuzz about the implications of the Mayan calendar for the year 2012, and a Hollywood movie, "2012," already has been made to commercialize the interest. Do you think scenarios of the second coming or the end of the world that you see in movies, on cable channel programs, and in the popular press reflect well John's vision of believers as "a kingdom, priests"? Just what does a believer's salvation involve anyway? What is your fundamental sense of call as a Christian, that is, do you feel "called" to do anything? Why or why not?

- Listen to a broadcast of CNN's "Headline News," Fox News, or any of the major television networks. Make a record of the news stories reported. After you have your list, work through each story asking yourself, if God were to set up the final judgment right now, how would these news stories be impacted? Do you think God already is judging these events right now? Why or why not? If so, in what ways?

- If you would like to investigate how pervasive is prophecy belief among Americans in general and its extensive impact on modern American culture, you might wish to read Paul Boyer's *When Time Shall Be No More.*

2

One Like a Son of Man

Contemplating Christology in Rev 1:9–20

GERALD L. STEVENS

THE CENTRAL VISION

THE FIRST VISION IN Rev 1:9–20 is the hermeneutical key to all the others. John's vision of Jesus on Patmos was not unique.[1] John, however, chose to paint his scene with symbol rather than prose.[2] To grasp this central vision's meaning, the reader must understand its central context and its central figure.

---

1. John was in an awakened sense of deeper spiritual perception ("in the Spirit," 1:10). Compare Stephen, who, under interrogation by the Sanhedrin, suddenly was "filled with the Holy Spirit" and saw the heavens opened and the enthroned "Son of Man" (Acts 7:55–56). Paul's Damascus Road would be another classic illustration of a vision of Jesus (Acts 9:1). Also, 1 Cor 12:2 regularly is understood by commentators as a self-reference by Paul. For rhetorical analysis of New Testament vision reports, see Humphrey, "In Search of a Voice," 144.

2. John's symbolism, however, should not be (mis)read as non-historical, as does C. Koester, who concluded toward the end of his commentary, "When Revelation moves people to faith in God and the Lamb, it brings them to the End for which the book was written" (*Revelation and the End of All Things*, 172). That is the "End" to which all of Revelation's convoluted drama points? Pretty anticlimactic for such a three-ring circus of complex images! If Revelation is nothing more than an existential journey of faith that sublimates all its imagery to personal experience, then history is rendered more meaningless than the infinite Greek cycles of the ages.

THE CENTRAL CONTEXT

When John turned to see the voice speaking to him, John saw "seven lampstands" (1:12), later explicitly identified as the seven churches (1:19).[3] The number seven is well known as a symbol for ideas such as perfection, completion, consummation, and the totality of the whole. The seven churches stand in for the whole church.[4] The churches John addressed were diverse congregations.[5] John chose *these* seven diverse congregations principally for their representative efficacy. John addressed not just these seven particular churches in Asia Minor during Domitian's reign but the church corporate, and any local church in any generation.

THE CENTRAL FIGURE

The local church is the central context of the inaugural vision and a defining parameter of the rest of the book. Onto that church stage the central figure is introduced, "one like a son of man" (1:13).[6] The rest of the inaugural vision is devoted to describing this person, marking this individual as the central figure of the entire book.[7] John emphasized four major truths about this central figure.

---

3. All translations in this chapter except where noted are the author's own from the standard edited Greek text.

4. Cf. Smalley, *The Revelation to John*, 55.

5. One runs the gamut from the large and wealthy to the small and poverty stricken, from the troubled and persecuted to the spiritually lukewarm without any sense of conflict, from the outwardly active but spiritually static to the faithful ready for even greater opportunities, and, finally, those doctrinally pure but evangelistically challenged.

6. The rhetoric of simile seems odd, but simile is one of John's favorite stylistic penchants in Revelation. This stylistic trait is demonstrated quickly even in English translations with a concordance search on "like" or "as" in Revelation. Modulated out of his apocalyptic framing, John's expression in 1:13 becomes the near equivalent of Jesus' favorite self-designation in the Gospels, "the Son of Man," *ho huios tou anthrōpou* (ὁ υἱός τοῦ ἀνθρώπου). Without recognizing the phrase as an Aramaic circumlocution, one can make too much of the presence of the article in the Gospel form ("*the* Son of Man"), as does Grudem, *Bible Doctrine*, 238. Some argue that the indefinite form of the Greek in Rev 1:13 is a careful using of the exact phrase in Dan 7:13; see Bauckham, *Climax of Prophecy*, 295. Such an idea is much more likely than that John wanted readers to be aware of Jesus' metaphysical change from incarnation to ascension, Walhout, *Revelation Down to Earth*, 30.

7. Speaking in terms of rhetorical exigency; cf. Troeltsch, *Christian Faith*, 106. Even in Revelation's very first verse John introduced the name of Jesus before the name of

Truth 1: Who He Is

The first truth is who he is. Beloved Disney and Pixar characters teach children the significance of names for understanding characters and their contributions to the plot.[8] Names can be made to embody a character's essence, which then sets the background for what that character says and does. John named his central character "Son of Man."[9] This title alludes to the most common self-reference of Jesus in the Gospels, which Jesus used for himself more than all other names combined. In this name Jesus encapsulated his heavenly origin, suffering ministry, redemptive death, and resurrected glory—and along the way completely redefined "messiah" for Israel.[10]

God. One also should note that John presented the inaugural vision in chapter 1, whose central figure is Jesus, before he presented the heavenly vision in chapter 4, whose central figure is God ("one seated on the throne"). While these two figures of Jesus and God have a mutuality of operation and status on Revelation's stage, the reader should be careful to note that John spoke about Jesus first in order to speak about God. Theologically, all Christian speech about God is constrained by the reality of the incarnation, whose historical locus is Jesus of Nazareth. See Newport, *Lion and the Lamb*, 140.

8. Snow White's seven dwarfs had names for their personality traits. *The Lion King* (1994) character Simba's name means "lion" in Swahili, and Simba has to learn a lesson of taking on a lion's character of courage and wisdom. "Buzz Lightyear" in *Toy Story* (1995) is obvious for his spaceman character. "Hopper" also is obvious for the grasshopper villain in *A Bug's Life* (1998). Nemo's mother in *Finding Nemo* (2003) is "Coral," a clear allusion to the habitat where clownfish live and thrive. As with many racecar drivers, "Lightning McQueen" lives up to his moniker in *Cars* (2006). Finally, *WALL-E* (2008) is named for its robot main character, an inventive acronym for his job: Waste Allocation Load Lifter, Earth Class, and his robot romantic interest, "Eve," invoking a new beginning for waste-polluted planet earth. Outside Disney and Pixar, *Dances With Wolves* (1990) evokes the Indian name given to Lt. John Dunbar, played by Kevin Costner, as the Indians observed his close affinity for wild wolves while serving at an abandoned frontier fort.

9. The expression found only one other time in Revelation in 14:14; both occurrences seem derived from Dan 7:13.

10. Literature on "Son of Man" research is voluminous, and the study is fraught with ambiguities of background, oddities in linguistic data, and distinctive patterns of literary incorporation. Jewish canonical background focuses on Dan 7:13, with issues of individual, corporate, messianic, or mythic traditions. Jewish non-canonical background focuses on *1 En.* 37–71 and *4 Ezra* 13, with its issue of an apocalyptic, heavenly, universal, and exalted figure. Aramaic background focuses on linguistic data, with the issue of circumlocution, not title. The most current exhaustive review and analysis is Mogens Müller, *The Expression 'Son of Man' and the Development of Christology*. Müller (417–19) concludes that: (1) before the Gospel of Mark, the history of the term is impossible to trace; (2) even if no more than an Aramaic circumlocution ("man," "someone," "I"), the term still is imbued with specific contextual meaning in each Gospel;

Defining who Jesus is becomes crucial to defining who believers are. A disciple's identity is given by the one the disciple follows. More importantly, who a person is also determines how that person lives. John felt the suffering of believers in Asia Minor needed reimagining away from a random series of meaningless life events to a realistic appraisal of the path of faithful witness that could put one on an island such as Patmos. A name, then, is a destiny.

Truth 2: Where He Is

The second truth is where he is. This central figure is "among the lampstands" (1:13). The probable background of the lampstands is the menorah of the Jerusalem temple.[11] The perceptive reader begins to grasp that one truth predicates the other. Who Jesus is anticipates where he is. The lampstands of 1:13 together with the stars of 1:16 indicate that John's vision is a vision in the night. The darkness of the world seeks to overcome the light of Christ.

---

(3) the literary context of the term's inclusion is notably only in christologically-loaded sayings; (4) the term never is used, however, as a title for Jesus by someone else, never in a confessional saying about Jesus, and never predicative ("Jesus is Son of Man"). Müller's thesis is that the combined linguistic and background ambiguity but notable literary contextualization causes the term to precipitate like theological condensate on a cold glass pane the christological assumptions and arguments of any given Christian era. Of these assumptions, the most important to Müller in the history of interpretation are whether Christology is to be constructed on the assumption of a messianic self-consciousness by Jesus (with emphasis on "titles" research) or as the interpretive constructs of diverse early Christian communities. Müller opines, "The interpretation of the Son of man in the New Testament Gospels is in free fall until it is recognized that the expression does not have any special meaning before it receives it through its concrete context in the respective Gospels" (419). His only tangential comment on Rev 1:13 seems to discount connection to the Gospels, 283. For a shorter summary of Son of Man research, see Burkett, *Son of Man Debate*, 121–24. The work by Casey, *The Solution to the 'Son of Man' Problem*, does not advance the discussion; he simply reiterates the Aramaic solution for the life of Jesus, with the title usage a later invention of the evangelists (314–19).

11. Lampstands have Jewish associations with God's presence, deriving from the seven-pronged menorah with its seven oil-burning wicks representing the divine presence in the tabernacle, and later in Solomon's temple (construction detailed in Exod 25:31–40). This imagery also seems behind Paul's own allusive references, such as 1 Cor 3:16. A related Johannine thought is summarized in one of the "I am" declarations in John 8:12, "I am the light of the world," a theme already introduced in the prologue in John 1:4–5.

FIGURE 3. Triumphal Arch of Titus in Rome. The Arch of Titus celebrates the hard-won victory of the Romans over the Jews in the First Jewish War (photograph by Gerald L. Stevens).

John's image "among the lampstands" is the christological equivalent of Luke's ascension/Pentecost tradition.[12] After the resurrection, Jesus is not remote in some distant galaxy "far, far away" preoccupied in saving some other world, distracted from the needs of Christians under duress in Asia Minor. Jesus is "among the lampstands," providing his presence to the church.

---

12. Luke 24:48–51; Acts 1:8–11; 2:32–33. For Luke, Jesus transcended time and space limitations of the incarnation in the Spirit's descent at Pentecost. The Johannine equivalent for Jesus' presence in the church through the Spirit after the resurrection is John 16:7.

FIGURE 4. Arch of Titus in Rome Showing Jewish Menorah. This image of the interior of one side of the Arch of Titus in Rome shows a relief of the Jewish menorah taken from the Jerusalem temple after the First Jewish War (photograph by Gerald L. Stevens).

Jesus' presence is a saving presence. Jesus holds the church together, the guarantor of her survival in tribulation, her witness in persecution, her victory in the kingdom.[13] The flame of the Jewish menorah went out in the destruction of the temple in the First Jewish War (66–70 C.E.). In contrast, the One who lights the church has the power to preserve the flame. The tribulation overtaking John and his fellow believers in Asia Minor was not simply meaningless misfortune. If God in his mysterious way and miraculous power could transform the darkness of the cross in Judea into the salvation of the world, he also could transform the darkness of persecution in Asia Minor into the coming of the kingdom.

13. Matthew's equivalent is Matt 16:18. In his book, *The Book of Revelation: Apocalypse and Empire*, Leonard Thompson calls into question the commonplace description of Revelation as written in a time of "persecution" under Domitian. Thompson charges interpreters with an uncritical reading of Roman historians such as Tacitus who were wanting to aggrandize Trajan by defaming his predecessor, Domitian. Thompson, however, overstates his case; see deSilva, *Seeing Things John's Way*, 50–55.

Truth 3: How He Is Clothed

The third truth is how he is clothed. In describing the clothes of the Son of Man, John was saying clothes make the man.[14] Clothes often represent fashion, but they also can represent function—the kaki outfit of a soldier, the green scrubs of a physician, the white collar of a priest, or the blue uniform of a policeman. Function is John's point in describing the clothes of the Son of Man.

The Priestly Robe

John's brief description is significant: "In the middle of the lampstands was one like a Son of Man, clothed in a foot-length robe, and wrapped around the chest with a golden belt" (1:13). John's minimalist description mentions only two items because he focused on only two particular functions of the Son of Man.

A robe down to the feet was general apparel in the first-century world, but literary context indicates priestly activity.[15] Jewish priests served in the temple and mediated the sacrifices prescribed in the law for the sins of the people. The people of Israel came to the priests to approach God in making various offerings and in seeking forgiveness of sins. Early Christians understood that Jesus took on this function of Israel's priestly cultus in his own person. The author of Hebrews underscored the high priesthood of Jesus and the unique nature of a once-for-all sacrifice for sin through Jesus' death on the cross; that high priesthood also was connected to believers holding fast to their confession.[16] In Acts, Peter preached his message of salvation exclusively in Jesus' name in the shadow of the temple in the hearing of the ritually appointed high priest,

14. An intentional allusion to "Clothes Make the Man" by Henri Duvernois. In donning a police uniform to act as a decoy cop during a robbery in a Parisian neighborhood, Tango, one thief in a gang of three, gradually transitions in his mind from the role of criminal to the role of cop and unwittingly is responsible for his two companions getting arrested.

15. Aune's charge that the priestly view is "unfounded" is unnecessarily dismissive, *Revelation 1–5*, 93–94; more weight should be given to the broader narrative context, especially Rev 1:6 ("made us a kingdom, priests unto God"), as well as even the lampstands here evocative of the temple sanctuary. Others, however, agree with a non-priestly image; cf. Resseguie, *The Revelation of John*, 76; Beasley-Murray, *Revelation*, 66–67; Osborne, *Revelation*, 89; Murphy, *Fallen is Babylon*, 90. The priestly image is not without defenders as well; cf. Beale, *The Book of Revelation*, 208; deSilva, *Honor, Patronage, Kinship, and Purity*, 309n37; Smalley, *The Revelation to John*, 54, among others.

16. Heb 4:14, with 7:27; 9:12, 26; 10:2, 10. Cf. Rom 6:10 and 1 Pet 3:18.

Caiaphas, who only recently had condemned Jesus to death (Acts 4:12). If Jewish teachers had insisted that the messianic age would be characterized by the presence of God's forgiveness, early Christian tradition stressed that the kingdom reign of God's forgiveness began in earnest in Jesus.[17] This understanding derived directly from Jesus, who emphasized the centrality of forgiveness in his mission.[18]

John reflected this Christian emphasis on Jesus' priestly ministry in both units of his opening chapter. First, in the introduction in 1:1–8, John made clear the fundamental priestly reality of the kingdom Jesus established through his blood in Rev 1:5–6. Then, in the inaugural vision in 1:9–20, John enhanced this priestly kingdom theme in the imagery of the priestly robe of the Son of Man in Rev 1:13.[19]

The Kingly Belt

John then noted that the Son of Man was "wrapped around the chest with a golden belt" (1:13). With the golden belt, John turned to the office of king.[20] This function of the Son of Man is the Jewish issue of the promised Davidic ruler. A thousand years before Christ, God promised that David's throne would be established forever (2 Sam 7:16). Early

17. Peter so preached at Pentecost (Acts 2:38), and Paul used priestly sacrifice as a metaphor for Christian living in Rom 12:1. The confession in Col 1:13–14 is, "For he delivered us from the authority of darkness, and transferred us into the kingdom of his beloved Son, in whom we have redemption, the forgiveness of sins."

18. Seen in the answer to Peter's question about how many times to forgive (Matt 18:21–22) and in the famous petition in the model prayer for Jesus' disciples (Matt 6:12).

19. John then played out this priestly imagery of the Son of Man's clothing by describing those who follow faithfully with similar images of priestly purity. The Lamb's bride is clothed in fine, pure linen, the symbol of righteous deeds, in 19:8. The heavenly armies following the rider on the white horse in 19:14 also are described in this way. Daniel's eschatological description of the wise as "refined, purified, and cleansed" in Dan 11:35 (NRSV) is similar. Finally, one can note that Paul clearly envisioned his gospel mission as a priestly service to God (Rom 15:16).

20. The priest's sash was blue, purple, and crimson, not gold (Exod 39:29). The king's sash is royal (Job 12:18) and represents the power and authority of the entire royal house (Isa 22:20–22). Each of the seven angels with the seven last plagues that conclude Revelation's Judgment Cycle (6–19) has a golden sash (Rev 15:6), language clearly echoing the Son of Man's description in 1:13. This intratextual linkage implies that each bowl angel acts in the power and authority of the exalted Son of Man of the inaugural vision. The seven bowls of God's wrath as judgment are sublimated by this clothing linkage to the earlier inaugural vision of the Son of Man and how he engages the conflict. While rejecting that the robe is priestly, Murphy makes a strong case for the overall imagery as kingly (*Fallen Is Babylon*, 90).

Christians carefully preserved the tradition of Jesus' Davidic descent.[21] John picked up this Davidic emphasis of the earliest Christian witnesses and faithfully encoded the tradition into his imagery in Revelation.[22]

John incorporated Davidic kingship into the Son of Man's clothing to address the historical issue of the utter failure of kingship in Israel. The institution needed redemption for God's promise to have fulfillment. God desired that the king would reify God's theocratic rule over Israel, representing God to Israel and Israel to God.[23] However, from its beginnings in the united kingdom of David and Solomon on through the Herodian days of Jesus and the early church, kingship in Israel was an utterly bankrupt enterprise, a spiritual charade that never came close to fulfillment.

Kingship Before and After the Exile

Before the exile, the story of kingship in Israel devolves quickly into a tragic tale of the impudent flaunting of God's laws.[24] Theft, lying, deceit,

21. Jesus' Davidic descent was integral to the birth narratives (Matt 1:1; Luke 2:4); the birth narratives also give prominent position to Gabriel's Davidic announcement to Mary (Luke 1:32) and to Zechariah's prophecy about the consummation of Davidic promise in Mary's child (1:69). The sick who were healed confessed Jesus to be Davidic (Matt 9:27; Mark 10:47; Luke 18:38), and even Gentile pagans confessed Jesus' Davidic authority (Matt 15:22). During great festivals Jesus' messianic actions in Jerusalem did not fail to stir up debate about his Davidic heritage against the scandal of his Galilean origins (John 7:42). Jerusalem crowds hailed Jesus as Davidic in his triumphal entry into Jerusalem (Matt 21:9; Mark 11:10; Luke 19:38), which later was echoed by the children of Jerusalem (Matt 21:15). After the resurrection, Jesus' own brother, James, made clear to the Jerusalem church the fulfillment of Davidic promises in Jesus (Acts 15:16). Paul later quoted Roman church creedal material about Jesus' Davidic descent in addressing his letter to the Romans (Rom 1:3, which is echoed in 2 Tim 2:8). On the shift away from this Davidic emphasis in the earliest church traditions, see McGrath, *Christian Theology*, 277.

22. The tradition also surfaces: (1) in the seven letters following the inaugural vision in the court imagery of the royal key holder who has access even to the inner bedchambers and the security of the whole royal house (Rev 3:7; cf. Isa 22:2–22); (2) in the vision of heaven in the messianic imagery of the Lion of the tribe of Judah, "the root of David" (Rev 5:5); and (3) in the final testimony of Jesus himself in the book, "I, Jesus, sent my angel to you to testify these things for the churches. I am the root and the descendant of David, the bright morning star" (Rev 22:16).

23. A composite picture that can be derived from texts such as 1 Sam 8:7 and the climatic declaration of the enthronement psalm in Ps 2:6–7.

24. Including David and Solomon; David was not allowed to build a temple because of his warlike spirit (1 Kgs 5:3), and Solomon, though famous for his wisdom, in the end blended into the background of pagan kingship patterns with his political alliances,

adultery, idolatry, fornication, bribery, murder and more fill the pages of Kings and Chronicles, until the reader finally arrives at the dismal observation: "The LORD, the God of their ancestors, sent persistently to them by his messengers, because he had compassion on his people and on his dwelling place; but they kept mocking the messengers of God, despising his words, and scoffing at his prophets, until the wrath of the LORD against his people became so great that there was no remedy" (2 Chr 36:15–16, NRSV).

Matters hardly were any better after the exile. When the Jews regained political independence and consolidated a renewed kingdom under the Hasmonean dynasty after the Maccabean Revolt, the Hasmonean rulers remained as far away from God's ideal for kingship as did the kings of Israel and Judah before the exile. As client kings at Rome's behest, the Hasmonean royal house was an exercise in political harlotry that quickly took on all the Hellenistic trappings that the original Maccabean Revolt had determined to oppose.[25]

Kingship in New Testament Times

The story of Jewish kingship culminates in the accession of Herod the Great to the Jewish throne prior to the birth of Jesus. Herod ended the political hegemony of the Hasmonean dynasty. The political expediency of his Judaism should not be confused with genuine "piety."[26] He was an

---

many wives, and corrupt court (1 Kgs 11:1–11). In later generations, the notable cultic reforms of Hezekiah (2 Kgs 18:1–6) did not last even one generation, as the son who ruled immediately after him, Manasseh, was the most evil king Judah ever endured (2 Kgs 21:1–17), and the fleeting revival under Josiah was cut short by Josiah's untimely death in ill-advised battle with Pharaoh Neco (2 Kgs 22:1—23:30).

25. Josephus *Ant.* 12.5.1 (12.240–41); 13.9.1 (13.257); 13.11.1 (13.301–2); 13.11.3 (13.318). Cf. H. Koester, *Introduction to the New Testament*, 1:208–210. References to the works of Josephus will include two sets of numbers. The first set identifies Whiston's numbering system. The second set within parenthesis refers to Thackery's numbering system.

26. Herod circumvented the authority of the high priest, ignored the courts with great disdain, built icons of Hellenism even in Jerusalem itself, and built temples not only to his patrons, the emperor and Rome, but to pagan gods as well. To assert (Richardson, *Herod*, 184–85) that Herod's building of temples to the emperor and to Rome was just a logical "extension" of the daily prayers to God on behalf of the emperor in Rome by the Jewish temple priests is not persuasive. That Herod promoted Torah disobedience is not in question; even Richardson, who wanted to rehabilitate Herod's image, acknowledges this much (*Herod*, 32). Herod scrupulously made provision for the daily sacrifice offering to continue without interruption during temple construc-

Idumean, enthroned by the unilateral declaration of the Roman senate in 40 B.C.E.[27] As a result, Herod was rejected by many Jews as their legitimate ruler, and his rule was marked by his infamous insecurity over the security of his throne.[28]

Conditions with the Jewish throne did not improve with Herod's three sons, Archelaus, Antipas, and Philip, who ruled immediately after him.[29] Neither does the story change with the two later Herodians,

---

tion and that only priests worked on the sanctuary itself. Such actions, however, in no way were signs of Herod's "piety," regardless whether Josephus can so describe them. Such actions were political expediency to accomplish the project without riot; *contra* Richardson, *Herod*, 195. Herod was aggrandizing Jewish religion to aggrandize his reign as a patron of Hellenism and client-king of Rome.

27. Josephus *Ant.* 14.14.4 (14.385). The standard consensus that the Idumeans were Judaized by force in the time of John Hyrcanus I also has been challenged. The counter-proposal is that the Idumeans submitted willingly and later were considered full Jews, cf. Kasher, *Jews, Idumeans and Ancient Arabs*, 46–78; followed by Richardson, *Herod*, 55 (cf. note 12). Quoting Josephus *Ant.* 20.8.1 (20.273) [parallel in *J. W.* 2.13.7 (2.266)] in support is tendentious, because the Jewish crowds clearly were ready to argue anything with the Syrians to prove ownership of Caesarea, and the Syrians simply were distinguishing Greek and non-Greek.

28. Josephus *Ant.* 14.15.2 (14.403); 14.15.5 (14.430); 14.16.4 (14.489); 15.1.2 (15.8–10); 15.3.2 (15.42); 15.3.3 (15.56); 15.3.9 (15.87); 15.6.2 (15.173); 15.7.6 (15.237); 17.5.7 (17.133). Herod executed his own beloved wife, Mariamne, the beautiful Hasmonean princess, as well as the 80 year old Hasmonean high priest Hyrcanus II and Herod's two sons by Mariamne, Alexander and Aristobulus, whom he feared of their popularity with the people as offspring of Mariamne, and then his oldest son, Antipater, shortly before Herod himself died. Cf. Ferguson, *Backgrounds of Early Christianity*, 414; H. Koester, *Introduction to the New Testament*, 1:374. Burge, Cohick, and Green assert that, in all, Herod executed as many as forty-five of the royal Hasmoneans, *The New Testament in Antiquity*, 39.

29. First, Herod's son Archelaus, who ruled Judea, Samaria, and Idumea from 4 B.C.E. to 6 C.E., was so corrupt and brutal that he had to be banished to Gaul by Augustus after only ten years. Archelaus was the reason why the parents of Jesus had to return to Galilee after the sojourn in Egypt escaping Herod's wrath, rather than settling back in Bethlehem as they apparently had intended (Matt 2:22). Second, Herod Antipas, who ruled Galilee and Perea from 4 B.C.E. to 39 C.E., is infamous for his divorce of a Nabatean princess in order to marry his brother Philip's wife, Herodias. John the Baptist excoriated Antipas and Herodias for this adulterous liaison so publically that he earned Herodias's eternal hatred. She eventually repaid John the favor by having him beheaded (Matt 14:1–12). That story too, is full of evil and immorality. Salome, Herodias's daughter, so beguiled her drunken father with a seductive dance at a feast that Antipas rashly promised Salome anything up to half his kingdom. After advice from her mother, Salome asked Antipas for the head of John the Baptist on a silver platter (Mark 6:16–28). Third, Herod Philip, who ruled the Transjordan from 4 B.C.E. to 34 C.E., while having a more peaceful reign than either Archelaus or Antipas,

Agrippa I and Agrippa II, who ruled for brief intervals.[30] Even toward the end the First Jewish War while Jerusalem was in the death throes of her destruction, both Zealot leaders, Menaham and Simon ben Giora, each in turn had the audacity to claim to be Israel's rightful king.[31]

One should note in all this history of kingship in Israel that, whereas God acceded to the original cries of the people for a king "like the nations," he never desired that path as first choice for Israel. Sin would consume the kingship, and kingship would consume Israel—like a malignant cancer destroying the very body in which the disease resides. As the people cried out for a king in 1 Sam 8, God already began configuring Israel's storyline toward a future redeemer who could deliver Israel from the curse of kingship. In this sense, the coming of Messiah would not mark the historical apogee of Israel's glory but, rather, the historical nadir of Israel's fall.[32] Jesus Christ stands as God's greatest judgment against the institution of kingship in Israel. Indeed, the coming of

---

was thoroughly Hellenistic in all respects. One notable example was Philip's choice to build his capital at the ancient pagan site of Pan at the headwaters of the Jordan River. Numerous pagan cults had worshipped at Pan for generations. Pan preserved a large deposit of dedicatory shrines to pagan gods for pilgrims to visit and show homage. Philip did nothing about this pagan worship in his capital city. Philip renamed Pan as Caesarea Philippi, in honor of his patron, the Roman emperor, using his own name in addition to distinguish this Caesarea from the seaport harbor his father had built. That Caesarea Philippi was precisely where Jesus chose to confront his disciples with the penetrating question about his identity (Mark 8:27) seems no coincidence.

30. Herod Agrippa I, grandson of Herod the Great, became king of almost all the territories his grandfather had ruled (41–44). To ingratiate himself with Jewish leaders in Jerusalem, Agrippa attacked early church leaders, first killing James, the son of Zebedee, in Jerusalem (Acts 12:1–2) and then imprisoning Peter, who later was freed miraculously by God's angel (Acts 12:3–17). Agrippa's rule was cut short by his sudden death in the theater at Caesarea after receiving divine acclamations from the flattering crowds as he appeared in his regal finery. Both Josephus and Acts give similar accounts of this event, but the story in Acts is told as an act of divine vengeance (cf. *Ant.* 19.8.2; Acts 12:21–23). Herod Agrippa II was judged by the Romans too young to rule after his father's unexpected death in the theater in Caesarea. In the years leading up to the First Jewish War, Agrippa II eventually received various territorial grants, including Chalcis and Galilee. The Apostle Paul made a defense before Agrippa II in Acts 25:23—26:32. Agrippa II opposed the Jewish War and afterwards lived out the rest of his life in Rome as part of the Jewish aristocratic elite loyal to their Roman patrons. Cf. Josephus *J.W.* 4.1.3 (4.14).

31. Josephus *J.W.* 2.17.8 (2.434); 4.9.3 (4.508).

32. A reality proleptically foreshadowed in Amos's warnings in Amos 5:18–20 to the Northern Kingdom of Israel, whose inhabitants were not perceiving the Assyrian threat on the near horizon.

Messiah marked the beginning of the end for Israel as a nation among the nations, along with its institutions and leaders.[33]

When Messiah came, the temple was cleansed, and Israel judged and found wanting. Messiah established the only truly legitimate Davidic kingdom. As Jesus had asked the completely befuddled Pharisees, how could David call his own descendant, "Lord" (Matt 22:41–46)?[34] The only reason David had a legitimate lineage was not because of the seed in David's loins, but because of the Messiah who came and sanctified the entire line. Jesus as Messiah consummated the divine ideal of kingship in Israel and spiritually ordained this royal line both backward and forward, a stunning historical inversion from David's physical seed to the spiritual seed of Jesus.[35] With the imagery of the golden belt of royal rule, combined with the long robe of priestly intercession, John perfectly captured the picture of the spiritual ideal, the true and only king ever to occupy Israel's throne according to the divine intent when God granted Israel's original request for a king, the Lion of the tribe of Judah.[36]

Truth 4: What He Looks Like

The fourth truth is what he looks like. As one counts the features of the Son of Man, seven emerge (head/hair, eyes, feet, voice, right hand, mouth, face). As with the symbolic significance of seven lampstands, these seven features of the Son of Man helped John symbolize how

33. Interpreting historical events as divine judgment raises complex issues. Public discourse in the media, press, print, and Internet blogs after Sept. 11, 2001 is a case in point. A reasoned approach to this debate is given by Keillor's *God's Judgments: Interpreting History and the Christian Faith*. For the view that 9/11 was God's judgment, see Melon, *"Yet You Would not Return to Me,"* 205–09.

34. Recapitulated by Peter in his sermon to Jerusalem's Pentecost crowds (Acts 2:30–35).

35. Paul gives a compressed form of this inversion in quoting the Roman creedal formula of Jesus as God's Son, "who was born a descendant of David according to the flesh, who was declared the Son of God with power by the resurrection from the dead, according to the Spirit of holiness, Jesus Christ our Lord" (Rom 1:3–4).

36. Rev 5:5, which, combined with its slaughtered Lamb imagery also fuses together both priest and king functions. The Hasmoneans represent the only other historical attempt in the history of Israel to combine both priestly and kingly functions into one person, tracing back at least as far as the claim of Aristobulus in 104 B.C.E.; Josephus *Ant.* 13.11.1 (13.301). This failed attempt of the Hasmonean dynasty Jesus would consummate forever in his own person. For the authority of the exalted Jesus as enthroned king, cf. Matt 28:18–19; Eph 1:20–21; Phil 2:9–11.

perfectly Jesus fulfills his identity as Son of Man, his presence within the church, and his functions as priest and king, that is, the other three truths. John chose these particular features because they enhance principle themes already established.[37]

Lord of Judgment

The first Son of Man feature is the duality of head and hair, which are "like white wool, like snow" (Rev 1:14). Such imagery conjures ideas of heavenly origin, eternity, and purity. The likely allusion is to Daniel's vision of the Ancient of Days sitting in judgment:

> As I watched
> > thrones were set in place,
> > > and an Ancient One took his throne
> > his clothing was white as snow,
> > > and the hair of his head like pure wool. (Dan 7:9)

John's allusion conforms to other New Testament passages that imply Jesus' heavenly origins, purity, and equal status to God.[38] The Son of Man will declare at the end of the inaugural vision, "I am the First and the Last . . . I was dead, and behold, I am alive forevermore" (Rev 1:18, 19). The implication for judgment is clear: the judgment of the Ancient of Days anticipated by Daniel, John declared, had been realized in the Son of Man.

The second feature of the eyes are "like a flame of fire" (Rev. 1:14).[39] Such imagery conjures ideas of intimidating omniscience, infallible knowledge, and infinite insight. This feature of the eyes is coordinated closely with the theme of judgment in the first feature. The fire metaphor

37. Such as faithful witness concerning truths about Jesus and the gospel, truths about believers and salvation, and truths about judgment and the second coming from 1:7–8. John also used the features of the Son of Man to make literary and linguistic ties in the next section between the One addressing the church in the seven letters in chapters 2–3 and the Son of Man central figure of the inaugural vision. Note the opening identification section of each letter, as, for example, in the letter to Ephesus: "Thus says the one who holds the seven stars in his right hand, the one who walks in the midst of the seven lampstands" (Rev 2:1).

38. A sampling could include John 1:2; 3:13; Col 1:17; 1 Thess 4:16; Heb 4:15; 7:24–26, 28; 2 Pet 1:1.

39. Seen again in the letter to Thyatira (Rev 2:18) and the heavenly warrior on the white horse (Rev 19:12). Aune points out that ancient descriptions of the gods, as well as other figures, with fiery eyes is a frequent metaphor in Greek and Latin literature, Aune, *Revelation 1–5*, 95.

is about penetrating vision, a power to illumine even the darkest corners of the human heart. Even the deepest secret is transparent to the eyes of the Son of Man. Hence, the One addressing the seven churches in the seven letters knows both good and bad, and the churches come in for both commendation and condemnation.[40] As echoed in Hebrews, "No creature is hidden from his sight, but all things are open and laid bare to the eyes of him with whom we have to do" (Heb 4:13).

Such vision is imperative if Jesus is to function as "ruler of the kings of the earth" (Rev 1:5). Unlike the unjust administration of the Roman empire, in which corrupt procurators such as Felix often anticipated bribes (Acts 24:26), Jesus will see through every pretense and judge unerringly. Penetrating vision can be a threat regarding judgment but a consolation regarding salvation. John was telling persecuted believers of Asia Minor that they need not worry whether their suffering was observed.[41] At the same time, he was warning those who sinfully oppressed others about their own accountability and culpability.

In sum, the combined pictures of the heard/hair and eyes have presented Jesus as a glorious "Lord of Judgment" to believers in first-century Asia Minor. He functions in the role of Daniel's Ancient of Days sitting in judgment on the world.

Lord of Strength

The third feature of the feet are "like burnished bronze, when it has been caused to glow in a furnace" (Rev 1:15). Such imagery conjures ideas of strength and stability. Wherever the Son of Man stands, he stands unmoved. Since he is in the midst of the lampstands, the lampstands are unmoved, unless the Son of Man himself removes the lampstand (Rev 2:5). The doxology of Jude reflects a similar sentiment, "to him who is able to keep you from stumbling, and to make you stand in the presence

---

40. One can read intimations of this penetrating insight in the ministry of Jesus, as Nathanael is caught off guard at Jesus' knowledge of him before ever being introduced (John 1:48) or as doubters are answered before they even can speak their objections (Luke 11:17), or, even later, in the Spirit's disclosing of the secret conspiracy to lie by Ananias and Sapphira (Acts 5:1–10).

41. One familiar with Scriptures might think of the Chronicler's words, "For the eyes of the Lord move to and fro throughout the earth that He may strongly support those whose heart is completely His" (2 Chr 16:9, NASB). Paul's word to the Corinthians also seems in line with John's thought here, "Therefore, my beloved brethren, be steadfast, immovable, always abounding in the word of the Lord, knowing that your toil is not in vain in the Lord" (1 Cor 15:58).

of his glory blameless with great joy" (Jude 24). Deriving strength from Christ is encouraged in Ephesians, "be strong in the Lord, and in the strength of his might" (Eph 6:10).[42]

The fourth feature of the voice is "like the sound of many waters" (Rev 1:15). Such imagery conjures ideas of majesty and authority. Anyone who has stood at the base of a powerful waterfall and tried to make conversation understands the point. The focus of the imagery is on the strength of what the Son of Man says. The Son of Man has authority over the church and over peoples and nations. What the Son of Man says in judgment no one contradicts, with no court of appeal.

John's "sound of many waters" affirms and augments with different imagery common ideas associated with the heavenly voice.[43] John's particular point would be the authoritative words of Jesus both to the church (Rev 2–3) and to the world (Rev 4–19), which John preserved in his prophecy. In the context of the awesome power of the Roman empire, impressed upon local residents through inscriptions, coins, statuary, and architecture, John's picture of the strength of the Son of Man served as an important reminder to believers in Asia Minor.[44]

In sum, the combined pictures of the feet and voice have presented Jesus as a glorious "Lord of Strength" to believers of first-century Asia Minor. He functions in the role of the strong deliverer of the church and powerful executor of God's word.

42. Building to the climax of putting on the whole armor of God in order to *withstand* in the evil day (Eph 6:13).

43. A similar biblical metaphor for the heavenly voice is thunder. The Israelites at Mount Sinai heard the voice of God as thunder. In John 12:29 the voice from heaven responding to Jesus' prayer some of the crowd heard as thunder, while others speculated the heavenly sound was the voice of an angel. The context for the commanding voice from heaven often is eschatological, as in John 5:25, "an hour is coming and now is, when the dead shall hear the voice of the Son of God, and those who hear shall live." Although apparently combined with the voice of an archangel, a similar thought is in Paul's revelation in 1 Thess 4:16, "for the Lord himself with a shout, with the voice of the archangel and the trumpet of God, will descend from heaven."

44. To explore this topic in depth, including copious illustrations, see Zanker, *The Power of Images in the Age of Augustus*. For how imperial propaganda affected religion, see Elliott, *The Arrogance of Nations*, 124–25.

FIGURE 5. Colossal Statue of Emperor Hadrian. This large statue of the emperor Hadrian stands about fifteen feet tall. The emperor is depicted in traditional ceremonial military cuirass and takes a traditional victory pose that indicates subjugation of a conquered population, shown in disproportionate size for shame and humiliation (photograph by Gerald L. Stevens).

Lord of Witness

The fifth feature of the right hand actually focuses on what is held, "in his right hand he held seven stars" (Rev 1:16). Imagery of the right hand conjures ideas of strength, security, and honor. Biblical imagery is rich with statements and metaphors about the right hand.[45] What is important in John's imagery about the right hand is what is held—seven stars. John explicitly spelled out this symbolism in Rev 1:20. The seven stars are "the angels of the seven churches." Clear is that the number seven is derived directly from the immediate connection to the seven churches.[46]

---

45. For example, the right hand is the hand of inheritance blessing (Gen 48:14); the hand of God's power (Exod 15:6; Deut 33:2; Ps 18:35; 44:3; 60:5; 63:8; 73:23; 89:13; 98:1; 118:15; Isa 48:13; 62:8; Acts 5:31); the hand of a priest receiving the mark of the ram's blood (Exod 29:20); the place of honor by the king (1 Kgs 2:19; Ps 16:11; 45:9; 110:1; Matt 26:64; Luke 22:69; Acts 2:33; 7:55; Rom 8:34; Eph 1:20; Col 3:1; Heb 1:3; 8:1; 10:12; 12:2; 1 Pet 3:22); the hand of God's security (Ps 16:8; 139:10); the hand of God's salvation (Ps 17:7; 20:6; 60:5; 108:6; 138:7); the hand of God's righteousness (Isa 41:10); the hand for swearing an oath (Dan 12:7). As the psalmist prayed, "But let your hand be on the one at your right hand, the one whom you made strong for yourself" (Ps 80:17, NRSV).

46. Numerous astrological allusions have been supposed, such as the seven planets or certain constellations, such as Pleiades or Ursa Minor, etc.; the implication from the ancient worldview would be control of destiny (see Murphy, *Fallen Is Babylon*, 91; for more detail, cf. Aune, *Revelation 1–5*, 97–98). However, all such suggestions necessarily are speculative; the symbolic bottom line that John made clear was the connection to the seven churches.

STEVENS • One Like a Son of Man   33

What is not clear is the meaning of "angels" specified in Rev 1:20. The word for "angel" (*aggelos*, ἄγγελος) fundamentally means "messenger," usually bringing God's message from heaven to humans.[47] Every other time the word *aggelos* occurs in Revelation, context makes clear the meaning is "angel," not the generic "messenger." Such linguistic data complicates exegesis of *aggelos* in 1:20. The interpretive problem is the absence of early Christian teaching about "angels" associated with particular churches. Thus, John's statement in Rev 1:20 is without parallel in the New Testament, and in Revelation itself the only other connection is in the addresses to the seven letters in Rev 2–3 ("to the angel of the church in . . . write"). Interpretation of the meaning of Rev 1:20, therefore, inevitably is without definitive result.[48]

Of the proposals, that the "angels" in Rev 1:20 could represent the leading prophets of the local congregations of the seven churches, or their pastors, whether individually or as a group, is reasonable.[49] This

47. The name of the angel Gabriel is well known in this capacity; cf. Dan 8:16; 9:21; Luke 1:19, 26.

48. Aune provides a long excursus (*Revelation 1–5*, 108–12) on the meaning of the "angels" of the seven churches in Rev 1:20, but came to no conclusion, only writing that the issue "continues to be a major problem in the interpretation of Revelation" (108). Inexplicably, Smalley completely ignores the question of the meaning of the angels here in Rev 1:16, 20 (*The Revelation to John*, 55). To Aune's excursus we might add that Jesus tradition includes angels associated with the Son of Man's activity in judgment (Matt 13:41, 49; 16:27; 18:10; 24:31; 25:31; Mark 8:38; 13:27; Luke 9:26; John 1:51; cf. 2 Thess 1:7). This tradition, however, does not involve the idea of angels of churches. Jesus tradition also includes an idea of angels associated with "little ones" that Jesus used for illustrative purposes in Matt 18:10. However, this single verse is the only text on this topic, and its interpretive implications are uncertain. The text is unclear whether the angels to whom reference is made are meant to be understood as a distinct group in an assumed heavenly hierarchy of functions, or just another way to refer to the reality of angels in heaven in general (as is clear in Luke 15:10). Further, even if the reference is meant to play out some heavenly hierarchy of angelic functions, whether these angels act as a designated group together or discretely as individual angels assigned to individual "little ones" is even less clear. With such interpretive ambiguities, Matt 18:10 does little to inform John's meaning in Rev 1:20. Also to be considered are two statements of Paul in Galatians. In Gal 1:8 Paul, by way of hyperbole, referred to the possibility of an angel preaching another gospel to the Galatians. Then, in Gal 4:14, Paul, again speaking hyperbolically, referred to the original Galatian reception of him almost as if he were an angel of God, or even Christ himself. Not only do both of these texts, however, have the clear mark of rhetorical hyperbole, neither of these texts actually speaks directly to the idea of angels of particular churches.

49. Rejected by Newport, *The Lion and the Lamb*, 139. Walhout, *Revelation Down to Earth*, 32, loosely extends John's specific point to anyone witnessing gospel truths.

interpretation holds concord with John's general emphasis on prophetic leadership and its functions of testimony and witness. He would include himself in that number (Rev 1:9).

One possible collaborating detail for this association with prophetic leadership comes at the end of the vision of the Son of Man when John fell down as "though dead" (Rev 1:17).[50] John singled out specifically *the right hand* of the Son of Man (that held the seven stars = angels) as the hand that touched him to raise him up.[51] This wording might signal associating the seven stars with the prophetic leadership of the seven churches, of which John himself is a representative. This argument at best is only implicit. If allowed, then the idea is that the prophetic leadership of the church is held in the strong right hand of the Son of Man. Such an image would communicate that the destiny of the church's prophetic mission in the world is not in doubt.[52] While problems and persecution might silence the voice of a given prophet or congregation, the witness of the church corporate is not left without voice. As deSilva observes, "The maintenance of Christian witness—and the identification of the boundaries of confession and practice that maintain this witness—was of central concern to John."[53] Understanding the seven stars as representing the prophetic leadership of the church facilitates a logical connection between the fifth and sixth features of the Son of Man.

The sixth feature of the mouth actually focuses on what comes out, "out of his mouth came a sharp, two-edged sword" (Rev 1:16). Imagery

---

50. That the "as dead" image here literally has in view more than simply the stereotypical response of a seer to a heavenly vision or visitor is acknowledged by Aune, *Revelation 1–5*, 100.

51. Similarly in the transfiguration, Jesus reached out and touched his disciples (Matt 17:7).

52. In answering the question why orthodoxy persists, Thomas C. Oden has replied in a section on the divine will transcending temporary apostasies, "Thus the Spirit protects the continuity of the Word in history, ensuring that the whole church does not at any given time completely err, and that it does not err in the foundation, . . . " (*The Rebirth of Orthodoxy*, 46).

53. deSilva, *Seeing Things John's Way*, 331. The church will overcome until her mission of witness in the world is complete. Note how the conquering theme is prominent in the seven letters, especially the formulaic "to the one who overcomes" in every letter (2:7, 11, 17, 26; 3:5, 12, 21). As Jesus said, "I give them eternal life, and they never will perish; and no one will snatch them out of my hand" (John 10:28).

of the sword conjures martial ideas. A word of judgment is the usual context for such sword imagery.[54]

While the image is militant, John's point is neither radical revolt nor that Jesus will have to use institutions, methods, or instruments of human warfare to accomplish his goals.[55] Quite notably to the point, the sword is not imaged in the expected place of the right hand. Rather, in a grotesque way if taken literally, the sword comes out of the mouth. John's meaning is clear: the words of the Son of Man are his chosen weapon of offense. The imagery speaks to the power of Jesus' words as the revelation of God's will. This imagery ties into the Gospel of John's "Word theology," a Word that contains the power of creation and the promise of salvation and is light to the world (John 1:1–14).[56]

The sword in Rev 1:16 has two characteristics. First, the sword is sharp. Its cutting power is undiminished by the hardness of the material opposing its action. Christ's Word will cut through even the Roman propaganda of an inevitable and invincible empire.[57] Second, the sword is two-edged. The sword cuts two ways simultaneously. The same Word of God that cuts in judgment also cuts in salvation.[58] The difference in the type of cut is in the response of the hearer. The question Jesus asked his disciples, "but who do you say that I am?" (Mark 8:29) becomes universal to all humanity. An answer of faith means commendation (John 3:16). An answer of unbelief means condemnation (John 3:36). John's imagery in Rev 1:16 is given in more prosaic form in Hebrews, "For the

54. Cf. A. Hanson, *The Wrath of the Lamb*, 166–67.

55. Neither in the first coming nor in the second coming. David L. Barr, "The Lamb Who Looks Like a Dragon?" 205–6, demonstrates how John's martial imagery actually functions as subversive rhetoric. While acknowledging Revelation's martial language has been misunderstood, Newport insists that a balanced reading shows John intended the language to speak to Christian truths related to Jesus' own sacrificial death (*The Lion and the Lamb*, 121).

56. Cf. Smalley, *The Revelation to John*, 55. This theology is echoed in Peter's confession, "Lord, to whom will we go? You have the words of eternal life" (John 6:68). The author of Hebrews confessed, "he upholds all things by the word of his power" (Heb 1:3). Ephesians contains a description of the Christian's armor using language that is the practical equivalent of John's image, "the sword of the Spirit, which is the Word of God" (Eph 6:17).

57. Such as Virgil's almost euphoric words hailing Augustus as savior of the world and bearer of peace in *Eclogae* 4, which, Ferguson points out, "shows the almost 'messianic' aura that surrounded the expectations of people in the Augustan age," *Backgrounds of Early Christianity*, 114. Cf. Perriman, *The Coming of the Son of Man*, 163.

58. Cf. Reddish, *Revelation*, 41.

Word of God is living and active and sharper than any two-edged sword, and piercing even as far as the division of soul and spirit, of both joints and marrow, and able to judge the thoughts and intentions of the heart" (Heb 4:12). The seven letters that follow this inaugural vision show that this sharp sword out of the mouth of the Son of Man also cuts two ways within the church. John was on Patmos because of the Word of God and his testimony about Jesus (Rev 1:9). He expected believers in Asia Minor to fulfill the same mission of faithful witness.[59] The war the imagery envisions is a war of words.[60]

Through this sword imagery John connected the heavenly Son of Man of the inaugural vision to the heavenly rider on the white horse in Rev 19. The emphasis is on witness because the heavenly warrior in Rev 19 who "judges and makes war" (19:11) has the name "Word of God" (19:13). In a direct allusion to the inaugural vision, only one weapon is described, "from his mouth comes a sharp sword" (19:15). Notably, those defeated are slain exclusively by the "sword of the rider on the horse," which, to seal the symbolic deal, John explained redundantly, "the sword that came from his mouth" (19:21).[61]

In sum, the combined pictures of the right hand and mouth have presented Jesus as a glorious "Lord of Witness" to believers of first-century Asia Minor. He functions in the role of securing the prophetic destiny of the church and enabling the witness of believers to God's Word.

Lord of Deity

The seventh and last feature of the face is described "as the sun shining in its strength" (Rev 1:16). Such imagery conjures ideas of deity. The sun in its strength is the sun at noonday, too bright to look upon directly. *A*

---

59. Cf. Beale, *The Book of Revelation*, 213.

60. Note that the expected Davidic ruler in Isa 11:4 will "strike the earth with the rod of his mouth" and will vanquish the wicked "with the breath of his lips" (NRSV). This Isaiah passage and John's imagery in Rev 1:16 may elucidate the oddly phrased destruction of the lawless one in 2 Thess 2:8, "whom the Lord Jesus will destroy with the breath ["spirit," *pneuma*, πνεῦμα] of his mouth." Though not making a connection to John's imagery in Rev 1:16, Perriman suggests 2 Thess 2:8 "would seem to signify a spoken truth," *The Coming of the Son of Man*, 161.

61. Thus drawing together in the one figure of Son of Man both suffering humility and conquering victor to encourage the community of Asia Minor believers. Järvinen in his narrative analysis of Q material sees a similar role to the Son of Man sayings for the ostracized Q community in its failed mission to Israel ("The Son of Man and His Followers," 182).

vision in the night suddenly transforms into a vision at noonday. The face of the Son of Man bedazzles all the stars of the universe in its glorious splendor and majesty. Seeing Christ for who he really is transfigures the reality of this life. The light of Christ overcomes the darkness of this world. John's image of brilliance is allusive of divinity and characteristics of God.[62]

In sum, the singular picture of the face has presented Jesus as a glorious "Lord of Deity" to believers of first-century Asia Minor. He functions in the role of God's unique representative with equal status to God.

THE CENTRAL REVELATION

Words of Jesus conclude this inaugural vision of Revelation. These words become the revelation within the Revelation. The sayings are framed similarly to the "I am" formulations of the Gospel of John, and likewise function as self-designations by Jesus.[63] The phrasing connects to earlier elements of John's introduction, but especially Rev 1:5.

> I am the First and the Last, and the Living One. I was dead and behold, I am alive forever, and I have the keys of Death and Hades. (Rev 1:17–18)

62. Commentators often point to the transfiguration experience of Jesus, which Mark described as a change in the appearance of Jesus' clothes, "his garments became radiant and exceedingly white, as no launderer on earth can whiten them" (Mark 9:3); Matthew included Jesus' face, "he was transfigured in their presence, and his face began to shine as the sun" (Matt 17:1–2). Matthew may be more focused on the Sinai experience of Moses, who was warned he could not see God's face and live (Exod 33:20), and when Moses came down from the mountain, his face shone such that he had to wear a veil before the people (Exod 34:29–35). The theme of divine light, radiance, and glory that believers will share (as Moses shared a light on his face after being with God on Sinai) surfaces regularly in the New Testament. Paul was confronted by a bright, heavenly light on the Damascus Road later identified as Jesus (Acts 9:3–5). The affirmation in Colossians that "in him all the fullness of deity dwells in bodily form" (Col 2:9) is echoed in Hebrews in the words, "he is the radiance of his glory and the exact representation of his nature" (Heb 1:3). In 2 Thess 1:7 Jesus returns "in flaming fire." Paul said that believers would be transformed "into conformity with the body of his glory," a thought echoed again in Col 1:12, "he has glorified us to share in the inheritance of the saints in light," and similarly in Col 3:3–4. On deity, see Resseguie, *The Revelation of John*, 79.

63. Aune, *Revelation 1–5*, 100–101, notes that the "I am" self-predication formula occurs forty-eight times in the New Testament, almost always related to God or Christ, therefore weighted with christological or theological significance.

The titles First and Last suggests the divine title Alpha and Omega in Rev 1:8 (cf. 21:6).[64] The title Living One, a typical Jewish description of God further elaborated here as "dead . . . alive forever," suggests "first-born of the dead" of Rev 1:5, the crux of the gospel message of death and resurrection. Alive forever in Revelation is exclusively God's domain.[65] Thus, as a type of double entendre, these words of Jesus combine the reality of God's life with the reality of Jesus' resurrection.[66] Having the keys of Death and Hades represents the power behind being "ruler of the kings of the earth" in Rev 1:5 and is suggestive of the plot to come that will culminate in the destruction of rebellious kings of the earth.[67] Hades is the Greek equivalent of the Hebrew concept Sheol, the place of the dead. In Rev 20:13–14, Death and Hades give up their captives and are thrown into the lake of fire, a final destiny.[68] The key to this climatic action in the drama is the powerful Son of Man of the inaugural vision. With these concluding words of Jesus, John has left no doubt of his high Christology. As Smalley observed, "The Son of man figure seems to merge with God."[69]

64. The likely background is Isa 44:6; 48:12, titles through which God indicated his control of history; so Murphy, *Fallen Is Babylon*, 93; cf. Aune, *Revelation 1–5*, 101.

65. Rev 4:9; 15:7.

66. Aune, *Revelation 1–5*, 101.

67. Rev 6:15; 10:11; 16:12, 14; 17:2, 9, 12, 14, 18; 18:3, 9; 19:18, 19; rhetorically subverted by the eventual blessing of faithful kings in 21:24. These suggestive connections also create a literary *inclusio* for John's introductory material marked by the opening epistolary style beginning in 1:5 (*inclusio* is a set of bounding phrases that mark off a block of material as a distinct literary unit). The *inclusio* indicates that John is ready to move to a new literary unit, which the reader encounters as the letters to the seven churches in Rev 2–3. These letters themselves are integrated back into the inaugural vision of 1:9–20.

68. The scenario here is compatible with Paul's thoughts in 1 Corinthians, in which the last eschatological enemy destroyed is death (1 Cor 15:26); cf. Murphy, *Fallen Is Babylon*, 95. That Death and Hades are characters thrown into the lake of fire in 20:13–14 seems to argue that the genitives "of death" and "of Hades" in Rev 1:18 are objective genitives (keys that are death and Hades), not possessive genitives (keys that death and Hades hold), against Aune, *Revelation 1–5*, 104, who points to the popular myth of the goddess Hekate holding the keys to the gates of Hades, a myth that originated in Asia Minor. Beale suggests both objective and possessive genitives might be in view, *The Book of Revelation*, 214, but this idea obfuscates the clarity of the later narrative development.

69. Smalley, *The Revelation to John*, 53.

CONCLUSION

In the inaugural vision of Rev 1:9–20, a vision of Christ as the Son of Man means that a believer's circumstances, perspectives, and values encounter a radical metamorphosis into deeper kingdom realities. John's vision resonates with the admonition in 2 Tim 4:1–2, "I solemnly charge you in the presence of God and of Christ Jesus, who is to judge the living and the dead, and by his appearing and his kingdom: preach the word; be ready in season and out of season; reprove, rebuke, exhort, with great patience and instruction."

Two conclusions surface in the process of contemplating the Christology of Rev 1. The first conclusion is that the reader does not learn anything about Jesus in the opening chapter of Revelation that cannot already be ascertained as fundamental Christian truth in other New Testament authors. The implication is that John's allusive imaging of traditions common to Israel and the early church keyed to gospel truths in chapter 1 ought to be a guide for reading all the visions that follow. That is, the epistolary opening and closing of the book centered on the Jesus who is identified as the Son of Man is the hermeneutical key sandwiching all the visionary meat in between. The second conclusion is that in the imagery of the inaugural vision, John gave voice to one of the highest christologies in the New Testament, even though shrouded in allusion. For its Christology alone the book is worth studied attention and devotion, regardless what the future holds.

QUESTIONS FOR REFLECTION

• I have to admit that I am a Sci-Fi movie buff. The *Matrix* trilogy starring Keanu Reeves is now a classic and one of my favorites.[70] I always have been intrigued by the names of the characters in that series: "Neo," "Trinity," "The Oracle," "Zion," and others. Do you think these names are intended to be strong allusions, even metaphors? Why or why not? Give your own examples of movie characters whose names evoke a personal characteristic or plot element in the movie.

• Can you think of other names in Revelation that seem to evoke a characterization in the story that moves the plot along?

---

70. *The Matrix* (1999), *The Matrix Reloaded* (2003), and *The Matrix Revolutions* (2003).

- John used the name "Son of Man" elaborated in Rev 1:9–20 as a critique on the values of his own Greco-Roman society. If John were writing to us today how would contemporary American culture stand in the backlight of specific elements in his description of the "Son of Man"?

- What challenge does the name "Son of Man" present to you personally in terms of John's portrait in the inaugural vision?

- How might John's sword image for the "Son of Man" apply in today's Internet, Facebook, and Twitter world (think "war of words")?

3

Hallelujah, the Lord our God, the Almighty Reigns

The Theology of the Hymns of Revelation

STEPHEN N. HORN

INTRODUCTION

A COMMON COMPLAINT HEARD AMONG some today is the dearth of hymns in the local church context. The lament is that the other popular songs of the church today do not provide the theology found in hymns. The criticism toward these popular songs is probably unfair, but hymns are an appropriate place to glean theological conviction. The hymns of the New Testament are an appropriate place to understand the theology of the early church, because these worship elements encoded rich theological ideas with an economy of words. In particular, the hymns of Revelation, while challenging exegetical territory, seem to function in a similar way. Could John have intended to use the hymns as a means of expressing the main theological themes in the book for his reader?

Finding a place to begin in a book like Revelation is not an easy task. The apocalyptic nature of the book is notoriously difficult to interpret in comparison to the narratives of the Gospels and the pastoral style of the epistles. In addition, more times than not, the interpreter approaches Revelation with an exegetical bias formed by a particular millennial viewpoint. This confusion about the book of Revelation leads most people either to fanciful discussions about the symbols of the text or to a dismissal altogether of the book from its proper place in the canon. The serious student of the Bible cannot allow these difficulties to stand in the way of arriving at the proper understanding of the message, both original and contemporary, of the Revelation.

M. Eugene Boring suggests in a 1986 article that the last hymn of Revelation serves a summary role in the Book of Revelation.[1] The point of this essay is to expand Boring's analysis to all of the hymns of Revelation. This expansion will lead to the suggestion that the hymns play a pivotal role in understanding the theological themes of Revelation. The investigation will proceed along three lines. First, the hymns of Revelation need to be identified. Then, the general theological themes of these hymns need to be outlined. Finally, the importance of the hymns in providing a summary of the theological core of Revelation will be presented.

WHERE ARE THE HYMNS IN REVELATION?

The identification of hymns in Revelation is made easier by observing worship scenes in the book of Revelation. Rather than specific style characteristics, hymns better can be identified as those sayings of praise that appear within the context of worship. Though other passages exhibit certain hymnic qualities, the acclamations of praise in worship scenes constitute a distinct group of hymns.

A worship scene has specific participants involved in giving praise to God, the Father, or Jesus. The settings also contain specific worship imagery. Imagery in the worship scenes of Revelation includes actions such as falling down, praying, casting crowns, crying with loud voices, standing before the throne, wearing white robes, and waving palm branches. Worship imagery also includes objects to accompany worship such as incense and harps. The common component in the worship scenes is that all of the hymns are preceded with a form of the word "saying" (usually some form of *legō*, λέγω). The hymns in Revelation are marked by the author's use of an expression of liturgical praise preceding or succeeding the hymns. For example, most of the hymns are identified by words referring to other aspects of worship such as pos-

---

1. Boring, "Theology of Revelation," 257–69.

ture of worship, loud voices, or a throne scene.[2] When identifying the hymns of Revelation, stylistic characteristics, such as parallelism and grammatical peculiarities are helpful, but the real marker is the scene around the hymn. For the purposes of this essay, the hymns identified as part of worship scenes are Rev 4:8–11; 5:8–14; 6:10; 7:9–12; 11:15–18; 12:10–12; 15:2–4; and 19:1–8.

SURVEYING THE THEOLOGY OF THE WORSHIP SCENES

Worship Scene 1 (Rev 4:8–11)

The first worship scene is in Rev 4 and contains two different hymns. The overall description in Rev 4 reveals the majesty of the one sitting on the throne. Added to this description of the majesty of heaven is an important image in heaven—the throne. John had already alluded to a throne on three occasions before Rev 4. In chapter one, seven spirits are before the throne of the one "who is, who was, and who is to come" (1:4). In Rev 3:21 in the letter to the church at Laodicea, the ones who overcome to the end are given authority to sit with Jesus on his throne. These two references give evidence that the place of God's rule is from his throne. Another reference that aids in interpreting the symbolism of the throne is in the message to the church at Pergamum. In that letter, Jesus told them, "I know the place where you live, where Satan's throne is" (Rev 2:13).[3] The implication is that the throne symbolizes a place from which the one in control reigns. Therefore, in John's vision of heaven, God is pictured as the one who has supreme reign. As Mitchell Reddish notes, "Even though chaos and confusion may seem to be rampant, John asserts that the heavenly throne is not empty—God is in control."[4] Before John is allowed to see anything that will shortly take place, the overwhelming focus is on God, the One who reigns.

---

2. O'Rourke, "The Hymns of the Apocalypse," 402.

3. All translations are the author's own from the standard edited Greek text.

4. Reddish, Revelation, 93.

FIGURE 6. Illumination Page from Ms. 180 (Douce Apocalypse). This beautiful illumination from the Douce Apocalypse depicts the worship scene of Rev 4 in which two hymns are sung (photograph by Gerald L. Stevens).

Important to this throne room scene are the two hymns of the worship scene. The first hymn is a triadic series, with each line having three parts:

> *Holy, Holy, Holy*
> *Lord, God, Almighty*
> *The one who was and is and is to come*

The triad of triads poetically set God apart from all living creatures. The triadic holy chant presents God as transcendent above all things. The middle line, especially in its description of God as Almighty, establishes God as transcendent in all things. Not only is God omnipotent, but more specifically, he is transcendent in all things.

Some have made much of the poor grammar of the last phrase of this hymn. Leon Morris, however, claims that the grammatical irregularity calls attention to the importance of this phrase.[5] Theologically, the impact of the phrase continues the idea of the transcendence of God and

5. Morris, *The Book of Revelation*, 48.

adds a temporal element. Not only is God omnipotent above all others and all things, but he is omnipotent at all times.

The second hymn, found in Rev 4:11, is longer and lacks the staccato style of the first hymn, but still has a grammatically poetic style. The theological importance in this hymn concerns what makes God worthy of receiving glory, honor, and power. He and only he is the One who has created the world. As in the first hymn, God is transcendent above all others. The theological implication of creation is God's sovereignty. Certainly the One who created the world is sovereign in the world regardless who may appear to be in control presently.

Theologically, the key point in this first set of hymns is God's sovereignty. The thrice-holy chant and the doxology are indicative of the sovereignty of God. Likewise, the title Almighty suggests that he is mighty in all things. God is described also as sovereign over creation. The first worship scene sets the tone for the continuing disclosure of the theme of sovereignty throughout the book.

Worship Scene 2 (Rev 5:8–14)

The worship scene of Rev 5 is actually an extension of the scene in Rev 4, but worship shifts from God to the Lamb. John returned to the One sitting on the throne. John saw in his right hand a book with seven seals with an angel announcing that no one was worthy to open the seals. While John wept because of this predicament, the elders announced that someone was worthy to open the seals. Thus, the three hymns of Revelation 5 are framed in the report and resolution of this tremendous tension.

The scene reveals a dramatic tension since John is told in 4:2 that he is about to see what will take place. Implied in the absence of one worthy to open the seals is that history cannot move forward until one is found worthy. The tension quickly comes to a halt with the acknowledgement that one who is worthy has been found. Breaking further the tension is the declaration that the overcomer is not an aggressor but a Lamb who has been slaughtered. The description of the Lamb echoes the description of Christ in Rev 1, making clear that the one worthy is Jesus. In celebration of Christ, a worship scene develops with the appearance of yet three more hymns.

The work of Christ in redemption is the central aspect of the first hymn of the second worship scene. No one is found worthy to open the seals until Christ's sacrifice is announced as complete. As in the first worship scene that refers to God alone being creator, now Christ alone is redeemer. He has done what no one else could do or has done. The Lamb, like God, is worthy of worship. God is praised in the first scene for his sovereignty; Christ is praised in the second scene for his work of salvation, which also makes him sovereign.

The other two hymns in the second worship scene are similar and continue this theme of the worthiness of the Lamb. The most significant theological feature of these two hymns is that the same praise offered to God is offered to the Lamb. In Rev 4:11, the twenty-four elders lavish praise on God because he has created the universe. In Rev 5:13, in similar language, every created thing bestows praise on the Lamb because he has redeemed the universe. J. Ramsey Michaels highlights the importance of these two hymns: "What was implicit now becomes explicit: God on the throne and the Lamb in the center of the throne are inextricably joined together as objects of Christian worship. Again and again throughout John's visions they will be seen together as equals sharing the same throne, both as objects of fear or worship and as the decisive actors in the drama of salvation."[6] As an understanding of the theology of the hymns develops most important will be this assertion—worship due God is also due Christ.

Worship Scene 3 (Rev 6:10)

The third worship scene contains only one hymn. In comparison to the hymns of Rev 4–5 and in comparison to how a contemporary audience views hymns, one might wonder whether Rev 6:10 is even a hymn. Granted, the hymn of Rev 6:10 is not in an elaborate worship setting. However, the characteristic formula of a worship saying, "They cried with a loud voice saying," precedes the hymn. Furthermore, the hymn directs attention toward God, attributes praise toward God, and makes a request of God.

The hymn contained in Rev 6:10 is in the fifth of seven seals. The opening of the seals is the first cycle in the main Judgment Cycle (6–19). Unlike the other hymns examined so far, the reasons for worship are more implicit. In fact, rather than praise, the hymn appears to be more of a prayer. The context of prayer, or petition to God, is an enticing place to view John's theology. What a person might ask God is instructive in

6. Michaels, *Revelation*, 97–98.

understanding what that person believes about God because the prayer acknowledges divine power to accomplish the request.

The prayer begins with the phrase, "How long?" Addressing God in this temporal way acknowledges that the suffering being experienced is not permanent. Calling to God is an acknowledgement of his sovereignty because the worshippers believe that God is capable of ending the suffering and bringing justice to those responsible for the ones being martyred. The acknowledgement of God's sovereignty is exemplified by the temporal question and the plea for justice.

The main theological significance in this brief hymn comes in the address to God. He is addressed as "Lord, holy and true." The Greek word for Lord in this instance is not the usual *kyrios* (κύριος) but instead *despotēs* (δεσπότης), a word that is much less used in the New Testament.[7] In fact, when used, the word has the connotation of a master/slave relationship. The implication could be one of complete authority or control. Thus, the point of the hymn in Rev 6:10 is again one of sovereignty. John has used the hymns to indicate God's sovereignty in creation, his sovereignty in salvation, and now his sovereignty even in distress.

The other two parts of the address to God, holy and true, indicate how God uses his sovereignty. He exercises sovereignty and brings about justice in a holy and true way. Both of these words are frequent in the book of Revelation. Both are used interchangeably of God and Jesus, making stronger their oneness. In addition, both of these terms speak of the uniqueness of God and Christ.

The theological impact of the hymn in the third worship scene can be summarized in three ways. First, the sovereignty of God continues to be at the core of the hymns of Revelation. Second, because of the language used to address God, the reader is alerted to similarity in the worship of God and Christ. Third, the worshippers' plea and the manner in which the request is made continues to implore God's goodness, holiness, and distinctiveness from all other beings.

Worship Scene 4 (Rev 7:9–12)

John's vision of the fourth worship scene happens in an interlude between the opening of the sixth and seventh seal. The first hymn in this unit is

7. Luke 2:39; Acts 4:24; 1 Tim 6:1, 2; 2 Tim 2:21; Titus 2:9; 1 Pet 2:18; 2 Pet 2:1; Jude 4; Rev 6:10.

a short utterance that makes one foundational point. The other hymn is a repetition of the seven-fold blessing of God. The hymns of Revelation reflect a variety of reasons to praise God, but in the first hymn of the fourth worship scene only one thought, salvation, is important.

Confessing that salvation belongs to God and the Lamb is recognizing that salvation is only God's to give. This recognition draws its power from its placement on the lips those who just have come out of the tribulation. They acknowledge that they have their salvation not of their own might, but of the working of God and the Lamb. The other issue of importance in this hymn is the link again between the worship of God and the Lamb.

Worship Scene 5 (Rev 11:15–18)

Compared to the paired worship scenes of Rev 4 and Rev 5, the fifth worship scene has relatively few details. The characteristics which make the passage a worship scene are the loud voices and the elders falling down before God. The worship scene contains yet two more hymns. Each hymn proclaims the work of God and offers thanksgiving for that work. The theology of Revelation continues to be developed in both hymns.

The initial hymn of this worship scene is a proclamation of God's character. The hymn's first proclamation is that God is sovereign over the evil of the world, which is an expansion of God's reign. The hymn's second proclamation is that God's sovereignty over evil is a result of the cross. The hymn's third proclamation is an elaboration of the non-temporal nature of the reign of God and his Christ.

If the first hymn is a proclamation of the work of God, the second hymn is a cry of thanksgiving for his great power. The greatest theological impact in this hymn may not be in what the worshippers say, but in what they do not say. Here, God is referred to as the "one who is and who was," but the expected "who is to come" from earlier occurrences of this phrase is absent.[8] The theological impact could not be greater. The worshippers no longer have need to say "who is to come," because the kingdom has come and is now.

8. Rev 1:4, 8; 4:8.

Worship Scene 6 (Rev 12:10–12)

Curiously the sixth worship scene does not contain the same worship imagery that appears in the other scenes. However, the literary feature that suggests the worship nature of this passage is the characteristic "loud voice" that utters the hymn. In addition, the important verbal form of "saying" that occurs in all of the other hymns introduces the hymn of Rev 12:10–12.

The sixth worship scene is most important to the theology of the book.[9] Coming in a long interlude between the trumpets and bowls that is notoriously difficult to interpret, the simplicity and exactness of the hymn is welcomed.[10] The hymn seems to fall into three distinct parts with each of the parts being divided by a verse in the text. The opening is a four-fold statement of what belongs to Christ. Following this theologically packed statement is an equally significant statement that these things were established by the blood of the Lamb, the witness of the believers, and the endurance of the believers. This witness and endurance of the believers does not mean that believers had anything to do with accomplishing the victory for God, but that God's victory is realized only for those who believe until death. The final part of the hymn is a call to worship as well as a word of warning concerning the present situation of the ones on earth. They have reason to celebrate the work of Christ, but live with the reality that Satan is allowed a temporary reign on earth.

Worship Scene 7 (Rev 15:2–4)

The seventh worship scene comes at a strategic time in the book of Revelation. Serving as an introduction to the revelation of the seven and final bowls of wrath, the scene's significance is related to the pastoral impact of the worship. Always striving to maintain a pastoral concern, John revealed the worship scene in order to bring a theological perspective to the revelation of God's most severe and culminating wrath.

In the first part of the hymn God is praised for his great and marvelous works and for being righteous and true. The names by which he is addressed are Lord Sovereign God and King of the Nations. The first title

9. Fee and Stuart call chapter 12 "the theological key to the book." *How to Read the Bible*, 261.

10. Witherington, *Revelation*, 21, comments that chapters 12–14 present "one of the great structural puzzles of Revelation" because of its abrupt beginning and flashback to an earlier chronological time than anything before Rev 12.

is familiar to Revelation; the second title is new. The second title amplifies the meaning of the first title to specify now that God is sovereign over the nations. This concept of God's sovereignty over the nations is certainly not new, because throughout Revelation God has been praised for being sovereign over all. John structured the second part of the hymn around a rhetorical question that is answered by three convincing proofs. God is worthy of reverence because: he alone is holy; he is sovereign over the nations; and his righteous acts have been revealed.

Worship Scene 8 (Rev 19:1–8)

This final worship scene is more fragmented than the other worship scenes. If the brief, "Amen, Hallelujah," in Rev 19:4 is counted, then the scene contains five distinct hymns. All participants of prior worship scenes emerge for this final time of worship. The content of the hymns is reminiscent of the hymns of the first seven worship scenes.

The first hymn of the worship scene revisits the theme of salvation belonging to God. The content of the second hymn reiterates the Hallelujah of the first hymn and continues, "her smoke rises up forever." Just as God's reign is forever, the overthrow of the forces of evil is a permanent action. An unidentified voice coming down from the throne produces the next hymn fragment. The voice is peculiar because every other mention of the throne suggests that God is on the throne. Since the hymn calls for praise to God, the voice probably is not God's voice. Because the emphasis is on the worship bearers rather than on God, the theological nature of this song is not as apparent.

The final hymn conjures thoughts of previous themes. A simple hymn, "Hallelujah, because our Lord God, the Almighty, reigns," includes three important aspects of the revelation. First, the title by this point in the Apocalypse refreshes the memory of all that the Lord God is and what he has done. Second, the title Almighty reminds the reader of the omnipotence of the Lord God. The aspect of reigning suggests God's sovereignty in the present world and in the world to come. The last worship scene's theological impact is in the last hymn. Captured in this final hymn is God's sovereignty, his omnipotence, his holiness, and his rule. Missing from this hymn is a direct link between the worship of God and Jesus. Present, however, is the constant reminder of the Apocalypse that the Lord God reigns.

SUMMARY OF THEOLOGICAL THEMES IN HYMNS

Several theological themes emerge in the hymns of the worship scenes. The theology of the hymns of the worship scenes can be described by the references to the character of God, the work of God, and the unity of God and Jesus. God's character in the hymns centers around his sovereignty and holiness. His sovereignty is related to his power over the world, including evil, and his eternal reign. The work of God in the hymns concerns his work in creation and his work in redemption. John's vision unified God and Jesus in the hymns to the extent that to offer praise to one was to offer praise to the other.

As for the conceptual frequency of theological themes, the most frequent theme is the sovereignty of God, which appears in all but the second worship scene. The next most frequent theme is the holiness of God, which appears in four of the hymns. Also significant in the theology of the hymns is the work of God. The most frequent allusions to the works of God are redemption and reigning. Other works that appear in the hymns are God as creator and God as judge. The most significant feature of the theology of the hymns when observing the frequency with which the themes appear is the unity of God and Jesus. In every worship scene, at least an implied relationship exists between God and Jesus. In the second, fourth, and fifth worship scenes, the relationship is a direct link held together by the conjunction "and."

Another way to compare the theology of the hymns with the remainder of the book is theme elaboration. The point of comparison is to determine whether the specific themes are elaborated in the same way. In order to do this comparison, theological themes discovered in the hymns must be analyzed for the specific statement that they make.

God's sovereignty is far reaching as developed in the hymns. The one word, almighty, establishes the parameter of God's sovereignty as over everything. This general description of God's sovereignty is defined more clearly as over creation (worship scene 1), over evil (worship scenes 3 and 5), over salvation (worship scenes 2, 4, 6, and 8), and over the world (worship scene 5). That God's sovereign rule never ends is described in worship scenes 1, 5, and 8. John communicated in these worship scenes who really is in control of the world.[11] Surely, the reminder

11. Ibid., 113–14.

that God is really in charge was welcomed by the original hearers, just as that knowledge is welcomed by every subsequent generation.

A second important theological statement concerning God is his right to judge. The hymns present God as the holy and just judge, which is indicative of the way that he judges. According to the hymns, the length of his judgment is forever, and the results are disastrous for the wicked. However, God is praised in the seventh worship scene, because the nations worship him as a result of the judgment. This worship indicates the persuasive nature of God's wrath.

Christology is another major theological element of the hymns. Christology is elaborated in terms of the slaughtered Lamb. The death of Jesus, rather than his life or ministry, is the primary focus of John's Christology. As indicated in the hymns, Jesus' slaughter results in the redemption of people for God, and his death is the means by which believers overcome. The second worship scene indicates Jesus being worshipped in the same way as God, which implies that Jesus is just as worthy to receive praise. His worthiness is specifically related to his death on the cross.

The human response of overcoming is a fourth theological feature of the hymns. Overcoming is detailed in the sixth worship scene. In this hymn, believers are said to overcome by the blood of the Lamb, by the word of their testimony, and by their commitment until death. This brief elaboration indicates that overcoming is nothing short of remaining faithful to the testimony of Christ for the duration of one's life.

REFLECTING ON REVELATION'S THEOLOGY

The question still remains, "What is the purpose of the hymns of the Revelation?" Did John have a particular reason for using the hymns? Do the hymns have rhetorical purpose? One of the inescapable conclusions from an analysis of the hymns is that hymns are loaded with theological content. Although space does not allow a comparison between the theology of the hymns and the theology of the whole book, one would expect that further study would confirm the link between the two.

A quick look at the theological development of the sovereignty of God in the whole book can serve as a good example. The theme of God's sovereignty is by far the most frequent theme in the entire book and the most frequent theme in the hymns. The sovereignty of God and Jesus is developed in the titles given for each in the first chapter. In chapters two and three, Jesus' ability to assess the churches and carry out promises to them emphasize his sovereignty. In the worship scenes of Rev 4–5, God's sovereignty is emphasized by his position of control before the description of the judgment to come. Jesus' sovereignty is emphasized in his worthiness to open the seals. The sovereignty of God is displayed in the Judgment Cycle of Rev 6–19, because he is in total control of the commencement, outpouring, purpose, length, and effects of judgment. God's sovereignty also is assumed in the last part of Revelation simply by the consummation of his kingdom.

After analyzing the theological content of the hymns of the worship scenes in Revelation and developing a theology of the whole book, the first conclusion is that a summary relationship exists between the theology of the hymns and the whole book. John used these hymns deliberately and with careful calculation and placement that reveal significant purposes. These purposes potentially are unlimited, but include brevity of expression, elaboration of themes, and encouragement of believers. Though the book poses interpretive problems because of apocalyptic imagery and symbolism not easily ascertained by the modern reader, the hymns are an easier literary window through which to study Revelation's theological impact.

Second, the summary relationship between the theology of the hymns and that of the whole book implies that John intended to frame the main focus of this theology in a literary unit that would continue to be used by the church. By continued use of these hymns, the church would learn these most important theological concepts. One of the greatest examples in the Western church is Handel's famous oratorio, "Messiah," whose "Hallelujah" chorus is inspired by two of Revelation's worship scenes.[12]

Finally, John provided his audience that essential encouragement to persevere to the end in these hymns—an understood Biblical use of hymns for the church.[13] As a contemporary hymn writer concludes, "If you know what hymns a person loves most, or what hymns a congregation is most addicted to, you will be able to infer what, in Christianity, means most to that person or that church."[14]

---

12. Worship scenes 5 and 7 (Rev 11:15; 19:6, 16).

13. See Eph 5:19.

14. Routley, *Christian Hymns Observed*, 3.

QUESTIONS FOR REFLECTION

- G. K. Beale in his commentary on Revelation says, "the main idea of the Apocalypse could be roughly formulated as follows: the sovereignty of God and Christ in redeeming and judging brings them glory, which is intended to motivate saints to worship God and reflect his glorious attributes through obedience to his word."[15] If Beale is correct, what part of this main idea is found in the hymns of Revelation?

- In what ways specifically do the hymns indicate God's sovereignty?

- Make a list of the theological ideas expressed in the hymns of Revelation. Rank the importance of these ideas. How do these ideas correlate with others in the book of Revelation?

- If you have access to commentaries on Revelation, compare and contrast what authors declare as the overall theological message of the book with the theological statements contained in the hymns. To what degree do you agree that the theology of Revelation is summarized by the hymns of Revelation?

- Share an occasion in your personal experience in which a hymn or praise song had a significant impact on your worship experience. What were the reasons or circumstances for this memorable experience?

- Identify specific ways the worship scenes of Revelation could impact contemporary worship today.

15. Beale, *The Book of Revelation*, 174.

4

Blessed Are the Peacemakers

The Theology of Peace in the Book of Revelation

Sylvie T. Raquel

INTRODUCTION

THE BOOK OF REVELATION continues to puzzle Christians and non-Christians alike and challenges the peace-loving Christian. Its most intriguing character, Jesus, appears as a priestly figure bringing judgment on seven churches (Rev 1), a slain lamb unleashing plagues on earth (Rev 5, 6), and a fearsome warrior thirsty for the blood of his enemies (Rev 19), or so it seems. These portraits of Christ look foreign to the Gospels' account of Jesus. The message of the book also seems distant from Jesus' message of peace. Indeed, many believe that Revelation justifies violence for implementing God's justice on earth. How can one reconcile the Gospels and Revelation's portraiture of Christ? As Bredin showed, two responses emerge.[1] First, Revelation legitimizes a call for vengeance against the oppressor; the believer is not asked to kill but hope that God will slaughter the believer's enemies. The second response focuses on the image of the slain Lamb, therefore on the Gospels' message; Revelation confronts yet seeks the conversion rather than the destruction of God's enemies.

---

1. Bredin, *Jesus, Revolutionary of Peace*, 25.

If the Jesus of the Gospels and the Christ of Revelation cannot be reconciled, Christians end up with either a schizophrenic Savior or a schizophrenic church. Since Jesus promoted in his life and teaching a message of peace and reconciliation,[2] the cosmic Christ of Revelation must follow this premise. The general consensus of early Christianity was to interpret the whole Bible in light of Jesus' law of love.[3] Indeed, the New Testament writers and early Church Fathers promoted peace and non-violence as an expression of their commitment to Christ.[4] The most prolific and prominent early Church Fathers accepted Revelation as canonical.[5] The Apocalypse fit into their theology. Therefore, one must strive to rediscover the elements of peace in this complex work. How strongly is the theology of peace substantiated in the Apocalypse? Are God's people in the book called to be a band of warriors or an assembly of priests? Is Christ a vengeful Lord or the agent of good news? Does God's justice require violence? This article will attempt to answer these questions.

Chapter 1 sets the tone of the book. John is about to unveil a word from Jesus to the churches. He first declares a state of emergency: things "must soon take place" and "the time is near." John sounds the trumpet to gather his people by formulating a blessing for those who read, listen

2. Raquel, "Perspectives on a Biblical Theology of Peace," 84–86.

3. Ibid., 78.

4. Clement of Rome (ca. C.E. 95) prayed for peace in all the world (*To the Corinthians* 19). For Ignatius of Antioch (c. 110), "Nothing [was] more precious than peace" (*To the Ephesians* 13). Justin Martyr (ca. 150) also defended nonviolence and advocated martyrdom over resistance (*First Apology* 34). Clement of Alexandria (ca. 150–215) called Christians a peaceful race (*The Instructor* 1.12). Irenaeus (ca. 180) declared that Christian nations used their swords for peaceful purposes (*Against Heresies* 4.34, Logos). For Tertullian (ca. 155–240), Christians could not carry the sword without violating the teachings of Jesus (*Apology* 30). Athenagoras (2nd c.) proclaimed that Christians detested cruelty in any forms (*Plea for Christians* 35). Origen (ca. 185–254) proclaimed that Christians fought their enemies by prayer to God (*Against Celsus* 3.7; 8.73–75, Logos). Ambrose (ca. 339–397) insisted on justice and compassion in the conduct of war (Holmes, *War and Christian Ethics*, 55). Augustine (354–430) recognized that war should be waged only as a necessity for the obtaining or preserving of peace (*Letter* 189.6).

5. By the second century, the Western Fathers embraced the book of Revelation, although the church was more restrictive in its process of canonization. The Eastern Church, on the other hand, debated its canonicity for at least two more centuries. Eusebius recorded this dilemma and listed Revelation as part of the books agreed upon and also part of the absurd and impious writings.

to, and take the account to heart. He boosts the morale of the troops by exalting Jesus as the supreme commander over all powers, even death. Christ is the faithful witness (v. 5) who has been pierced (v. 7) but rose from the dead (v. 5) and consequently was given authority over the kings of the earth (v. 5). Nothing is to be feared and victory is assured. So far, this "pep rally" uses much war rhetoric. As commander in chief, is Jesus not given military authority? Is he not preparing for an attack? John's subsequent depictions of Christ qualified his message: Jesus is the priest of priests (the faithful witness, Rev 1), the ultimate sacrifice (pierced in Rev 1, the slaughtered lamb in Rev 5) that brought life and victory (the lion of Judah of Rev 5), the almighty (the victorious rider of Rev 19). This is the story of the Gospels in a nutshell. So, what kind of battle were God's people preparing?

THE CHURCH AS PEACEMAKING INSTRUMENT

God's People in Revelation

John's Apocalypse served as a circular letter to seven congregations.[6] Each church would become aware of the warnings and blessings of the other six. Therefore, the purpose of the revelation was preventive as much as curative. All seven letters displayed the exact same literary structure: a positive account of the churches' performance, an assessment of their negative deeds, an exhortation to repent, attached to a promise, and a prophetic summation. What is of interest for the purpose of this article is the content of the commendations and rebukes because they mirror the activity of God's people.

Jesus commends the deeds and steadfastness of six congregations. Although the church of Ephesus endured hardships from evil men and false prophets, its members continued to work hard for Jesus' sake. The church of Smyrna already suffered economic pressure and was about to experience more tribulation. The church of Pergamum remained faithful to its Lord despite the death of one of its members. The church of Thyatira also persevered in deeds, love, and faith and gained spiritual strength. The church of Sardis gained a great reputation for its works. The church of Philadelphia was overpowered by those of "the synagogue of Satan." Yet, little Philadelphia remained faithful and did not deny Jesus'

---

6. Reddish, *Revelation*, 40.

name. The church of Laodicea is the only one that did not receive positive comments. In summary, all six communities persevered in faithful witnessing when facing various types of social, religious, or economic pressure, perhaps persecution.

Five of those assemblies received a word of rebuke. Smyrna and Philadelphia, the two congregations that are only commended, faced or will face stronger times of tribulation because of their testimony. The church of Ephesus lost its compassion for one another and for the "outsiders." The church of Pergamum allowed two groups of false teachers to flourish in their midst and did not have the courage to reprimand them. The church of Thyatira was divided; some remained faithful to Jesus while others tolerated and followed the immoral and idolatrous practices of a false prophetess. The church of Sardis did not produce worthy deeds and was already labeled as spiritually dead. Finally, the church of Laodicea, like Sardis, was satisfied with its status but lost its effectiveness in the community. In summary, the churches were reprimanded for four reasons: (1) a lack of church discipline that allowed false teachings to infiltrate some assemblies; (2) a lack of zeal for evangelism; (3) a lack of fervor in service to God and one another; or (4) an inclination toward apostasy.

The rest of Revelation emphasizes the testimonial involvement of God's people. In chapter 6, the faithful are slain because of the word of God and the testimony they have maintained. This testimony has the power to defeat the accuser (Satan) and his angels (Rev 12). Some were imprisoned; others died as a witness to their endurance and faith (Rev 7, 13). A special group is redeemed from the earth because they have remained undefiled, i.e., faithful (Rev 14). In chapter 16, God avenges the martyrs of the faith. The blood of God's saints and prophets inebriated Babylon, the mother of the prostitutes who slaughtered them (Rev 17:6; 18:24). Chapter 19 is a summary of the essence of prophecy that gives witness to Jesus. Although the book confuses the reader with its heaven/earth and past/present/future roller-coaster motion, one component remains: throughout time and circumstances, the church testifies and suffers as a consequence of its witness, even to the point of death. As a result, God's people are enthroned, reign with God, and serve Him as priests.

So far, God's people testify of the Word of God, worship God, pray, prophesy, endure, remain faithful, and do not compromise. As a response, they are slain, accused, killed, imprisoned, and even slaughtered. The book is not clear how they responded to the false prophets, but a fair assumption is that they ventured in debates, possibly verbal contentions, but not physical altercations. The only hostility they show toward their enemies is to ask God to avenge them and rejoice when he does. The overall picture depicts a people group who were persecuted or perceived to be so.[7] John was trying to regroup and encourage the communities to stand fast. Witnessing, not dying, was the goal he sought out for them.[8] Michael Cooper gave a recent example of how the wrong perception of worldview can bring disputatious relationships between two people groups and lead to violence, even war.[9] In the same way, perceived persecution can lead people to react negatively and draw aggression unto themselves.[10] The tension between the churches of Rev 2–3 and the "outsiders" possibly may have been the result of such mutual misunderstanding. To establish whether God's people in Revelation engaged in violence in any form or fashion, either privately or collectively, one has to determine what their witnessing and testifying encompassed. Did they participate only in verbal exchanges with the "outsiders" or did they engage in incarnational evidential evangelism that led to brutality? Did they face a real or perceived persecution?

Their Environment

Based on works by Thompson and Jones, who argued that Domitian was not a tyrant,[11] Mark Bredin claims that no clear evidence exists for a full-fledged persecution of Christians at the time of the Apocalypse.[12] However, even if the emperor was not a despot, he still imposed social and economic pressures that could have been perceived as persecution. Suetonius mentioned that several intrigues during Domitian's reign led the emperor to develop paranoia.[13] He became inconsistent, greedy, and

---

7. See A. Collins, *Crisis and Catharsis*.

8. Blount, *Can I Get a Witness*, x.

9. Cooper, "Necessity of Worldview Understanding."

10. Heller, "Psychological Perspectives on Peace."

11. Bredin, *Jesus, Revolutionary of Peace*, 105.

12. Ibid., 125.

13. Suetonius *Dom.* 12.

cruel.[14] Domitian's spirit of distrust increased with unrest in Asia Minor. Other early writers detected evidence for some type of persecution of the churches in Asia Minor.[15]

FIGURE 7. Colossal Flavian Statue at Ephesus. Recovered from the ruins at ancient Ephesus are the only surviving pieces of a colossal Flavian statue of either Titus or Domitian set up in the Imperial Temple as part of the emperor cult in that city. A normal size person standing next to this display would reach to the bottom of the statue's chin (photograph by Gerald L. Stevens).

14. Suetonius *Dom.* 3.

15. Melito, bishop of Sardis (ca. 170), mentioned that since Domitian's reign, Christians had been falsely accused (Eusebius *H.E.* 4.26.9). Tertullian and Eusebius indicated that Domitian showed cruelty toward Christians (Tertullian *Apology* 5; Eusebius *H.E.* 3.17; 20.9). Pliny's letter to Trajan mentioned that some Christians had abandoned the faith up to twenty-five years earlier—during Domitian's rule (*Ep. Tra.* 96). Other external evidences point to sporadic/localized persecution: Clement spoke of calamities befallen on Christians (*1 Clem.* 1:1, Holmes, *Apostolic Fathers*); Claudius's edict forbade Jews from showing contempt of other faiths (Josephus *Ant.* 19.5.3). Internal evidence also indicates the presence of persecution: Antipas died for his faith; the saints are slaughtered (Rev 6:9–11). Paul's letters and Acts also show how local synagogues violently resisted the Christian missionary movement (see 2 Cor); the material in 1 Peter and Hebrews clearly evokes a persecution background.

FIGURE 8. Temple of Domitian at Ephesus. These are the only surviving ruins of the Temple of Domitian in ancient Ephesus. The brick arches into the hillside actually formed part of the supporting structure of the temple's expansive foundation. The Ephesians prided themselves in being one of the official "temple wardens" (*neokoroi*) of Asia Minor, a city hosting a provincial imperial cult[16] (photograph by Gerald L. Stevens).

Beale and Witherington have challenged the perspective of no Domitianic persecution, asserting such a view needs revision.[17] If "Christians were not persecuted as Christians,"[18] they were victimized for other reasons, e.g. for being traitors or anti-social. In light of Domitian's atmosphere of suspicion, both Gentile and Jewish Christians were viewed as traitors for two reasons: (1) they did not participate in the Emperor cult, and (2) they did not pay the Jewish tax. The imperial cult was popular in Asia Minor, particularly in the cities of the seven churches.[19] Sacrifices were offered to or on behalf of the emperor. Most

16. [Ed.] For more information on this important *neokoros* city title, see Burrell, *Neokoroi*. A helpful blog on this and related topics, called "Religions of the Ancient Mediterranean," and maintained by Phil Harland of York University, Toronto, is located at http://www.philipharland.com/Blog/category/greco-roman-religions/emperor-worship.

17. Beale, *The Book of Revelation*; Witherington, *Revelation*.

18. Heemstra, *Rome's Administration of the Fiscus Judaicus*, 116.

19. Price, *Rituals and Power*.

Christians refused to engage in such idolatrous rituals, but this refusal to pay homage to the emperor was considered a symbolic gesture of protest toward the imperial religion. As the church challenged the claim of a divinely ordained empire, the suspect community was labeled as traitor. This labeling may have caused some to become apostates or to compromise with polytheism.[20]

Concerning the Jewish tax, Domitian wrote an edict widening its practicality for people who escaped the levy on the technicality of its terms:[21] (1) people who did not profess Judaism but lived a Jewish life, and (2) people who dissimulated their Jewish origin. Gentile and Jewish Christians fit both categories. As Bredin notes, the tax was a public humiliation because the levy showed subjugation to Rome, fed the emperor cult, and was a financial burden.[22] Gentile Christians evaded the tax by following the decision of the Jerusalem Council (Acts 15). They did not have to convert to Judaism but only abide by its ethics. In the same way, Jewish Christians no longer had to participate in the ritualistic Jewish tradition. For the governing authorities, this absence of public confession was connected to the desire of not paying the tax. Conversely, most Jews were willing to compromise with Rome for lucrative purposes.[23] Some Jews even gloried in being able to pay a tax that showed their affluence. They perceived Jewish Christians as antisocial and a threat to their economic well-being.

Christian Response

How did Christians respond to these accusations? Blount believes that John was asking his readers to adopt an active, non-violent resistance.[24]

20. Heemstra agrees with Hemer that "identification with pagan society . . . was most probably a way out for non-Jewish Christians under the pressure of persecution. This would lead to their apostasy" (*Rome's Administration of the Fiscus Judaicus*, 134).

21. The Jewish tax was introduced by Vespasian: "He [Vespasian] imposed a poll-tax of two drachmas, to be paid annually into the Capitol as formerly contributed by them to the temple at Jerusalem" (Josephus *J.W.* 7.6.6). Under Domitian: "Besides other taxes, that on the Jews was levied with the utmost rigour, and those were prosecuted who without publicly acknowledging that faith yet lived as Jews, as well as those who concealed their origin and did not pay the tribute levied upon their people" (Suetonius *Dom.* 12.2).

22. Bredin, *Jesus, Revolutionary of Peace*, 113.

23. Asia Minor was a wealthy province and the Jews needed to keep the trade up to be able to earn money.

24. Blount, *Can I Get a Witness*, 39.

The word *martys* (μάρτυς, the Greek root for the words "witness," "testimony," or "testify") is an active word that indicates an "active engagement, not sacrificial passivity."[25] Blount parallels this approach with the emergence of the black churches at the time of slavery. Any expression of unauthorized worship by slaves was an expression of resistance and political defiance.[26] Eventually, the gatherings led to the establishment of religious doctrine that challenged the political order. In a sense, the black churches "provided the ideological and theological underpinning for the [civil rights] movement."[27] For Blount, "John was interested not so much in creating a church of martyrs as he was encouraging a church filled with people committed to the ethical activity of witnessing to the lordship of Jesus Christ . . . It was a highly social, economic, and political [act] . . . John was asking his people to pick a social and religious fight."[28] Bredin also sees the nature of Revelation as "political and anti-Domitian, rather than concerned with religious sensibilities."[29] John presented the church as the challenger.

Were the hearers and readers of Revelation called to political defiance, religious provocation, or theological challenge? Although Jesus' followers jeopardized the interests and social standing of the Roman Empire and the synagogue,[30] these followers mainly challenged any obstacles to worshipping the one true God. If the book of Revelation was read as a call for resistance, that call was more than a political manifesto. John's message was christologically centered.[31] The picture of the slaughtered lamb in chapter 5 is the homeopathic medicine to enthuse the churches' confidence in and faithfulness to Christ.[32] As in 1 Peter, Revelation "holds up the suffering of Christ as a paradigm for Christian faithfulness (1 Pet. 2:21, 23; 3:17–18)."[33] The picture of the slaughtered

25. Ibid., 47.

26. Ibid., 54.

27. Ibid., 43.

28. Ibid., ix.

29. Bredin, *Jesus, Revolutionary of Peace*, 125.

30. Ibid., 55.

31. See Stevens's essay, "A Vision in the Night," in the present volume.

32. Blount explains: "The slaughtered lamb is . . . the prototypical witness figure, who models the ethic of confrontation . . . God deploys the violently slaughtered lamb as a homeopathic cure for the very violence that slaughtered him and now threatens those who follow him" (*Can I Get a Witness*, x).

33. Hays, *The Moral Vision of the New Testament*, 332.

people in Rev 6:9–11 may be a "visceral call for prophetic engagement" that can "shore up and ignite a furious and active resolve,"[34] but in light of Rev 5, the message inspires a religious wonder and gives an eternal and cosmic dimension to the churches' stand. Revelation's word articulates a crucicentric call for a christocentric liberation.

Blount asks, "Were they working for this liberation through their suffering, or were they witnessing so actively for this liberation that suffering was bound to occur?[35] This question presents a false dichotomy. The pivotal verse to understand the impact of faithful witness (Rev 12:11) includes both facets: "They conquered [the dragon] by the blood of the Lamb and by the word of their testimony since they did not cling to life in the face of death." Christ, their ultimate example, won the victory and brought spiritual freedom to all human beings through his death and resurrection.[36] On one hand, the religious, political, or social pressure and ostracism the Asian Christians experienced served for the advancement of the gospel as their case was seen and heard in the larger community; on the other hand, the gospel advance intensified their accusers' zeal.[37] John did not call for political liberation but for spiritual victory in spite of and through suffering.[38]

The Asian Christians' theological challenge may have had social implications, yet the goal was heavenly. Revelation more than any other New Testament text "depicts a symbolic world in which the real struggle is not against flesh and blood, in which the only weapons that the church wields are faith and the Word of God. . . . The power of violence is the illusory power of the beast, which is unmasked by the faithful testimony of the saints."[39] Revelation's saints did not engage in retaliation, fighting, war, or in passive passivism, just awaiting to be slaughtered, but in what Clifford Williams called active passivism, acting as a prophetic voice

---

34. Blount, *Can I Get a Witness*, 53.

35. Ibid., 45.

36. See Phil 2:5–11.

37. The word *martys* bears a forensic meaning. Jesus himself said in John 16:2: "A time is coming when anyone who kills you will think he is offering a service to God" (NIV).

38. Other New Testament passages speak of the Christian community being called to suffer and what its response to tribulation should be: Heb 10:32b–34; 1 Pet 1:6–7; 3:13–18; 4:12–19; 5:8–10.

39. Hays, *The Moral Vision of the New Testament*, 340.

against and on behalf of the society in which they lived.[40] Jesus' army was made up of priests unto God (Rev 1:6). The function of priests was not to wage war but to mediate the deity's blessing to the worshippers. God's people were not called to be a band of warriors but an assembly of priests bringing a message of reconciliation and peace to the world by the testimony of their life and the word they share.

JESUS AS PEACEMAKER IN REVELATION

Mark Bredin develops a non-violent Christology in the book of Revelation. However, he sees Jesus more as a political figure, a new type of Guevara whose purpose is to challenge the oppressing political power, although his weapons are love, martyrdom, and non-violence. Revelation may be one of the most political books of antiquity, yet John's main purpose was again more theological than political.

The Priest

In chapter 1, John first described Jesus as "clothed in a robe reaching to his feet, and girded across his chest with a golden sash." This attire was reserved to priests.[41] The king of kings is first and foremost the priest of priests who leads, advises, absolves, teaches, sanctifies, and intercedes for his people. Jesus stands in the midst of the churches, assuring them of his constant presence, and he holds them in his hands, assuring them of his steadfast intercession, care, and control over any situation. His only "weapons" are: (1) the seven stars which are the seven messengers of the churches, and (2) the double-edged sword that comes out of his mouth. Those messengers can represent angelic beings, the leaders of the communities, the churches themselves, or, most likely, the heavenly counterpart to the churches' earthly reality.[42] The double-edged sword symbolizes the Word of God that either can bring life to those who abide by its commands, or destruction to those who refuse to respond to

40. Williams, "A Philosopher's Reflections," 97–98.

41. On this debated point, see the essay in this volume by Stevens, "One Like a Son of Man." Also, Delebecque, *L'Apocalypse de Jean,* 164; Mounce, *The Book of Revelation* (1997), 56–58.

42. For angelic beings representative of the church: Beale, *The Book of Revelation,* 218; for bishops of local communities: Manns, "L'Évêque, ange de l'Église," 176–80; for the congregations: Reddish, *Revelation,* 42; for the heavenly dimension of the churches, see Beasley-Murray, "Revelation," NBC, 1427 and Resseguie, *The Revelation of John,* 81.

the truth of its message.[43] Neither one of those weapons describe lethal instruments.

The realm of Christ's dominion is clearly spiritual.[44] His source of power and authority is that he was dead and is alive forevermore (1:5–6). He was found worthy to receive power and riches and wisdom and might and honor and glory and blessing (Rev 5:12). As a result, he received the keys of death and Hades. Hence, John disclosed the mission: Jesus is not rallying his troops to engage into battle against people but to participate in a quest to lock both death and Hades forever. The strategy is to engage in faithful witnessing.

The Lamb That Roars

The other two descriptions of Christ challenge Revelation's theology of peace because they contrast drastically with the Gospels' portrayal of Jesus. Two of his deeds and sayings also are problematic because they seem to contradict the message of peace and reconciliation underlined in the Gospels. In Rev 5, Jesus is portrayed as a Lion and a Lamb with seven horns and seven eyes.[45] The main problem is that the creature opens the seals that unleashed war, terror, famine, and devastation on earth (Rev 6). What happened to the humble, innocent sacrificial lamb that John portrayed in his Gospel? More so, at the end of the fifth seal, the Lion-Lamb announced that the calamities will not stop until the number of martyrs is complete. Why would God allow his people to suffer even if he promises to vindicate them (Rev 7)?

The Lamb purchased for God, with its blood, people from every tribe and tongue and nation (Rev 5:9–10). The picture of the Lion and horned-Lamb does not evoke ferociousness and aggressiveness but nobility and assertiveness. The Lamb expresses the means of atonement while the Lion symbolizes the goal of reconciliation. The sacrifice of the Lamb is its power and strength. The innocent one has become the vic-

---

43. Heb 4:12.

44. See the dialogue between Jesus and Pilate in John 18.

45. Jesus is called *arnion* (little lamb) 29 times in the entire book. (Frequency statistics are derived from Logos Bible Software.) The seven horns represent perfect power (omnipotence), the seven eyes perfect wisdom (omniscience), and the seven spirits in all the earth perfect presence (omnipresence). These are the attributes of God. The Lion of Judah refers to Gen 49:8–10 when Jacob made Judah the tribe of kings. Jesus is also called the Root of David in the same chapter of Rev 5, referring not to his humanity (root in David) but to his divinity (see Wiersbe, *The Bible Exposition Commentary*).

torious one. The victim has become the victor. The sacrifice has become the sacred one. Revelation does not support a sacrificial scapegoat interpretation of the slaughtered lamb. Victory has not come through war and conflicts but through a self-willed sacrifice, a calculated, resistant weakness.[46] Non-violence is extracted from violence and then set out as its antidote.[47] The claim is again spiritual.[48]

Why did the Lamb have to open the seals? Most commentators understand the breaking of the seals to represent, one way or another, the sentence and judgment of God poured out on earth, or the purpose and design of God.[49] With this type of interpretation, one hardly can escape envisioning Christ as a vengeful deity. So much for peace! The nature of the scroll may include "God's plan of redemption and judgment,"[50] but the written words on the scroll are conceivably not God's will or purpose, but the totality of all evil human acts. The scroll is written inside out,[51] filled to the fullest,[52] indicating that all possible evil deeds have been committed. Once the Lion-Lamb opened the scroll, all kinds of calamities spilled out. The breaking of the seals unleashed and revealed what the human race has brought to earth: conquest, war, famine, death, persecution. As a surgeon who carefully incises a wound to remove its infection, Christ breaks each seal to extract the ignominy of war, violence, pestilence, and persecution from the earth. The Lion-Lamb operates as a kinsman redeemer (Lev 25:25) who reclaimed the earth and brought new life through his own sacrifice. Therefore, he is not the author or the cause but the redeemer of all violence described in Rev 6.

46. Barr, "Towards an Ethical Reading of the Apocalypse," 361; Blount, *Can I Get a Witness?* 30.

47. Blount, *Can I Get a Witness?* 81.

48. Revelation contains 18 combat-oriented circumstances in which John uses the Lamb. Half of these occurrences are in proximity to the mention of God's throne.

49. The scroll has been interpreted to be: a book of redemption (Niles, *As Seeing the Invisible,* 55); the Old Testament (Prigent, *Apocalypse et Liturgie,* 46–79); a book containing events of the future great tribulation; a book containing God's plan of judgment and redemption (Beasley-Murray, "Revelation," 1434); the book of a testament to be understood against the legal background of Roman wills (Beale, *The Book of Revelation,* 340).

50. Beale, *The Book of Revelation,* 341.

51. Most commentators agree that the book is a scroll and not a codex.

52. Seven represents fullness in Revelation.

The Wrath of God and the Lamb

The twenty-four elders of Rev 11 declared that the time for God's wrath had come. The third angel of chapter 14 announced that the recipients of this wrath are those who worship the beast and its statue. They "will be tormented with fire and burning sulfur" in the presence of the angels and the Lamb.[53] The Lamb does not engage in coercive behavior but his passivity in the presence of this horrific spectacle looks repugnantly unjust. Furthermore, as the story unfolds, an angel comes out from the temple to harvest "the clusters of grapes into the winepress of God's wrath." Blood flowed 180 miles long and at a horse bridle's height (14:14). "The 'wrath of the Lamb' in Revelation . . . has been considered either as 'affective,' i.e. the personal attitude of God and the Lamb towards sinners, or 'effective,' i.e. impersonal and in no way an activity of God, but the calculable effect of certain behavior."[54]

The material in chapter 16 and following explains the cause of this wrath. God avenges the martyrs of the faith with "true and just" measures. "Babylon the great, mother of prostitutes and of the abominations of the earth" was drunk with their blood (Rev 17). In her immorality, adultery, and love for luxury, she even traded human life (Rev 18). The blood of the prophets was spilled in her streets and she slaughtered God's people. So, the cause of God's wrath is the escalation of the world's violence, immorality, and disregard for his instruction. "The gradual dissolution of the world is replicated in the mounting wickedness of the inhabitants of the world."[55] In a word, "God is fed up with human disregard of God's commands and beneficence and with the mistreatment of God's faithful clients."[56] In chapter 19, a vast crowd in heaven rejoiced because God had avenged the murder of his servants. For God, victims have rights, an idea Greek or Roman functionaries would have found incomprehen-

---

53. The beast is probably the one tormenting them.

54. Bredin, *Jesus, Revolutionary of Peace*, 194. He footnotes the following scholars: "Affective": Chilton (1990): 198; A. Collins (1979): 48–49 argues that it is the response to the cries of the martyrs for vengeance. "Effective": Dodd (1954): 23–24; A. Hanson (1957): 170; Hillyer (1967): 234; Mounce (1997): 162; Caird (1984): 91; Sweet (1979): 144; Harrington (1993): 96.

55. Malina, *The New Testament World* (2001), 239. He cites *Jub.* 23:13–15; Matt 24:5–12; 2 Tim 3:1–5; 2 Esd 6:24; and *2 Bar.* 48:32–38).

56. deSilva, *Seeing Things John's Way*, 210.

sible.[57] "It is Jesus' identification with victims and with those most likely to be scapegoated that is the key criterion for judgment."[58]

If Revelation clearly states the cause of God's wrath, the book does not articulate its content precisely. Is that wrath the ceasing of mercy and forgiveness? If so, is God unfair to humanity? Can he not redeem all people? Ladd would give a negative answer; Revelation simply presents no repentance of the wicked.[59] Although warned over and over, the wicked will refuse to comply with common sense and will continue in self-destructive behavior. They will be caught up "in their own spiral of conflict and violence."[60] As Schillebeeckx explains, "God does not take vengeance; he leaves evil to its own."[61]

The Rider

At first glance, Rev 19 also includes troublesome pictures. Jesus appears as a bloodthirsty ruler who delights in the blood of his enemies.[62] After all, the glorious picture of Christ riding a white horse alludes to the Roman emperor's triumphal entry upon his return from a successful campaign.[63] Robert Mounce believes that the iron scepter means destruction.[64] Yet, a scepter was not used for combat but for ruling. Therefore, the iron scepter indicates only the certainty of God's divine resolution. Fundamentally, the vision of the warrior-like figure can be understood only in light of the Lamb figure. First, the name of the rider is "Faithful and True." Throughout the entire book, faithfulness has been tied up with testifying to the Word of God, even to the point of death (1:9; 2:10, 13). Jesus is God's prime witness, not only through his life but also through his death and resurrection (Rev 1:9). The blood on his robe is his own.[65] His weapon is the sword of his mouth, already defined as

57. Heim, *Saved from Sacrifice*, 262.

58. Ibid., 266.

59. Ladd, *Revelation of John*, 28–29.

60. Heim, *Saved from Sacrifice*, 265.

61. Schillebeeckx, *The Church*, 138–39.

62. The rider makes war, strikes the nations with the sword coming out of his mouth, rules with an iron scepter, and treads the winepress of the fury of the wrath of God. An angel invites all the birds to eat the flesh of all people.

63. Suetonius *Dom.* 2; See Aune, *Revelation 17–22*, 1051.

64. Mounce, *The Book of Revelation* (1997), 355.

65. This is also the view of Delebecque, *L'Apocalypse de Jean*, 245 and Newport, *The Lion and the Lamb*, 287.

the Word of God;[66] "the phrase means "gospel," [or "good news,"] i.e., the Christian message of salvation."[67] Second, the rider makes war through justice (v. 11). Heim declared, "The description or prediction of an explosion of violence is not the same thing as a claim that God is the one who requires it. . . . A second distinction is the one between violence that is a disintegration of human factionalism and violence that is a war of cosmic revenge. And a third distinction is the difference between defining God's wrath as anger against violence and defining it as the righteous exercise of violence."[68]

Verse 19:19 unlocks the key to understanding the passage: the beast and the kings of the earth and their armies are the ones attacking Jesus and his army. The beast and its worshippers are confident of their victory as revealed in Rev 13:4 when they ask, "Who can make war against [the beast]?" John's answer to this rhetorical question is that Jesus, the true Messiah/King, can. Yet, "Christ does not actually engage in a physical destruction of God's enemies. Rather, he pronounces God's judgments against them."[69] Neither do his hosts participate actively in the slaughter.[70] "The army that overcame the beast by martyrdom (14.1–5) will now share Christ's final triumph."[71] The war of chapter 19 is really the final war between Christ and Satan and the ultimate defeat of the latter.

CONCLUSION

Revelation reveals that the violence of God's enemies will escalate toward his saints. The dissolution story identifies the direction in which their behavior is heading.[72] God has to operate as a surgeon and remove all human ignominy. In Revelation, God's people do not engage in battle and Christ does not initiate conflict. He is the priest of priests (Rev 1) who offered himself as sacrifice (Rev 5) to atone for the sins of all people and make a kingdom of his faithful followers (Rev 12). God's tactic is the

---

66.   Delebecque makes reference to Rev 1:16; 2:12, 16; 6:8; and 19:21.

67.   Aune, *Revelation 17–22*, 1058.

68.   Heim, *Saved from Sacrifice*, 265.

69.   Reddish, *Revelation*, 370.

70.   Keener, *Revelation*, 458.

71.   Ibid., 454.

72.   Malina and Pilch, *Social-Science Commentary on the Book of Revelation*, 238.

cross[73] and the persistent non-violent witness of his people. "The resurrection serves as God's decisive vindication of Jesus' authority to teach and guide the community."[74]

QUESTIONS FOR REFLECTION

- In light of Revelation's theology of the "faithful witness," how can the twenty-first century church be a non-violent resisting witness for Christ?

- What response can Christians expect to this kind of witness? Can you give actual examples known to you or current examples in the news or on the Internet? Can you find a YouTube video that would illustrate this point?

- How should this non-violent understanding of resistance affect the way we train children? For example, the book of Revelation has influenced many Christians with images of holy war. American children who grow up in Christian churches are raised at the cadence of "onward Christian soldiers," and "I'm in the Lord's army." Although such songs speak of spiritual battles, are children able to understand such a concept? Early childhood psychologists such as Piaget teach that children are concrete thinkers; they develop abstract ideas only later in life. Being brought up in the semantics of war, are children in our churches absorbing the rhetoric of retribution and vengefulness? Does this rhetoric faithfully represent the message of Revelation? What lyrics can Christians invent to teach children the concept of a priestly kingdom?

73. Heim wrote, "From the New Testament's point of view, the cross has changed the world. It has ended sacrifice, not in the sense that it can no longer happen, but in the sense that its viability is doomed" (*Saved from Sacrifice*, 264).

74. Hays, *The Moral Vision of the New Testament*, 322.

5

Women and Warriors

Character Development in John's Apocalypse

RENATE VIVEEN HOOD

INTRODUCTION

GREAT CHARACTERS MAKE GREAT movies. Who can forget the passionate tenacity of Erin Brockovich played by Julia Roberts in *Erin Brockovich* (2000) or the refined courage of Maximus played by Russell Crowe in *Gladiator* (2000)? These movies exemplify how actors in leading roles receive deeper character development and more resultant acclaim than actors in supporting roles. A movie would, however, not be the same without the supporting actors' roles. Each cast member uniquely captures the audience's attention and imagination as characters draw the audience into the movie's world. The audience cheers when crooked characters receive their due course. Emotions are felt when favorite characters are treated unjustly, achieve victories, or find that long-awaited love. Typically, people associate themselves with certain characters in the storyline based on factors such as their own life experiences, age, interests, gender, ethnicity, etc.

People associate themselves with characters in biblical literature as well. One thus may ask in what ways people respond to the characters in the Apocalypse of John. Do the readers' preconceptions, for example, affect the way in which they interpret the plot? How would a person traumatized by war experiences, for instance, respond to reading the Apocalypse? What about a person experiencing oppression from a harsh regime? Does such a person respond differently to the reading of the text than a person who enjoys a life of peace and freedom? Furthermore, do believers respond to the text differently than nonbelievers? One could expect anxiety among believers concerning a concept of martyrdom as a certain future for all faithful Christians.[1] In all, the reality of the ancient audience and the reader affect the response to characters in the Apocalypse.

The believers in the seven churches of Revelation identified with, and responded to, the major and minor characters in John's vision. However, the narrative, and thus the characters therein, does more than merely tell a story. As seen in many ancient apocalyptic communities, the narrative world in Revelation is one of sharp dichotomy—two realms existing side by side, the realm of God and the realm of Satan.[2] Each of the characters in the Apocalypse belongs to one of these realms.

READING THE APOCALYPSE AS A NARRATIVE

When reading Revelation from a narrative perspective, the viewpoint with which the text is engaged and the viewpoint which the text wishes for the reader to embrace work together. The viewpoint of the text is discussed first. When considering this viewpoint, one must realize that, much like moviemakers, story writers sometimes attempt to exert influence over their audience.[3] One therefore might ask what ideological or theological perspective John wanted the reader (hearer) to assume.[4]

---

1. The story of Revelation has in its plotline martyrdom as the destiny of all faithful Christians. However, as Bauckham notes, "The message of the book is that if Christians are faithful to their calling to bear witness to the truth against the claim of the beast, they will provide a conflict with the beast so critical as to be a struggle to the death" (*The Theology of the Book of Revelation*, 93).

2. Duff, *Who Rides the Beast*, 75. For an introduction to ancient apocalyptic literature see for example Reddish, *Apocalyptic Literature* and J. Collins, *The Apocalyptic Imagination*.

3. Two helpful resources for reading Revelation as a narrative include Resseguie's *The Revelation of John* in which Resseguie discusses the role of the author and implied author, and Barr's *Tales of the End* in which Barr discusses the reader and the implied reader.

4. Resseguie, *The Revelation of John*, 11.

FIGURE 9. Terracotta Masks. These terracotta masks from the 3rd century C.E. are evocative of theatrical character roles. Character masks used in the ancient stage indicate the keen awareness the ancient audience had toward characters and their development in a story, including the impact on the audience's thoughts and emotions, as well as the movement of the plot (photograph by Gerald L. Stevens).

Throughout the story of Revelation, characters and images play on the emotions, hopes, and conceptual worlds of John's contemporaries. John uses these points of connection with the audience to convey a prophetic message for the Christian community. These specific points of connection with the audience restrain the interpretation of symbols. The images and symbols in the Revelation story find their connections in the "real" world in first-century Asia Minor. However, these images and symbols, along with the characters in the story, are not detailed literary descriptions found in the landscape of the apocalyptic world of the seven churches. Rather, all elements of the story are part of the larger plot and, as Bauckham asserts, "must be read for their theological meaning and their power to evoke response."[5]

The narrative of Revelation goes beyond apocalyptic and includes rich rhetorical overtones.[6] The narrative induces a response and seeks to

---

5. Bauckham, *Theology of the Book of Revelation*, 20.
6. See deSilva, *Seeing Things John's Way*; and Witherington, *Revelation*.

persuade. Plot movement[7] and character placement are instrumental in these rhetorical endeavors. This apocalyptic narrative choice of genre for Revelation may seem peculiar from a twenty-first century perspective. For a target audience familiar with apocalyptic literature, however, conveying a narrative with apocalyptic imagery may just gain the hearing of those who otherwise might have little interest in the message.[8] An analysis of character development will prove helpful in determining how John's apocalypse seeks to spur on the reader.

Character Development in the Apocalypse

A character does not necessarily need to speak or speak often to impact the storyline.[9] For example, God speaks infrequently in Revelation. His voice is noted at the beginning and at the end of Revelation (1:8; 21:5–8), making the character placement highly effective as God's presence is noted everywhere in the narrative. Character placement at times may seem unstructured in narratives. The narrative of Revelation, for example, may appear like a series of detached units. Yet so-called "carried-over characters,"[10] in different parts of the plot contribute to the unity of the story. Tracing various main characters throughout Revelation will provide insight into their contributions to the narrative.

Main characters in Revelation include various witnesses, warriors, and women. These figures of witnesses, warriors, and women range from the divine to the diabolic, from flesh and blood to the deeply metaphorical. The witnesses include John (1:1–2), Jesus Christ, the faithful witness (1:5; 3:14; 19:11), Antipas (2:13), two witnesses who prophesy (11:3), and martyrs for Christ (17:6). The warriors are characters who belong to either one of two realms—the realm of God or the realm of Satan. These warriors include: the Lion of the tribe of Judah who has conquered (5:5), a conquering warrior on a white horse (6:2), a red

---

7. Barr discusses plot movement in Revelation, "The Story John Told," 11–23.

8. Duff, *Who Rides the Beast*, 72.

9. Resseguie, *The Revelation of John*, 39.

10. Barr, "The Story John Told," 19–20. A carried-over character is a character that reemerges in a different part of the narrative in which the character redirects the plot by emphasizing a different aspect of the character. For example, the Lamb in Rev 14 underscores the idea of readiness for a holy war, whereas the same Lamb reappears in Rev 19 as the one who will marry in the postwar victory celebration. The events in chapters 14 and 19 are connected by the character of the Lamb.

dragon whose tail swept away a third of the stars (12:4), a male child
who is to rule (12:5), Michael who waged war with the dragon (12:7),
the beast out of the sea (13:1–7), the Lamb with his followers (14:1),
the King of kings (19:11–16), and Satan (20:7–8). Among the characters
designated as female, who belong to either one of the two realms as well,
are: Jezebel (2:20), a woman clothed with the sun (12:1), the earth helping the woman (12:16), great Babylon (16:19), the great whore (17:1–6),
the bride of the Lamb (19:7), and New Jerusalem (21:2, 9–11).

Character development of warriors and women not only is dualistic in terms of their affinity either with the realm of God or the realm
of Satan, but also is dichotomous in regard to gender roles. All warriors
are described in male terms. However, some scholars suggest that the
woman in Rev 17 is dressed in military garb and thus embodies the distinctive features of a warrior—a female warrior.[11] Indeed, iconography
of the goddess Roma often is associated with Rev 17 and traditionally
shows a female in military tunic. However, the sheer dress of the goddess does not suggest that she is a warrior. Rather, as a divine patron
of the military she protects the warriors. Her army-like representation
functions as mere association. As part of the cult of Roma in Asia Minor,
Roma represented the power of Rome and facilitated worship.[12]

Female characters, as opposed to male warriors, are depicted with
stereotypical female qualities. Certain scholars consider the character
descriptions of the positive female characters in the story as problematic
as the negative portrayal of some female characters in the text. Pippin
and Kim, for example, recognize misogyny—a hatred of women—in
Revelation.[13] Concerning the portrayal of women in Revelation, Pippin
writes, "The making of archetypes of the female and the abuse of women's

11. This observation rests solely on ekphratic evidence, which is the understanding that images on art (including coins) of the time are conveyed in literary works. In
the case of Rev 17, the image is found on coins in circulation during the production
and reception of the Apocalypse. This image then would have been taken from statues
and other items of art. (For an extensive discussion concerning ekphrasis see Aune,
Revelation 17–22, 923–28.) Images on coins recovered show the goddess Roma seated
on seven hills with her toe touching the waters (17:1, 9). Hylen insists that the person
depicted actually is a male warrior ("The Power and Problem of Revelation 18," 215).
DeSilva refutes this argument and points out that the person's garment has an extra fold
over the girdle around the breasts, attesting to a woman's chest (deSilva, *Seeing Things
John's Way*, 204).

12. Price, *Rituals and Power*, 24, 40–43.

13. Kim, "Uncovering Her Wickedness," 61; Pippin, *Death and Desire*, 47.

bodies reveal a deep misogyny. Misogyny in the end of the twentieth century may be more technologically advanced, but the roots and results of woman-hatred are the same."[14] Other Revelation scholars, such as Elizabeth Schüssler Fiorenza and Adela Yarbro Collins, have a more positive outlook on the portrayal of female figures in the Apocalypse. However, Schüssler Fiorenza does concur with Pippin that Revelation, "engages the imagination of the contemporary reader to perceive women in terms of good or evil, pure or impure, heavenly or destructive, helpless or powerful, bride or temptress, wife or whore."[15] Indeed, as these characters are developed in Revelation, the question arises, "How are women to respond to the Apocalypse?"[16] Does a twenty-first century female read the text differently than a twenty-first century male? Moreover, does character placement play a role in the response of the reader? The significance of the characters in the Apocalypse is seen in their placement in the narrative.

Character Placement in the Apocalypse

The characters in the Apocalypse are situated both symmetrically and linguistically.[17] Besides using "carried-over characters," John employed corresponding qualities of characters as a device to unite various characters.[18] Thus, positive characters have qualities that correlate to God's attributes and negative characters have qualities that correspond to Satan's attributes. However, this concept of corresponding qualities at times is utilized literarily as well to signify equivalence of character qualities.[19] The use of these corresponding character qualities both to contrast and to signify equivalence is observed in the character placement of warriors and women in the Apocalypse.

With regard to the main four women in the story—Jezebel, the woman clothed with the sun, the great whore, and the bride—most scholars argue for the centrality of the woman with the sun.[20] Strategic

14. Pippin, *Death and Desire*, 53.

15. Schüssler Fiorenza, "Babylon the Great," 199.

16. Pippin, *Death and Desire*, 47. For a detailed treatment of gender concerns in the context of politics in Rev 17 and 18, see Schüssler Fiorenza, "Babylon the Great."

17. Duff, *Who Rides the Beast?* 84.

18. Thompson, *The Book of Revelation*, 78.

19. Duff, *Who Rides the Beast*, 76–79.

20. See for example: Beale, *The Book of Revelation* and Osborne, *Revelation*. Duff,

rhetorical patterns are observed. Rossing notes a two-women character placement,[21] where one woman first is introduced and described (Jezebel) and later a bride.[22] Metaphorical main female figures likewise appear as women character placements. These strategic placements inform authorial intent. Contrasts and comparisons in the character placements of Jezebel and the woman clothed with the sun form the first set of women character placements. Both female figures are cast as mothers. Jezebel is portrayed as a mother whose children are threatened with death by the Son of God (2:18, 23), while the woman with the sun gives birth to a male child who is threatened with death by the dragon (12:4–5). Jezebel is cast as a negative character, whereas the woman in chapter 12 is portrayed as a positive figure. Similar observations are made when contrasting and comparing the next two women character placements. Both the woman clothed with the sun and the great whore of Babylon are described as mothers as well. This is observed as the woman in chapter 12 gives birth to a male child (12:2, 4–5) and the female figure in chapter 17 is described as "the mother of whores" (ēmētērtōn pornōn, 17:5). The final main women character placement compares and contrasts the whore of Babylon with the bride in chapter 21. Both female figures are similar in that they both bear names of cities.[23] Both women—the whore and the bride—are adorned with costly jewelry (17:4; 21:2, 18–21). Thus, women character placements show deliberate contrast and similarities, and culminate in a call to leave the whore and come to the bride, the New Jerusalem.

Whereas female characters are placed as contrasting pairs, male characters, specifically main warriors, are placed throughout the Apocalypse. The first, and positive, warrior figure is the Lion of the tribe of Judah (5:5). Resseguie asserts that the image of a lion stands for "power and strength."[24] The Lion character is a main figure due to its primary placement in the text. As the reader follows the further character

---

however, parted with this view and saw the great whore of Babylon as the dominant figure among the main women with the other female figures situated to compare and contrast with her (Duff, *Who Rides the Beast*, 84).

21. Rossing, *The Choice Between Two Cities.*

22. deSilva, *Seeing Things John's Way*, 293.

23. The ancient city of Babylon was known as the enemy of Israel, the center of spiritual defilement. In contrast, Jerusalem was known as the city of God, the center of Israel's holiness.

24. Resseguie, *The Revelation of John*, 117.

development of the Lion, a Lamb next emerges in the story (5:6—6:1). The Lamb, a positive warrior character, reemerges in chapter 14 where the Lamb appears as a military leader (14:1–4). Two warriors appear on white horses, one as a negative and one as a positive rider. In chapter 6, a rider on a white horse appears as the first of four riders and thus is a prominent character among the four. The rider seeks to conquer and fits the description of a Parthian warrior, a negative character (6:2).[25] In chapter 19, a rider likewise appears on a white horse. However, in contrast to the rider in chapter 6, this rider wages war in righteousness (19:11–16). Chapter 12 introduces a male child who is to rule all the nations (12:5). This messianic character is presented first when the woman who is to give birth to him is in labor (12:2, 4–5). Next, the woman who gives birth to the child is persecuted by a dragon. The text specifically identifies this persecuted woman as the one who gave birth to the male child (12:13). Thus the male child emerges as a main character as well, one born to rule. The next main character, the beast out of the sea (13:1–7), likewise seeks to rule but has negative qualities. The beast wages war (13:4), utters blasphemy, and finally conquers every nation (13:7). Eventually, the divine warrior makes his triumphant entry (19:11). Thus, as seen, the main warriors are dispersed throughout the text.

Male and Female Images in the Apocalypse

Whereas witnesses are all positive characters in the narrative, both women and warriors are depicted both positively and negatively. After the introduction of Jesus Christ as the faithful witness, the Christian community is described as a community that is made a kingdom and priests (1:6). From thereon the use of the male and female imagery commences in the text as the initial vision of Jesus Christ walking among the lampstands speaking to his church sets "the scene for a relationship later developed in masculine/feminine imagery."[26] The subsequent first placement of a female character, Jezebel, is a negative one and sets a tone of rebuke. The appearance of the first warrior, the Lion, however, is

25. Parthian horsemen were notorious for having forced out the remnants of Alexander's empire from Persia and for having crushed the Roman army at Carrhae in 53 B.C.E. One specific reason for the latter historical and humiliating defeat was the specific tactic used by the Parthian cavalry of faking retreat and then using bows and arrows to deliver the famous "Parthian shot" (Hood, "The Parthians," forthcoming).

26. Humphrey, "A Tale of Two Cities," 83.

positive and sets the stage for further plot expectations. Thus, from the beginning of engaging the text, audience expectations of female images and male images might differ. Do the warriors in this story indeed give voice to success while the women are made to crouch in shame? Are negative female characters mere sexualized parodies of one half of the human race or does the typecasting of characters serve as a rhetorical device? If so, linguistic and metaphorical functions of this typecasting need further exploring.

Both linguistically and metaphorically speaking, sexual inferences are present in the text. Babylon is portrayed, as Duff writes, as "a woman who is out of control. She is a glutton and a sexual predator, enslaving 'the kings of the earth' with her lascivious power."[27] The two main negative female characters, Jezebel and Babylon, are linked linguistically by the repetition of the phrase "of her immorality" (*ek tēs porneias autēs*, 2:21; 14:8, NASB). The audience is warned against defiling associations with such women. Social distance must be maintained between themselves and Jezebel, and themselves and Babylon, so *porneias* is avoided.[28] The word *porneia* has a broad range of meaning. The noun *porneia* and the verb *porneuō* are used frequently in the Septuagint to translate the Hebrew word *zanah*.[29] Typically, *porneia* and *porneuō* are used to translate Hebrew terms regarding a woman's unfaithfulness to her husband (Hos 1:2; Ezek 16:23). This word group metaphorically referred to Israel's unfaithfulness to God and was likened to the sense of idolatry, *eidōlolatria*.[30] Examples of Israel's unfaithfulness are found in various places in the Old Testament prophets. In Hosea, harlotry is a metaphor for Israel's unfaithfulness (idolatry) to God. Isaiah uses sexual imagery to indict Tyre for unfaithfulness in economics (Isa 23:15–18). The prophet Nahum accused Nineveh of economic prostitution. Ezekiel portrays Jerusalem as an unfaithful wife who compromises with the surrounding culture. The actual woman Jezebel in the Old Testament was the queen of Phoenicia. She caused the king of Israel, Ahab, to practice syncretism. Ahab combined the worship of the God of Israel with the worship of Baal the pagan god (1 Kgs 18–20; 2 Kgs 9:22). Thus Jezebel

27. Duff, *Who Rides the Beast*, 111.

28. deSilva, *Seeing Things John's Way*, 226.

29. Except in Deut 23:18, in which *porneia* is used to translate the Hebrew word *qedeshah*.

30. Duff, *Who Rides the Beast?* 56.

became the perfect female poster child for spiritual unfaithfulness and idolatry. However, the female character representing the unfaithfulness of a people is not the unfaithfulness of a specific gender. This characterization of unfaithfulness of a people is augmented in the woman Babylon in Rev 17.

Beside main characters explored thus far, what about supporting characters, those so-called flat characters that contribute to the plot? Are all warriors powerful and authoritative males who are known for their success and all minor female images liabilities for shame? What about the puzzling description of the 144,000 gathered on Mount Zion with the Lamb, often considered supporting characters?

> No one could learn that song except the one hundred forty-four thousand who have been redeemed from the earth. It is these who have not defiled themselves with women, for they are virgins; these follow the Lamb wherever he goes. They have been redeemed from humankind as first fruits for God and the Lamb. (Rev 14:3b–4)

Are women in these verses cast as a source of defilement, that is, shame? Are male virgins of higher value to the Lamb than males who have lost their virginity? Is sexual activity cast in the realm of sin, or at least portrayed as less spiritual, in this narrative so as to elevate certain other virtues? Are males who remain virgins more successful in the eyes of the Lamb? Women appear not to follow the Lamb in this part of the narrative; they are but a source of shame. Interpretive restraint, however, is in order with regard to the character development and placement of these 144,000. The reference to the 144,000 as virgins contributes to an image of an army. The Greek word used for virgins, *parthenos*, is used either of a young girl of marriageable age, a woman who has not had sexual interaction with a man, or a chaste person. In addition, however, the term *parthenos* can refer to ritual purity. Temporary celibacy was part of the ritual requirement for holy warfare (Deut 23:9–14; 1 Sam 21:4–6). Holy warriors would abstain from sexual intercourse as part of readying themselves for God's battle. The 144,000 therefore are portrayed as warriors.

When comparing the main warrior character, the Lamb, and the supporting characters, the 144,000 (Rev 14:1–5), with the main warrior character, the King of kings, and the supporting characters, the armies of heaven (Rev 19:11–16), linguistic and thematic links are observed. Both passages start with the Greek phrase, *kai eidon*, "then I saw/looked," and contain a form of the word *akoloutheō*, "I follow." Thematically, connections are observed as well. The 144,000 have the name of the Lamb and the Father's name on their foreheads (Rev 14:1). The passage with the warrior in Rev 19 likewise makes mention of names in various parts of the text. The rider is called Faithful and True (Rev 19:11); an unknown name is inscribed on the Lamb's many diadems; the Lamb's name is The Word of God (Rev 19:13); and on the robe and thigh of the rider the name "King of kings and Lord of lords" is inscribed (Rev 19:16). Also, the 144,000 are described as blameless, *amōmos* (Rev 14:5). The word blamelessness conveys purity language. Those following the Lamb are pure. They are ritually pure and blameless. The armies of heaven following the King of kings are described as wearing white and pure linen. The riders following the King of kings therefore are supporting characters— warriors who appear not to fight but to depict the entry of a conquering king with his army following.

The Lord's army in Rev 19 is interpreted variably by scholars. Some maintain that the army consists entirely of angels, perhaps in particular led by Michael,[31] or believers,[32] or a combination of both.[33] Osborne likewise observes the literary connection by way of the verb "were following," *ēkolouthei*.[34] Indeed, similarities exist between the 144,000 warriors and the followers of the King of kings.[35] Resseguie argues that the army in Rev 19 does not consist of warriors since the battle has already been waged and won by the divine warrior.[36] However, this puts too much emphasis on plot chronology at the cost of character placement. A character does not cease to portray its role when one aspect of its character (fighting) is not emphasized. The heavenly entourage of warriors augments the main character in the scene—the divine warrior. The character placement builds on the parallels between the heavenly army in chapter 19 and the 144,000 warriors in chapter 14. This observation then puts a break on an overt focus on the male and female imagery. The imagery is one of warfare, not of misogyny. The 144,000 males are preparing for warfare;

31. Aune, *Revelation 17–22*, 1059.
32. Smalley, *The Revelation to John*, 493.
33. Osborne, *Revelation*, 684.
34. Ibid., 684.
35. Witherington, *Revelation*, 243.
36. Resseguie, *The Revelation of John*, 239.

they are not depicted as merely successful warriors. Likewise, the heavenly army following the divine warrior does just that—they follow. The might and success of the supporting male characters in chapters 14 and 19 is tempered by the main characters in these passages who truly are the foci. The warriors belong to the Lamb, having the name of his Father on their heads, or follow the divine warrior.

Just as male warriors are depicted positively and negatively, so are female characters. Both the woman clothed with the sun and the bride representing the New Jerusalem are positive depictions of female images in the text. For some scholars these images come a little too late in the narrative. Pippin maintains that the focus in the Apocalypse is on "the desire for and the death of the female."[37] Bothersome to scholars such as Pippin is the use of female archetypes of good and evil, virgin and whore, bride and temptress, wife and whore, etc.[38] Even the positive use of the imagery of a bride and the pure, New Jerusalem as the ultimate destination for all believers is seen as utilizing negative archetypes as they may be perceived as confinement to certain stereotypical female roles. Pippin writes, "Women in the apocalypse are victims—victims of war and patriarchy. The Apocalypse is not a safe place for women."[39] However, as seen, the image of the 144,000, for example, is understood better as war imagery, which tempers the potential negative portrayal of women in that setting. War imagery refocuses the plot to the victory eventually portrayed by the slain Lamb and the divine warrior. The characters are not the end all; the plot resolution is. The rhetoric of the narrative drives the plot forward. In the end, the reader is persuaded to be part of the good city, not of Babylon.

Women and Warriors

If the Apocalypse were not a safe place for women then, logically, female images would not have redemptive ability in the text. In chapter 12, however, the earth comes to the rescue of the woman clothed with the sun. The earth, a feminine noun and personified as a female character, helps the woman when the dragon, a negative male warrior character,

37. Pippin, *Death and Desire*, 16. To be fair, Pippin acknowledges that *both* male and female are silenced and destroyed in the Apocalypse; the focus of her monograph is on the clearly identified women in the text (*Death and Desire*, 47).

38. Pippin, *Death and Desire*, 47; and Schüssler Fiorenza, *The Book of Revelation*, 199.

39. Pippin, *Death and Desire*, 80.

seeks to sweep away the woman with a flood (12:15–16). The earth swallows up the flood and provides safety for the woman. The woman is not dependent on a male figure. Rather, she is kept safe by a female figure, earth, a redemptive force.

As seen in the portrayal of the women and warriors, stereotyping indeed is used in casting the characters in the Apocalypse. Yet the purpose thereof is theological and political, not pejorative toward gender or class distinctions. For example, the 144,000 are all males but the focus is not on those males or on their success as warriors. War imagery serves the overall plot's theme of conquering. Indeed, John used negative stereotyping of Greco-Roman women to depict the woman Babylon.[40] However, this stereotyping is based on the setting in Asia Minor. Vedia Marvia, for example, was an unmarried high priestess in Asia who lived in Ephesus,[41] providing the backdrop to understanding female images in the setting. Likewise, evidence exists of the presence of a priestess in a prominent temple, Otacilia Faustina, in Pergamum in the first half of the first century. She was a priestess of Athena and Julia Livilla. As such she was a *nikēphoros*, an object of worship.[42] This portrayal as an object of worship provides a context for understanding the woman Babylon as a depiction of culture.

John's Apocalypse, like other apocalyptic writings containing female imagery, is encoded with meaning drawn from its setting. Regular women are marginalized, humiliated, and often depicted as the abused. Yet such characterizations represented common reality.[43] Likewise, the characterization of warriors correlates to the realities of male honor in the very communities addressed in the Apocalypse. If not viewed as such, the warrior characters appear to relegate men to the realm of warfare in which success is achieved in battle only. Where is the character development of the caring male who kneels besides a wounded fellow

40. See Duff, *Who Rides the Beast*, 107–111, for a detailed analysis.

41. Her name was inscribed on a marble wall in the Prytaneion in Ephesus. The inscription was made between 97–100 C.E. to commemorate the end of her twelve-month service as *prytanis* of Ephesus. She was the high priestess in one of the provincial cults of the emperors (Friesen, "The Beast from the Land," 53).

42. Friesen, "The Beast from the Land," 56.

43. Humphrey, *The Ladies and the Cities*, 169. These circumstances either were social reality or were a matter of societal perspective. Examples of apocalyptic writings with such female imagery include: *Joseph and Aseneth, 4 Ezra*, and *The Shepherd of Hermas*.

warrior? Where are the nurturing, loving, and caring qualities of the males in this one-sided character portrayal? Is the Apocalypse guilty of misandry—a hatred of men? Indeed, an accusation of misandry could be leveled if one does not consider the ancient readers. With regard to the indictment of misogeny, Rossing points out that Pippin does not consider ancient readers.[44] In addition, Rossing asserts that Pippin interprets "desire" almost exclusively as "desire for sex and violence, ignoring the other desires—economic, political, and spiritual—evoked by the promises of Revelation's seven letters and by the New Jerusalem vision itself."[45] Certainly, when viewed in its broader context, one must conclude that the choice is offered to desire one of two realms represented by various characters—the realm of Babylon or the realm of New Jerusalem.

CONCLUSION

The reading of a narrative is balanced by understanding authorial intent. The audience is persuaded by rhetoric applicable to a specific audience. However, audiences in any age bring their own experiences and realities to the story. A woman always will read John's Apocalypse as a woman. Female imagery conjures female responses even if familiar with the ancient scene. Likewise, a man never ceases to be a male when reading the Apocalypse. Yet, awareness of the original life setting of the text's audience reassures and illumines the modern reader. One need not dwell on the shame of female characters or the success of male characters. Each character placement ultimately serves the plot in unique ways. Whether villain or hero, the Dark Knight or Princess Leia, all character traits assist in moving the plot to an outcome beneficial or else pleasing to the audience. Not everyone likes Sean Penn's or Susan Sarandon's characters in *Dead Man Walking* (1995). Still, this cinematographic portrayal of a true story is considered a great movie by many film enthusiasts. Even more so, regardless of the character trait *faux pas* in the eyes of modern readers, John's Apocalypse will shine in any age as a divine book of hope for those belonging to the Lamb.

44. Rossing, *The Choice Between Two Cities*, 14.
45. Ibid.

QUESTIONS FOR REFLECTION

- Do men and women respond differently to the portrayal of male and female images in John's Apocalypse?

- What character in the Apocalypse stands out positively and what character stands out negatively to you in the Apocalypse? Why?

- Does how you respond to or associate with characters in the Apocalypse affect how you understand the plot?

6

Pure or Defiled?

A Sociological Analysis of John's Apocalypse

RENATE VIVEEN HOOD

INTRODUCTION

> Blessed are those who wash their robes, so that they will have the right to the tree of life and may enter the city by the gates. Outside are the dogs and sorcerers and fornicators and murderers and idolaters, and everyone who loves and practices falsehood. (Rev 22:14–15)

FROM THE BEGINNING OF Revelation in the letters to the seven churches, the ultimate destiny of humanity is presented in the imagery of clean and unclean: those clean enter the heavenly city of God; those unclean remain outside. The one identified by John as one like the Son of Man (1:13) proclaimed to the church in Ephesus that those who conquered the corruption of "evildoers" (2:2) would eat from the tree of life (2:7), which stands in the city of God (22:14). The believers of the church in Sardis were told that those who had not soiled their clothes would walk in white robes (3:4), an indication of washed clothes (22:14). Moreover, those who did not fit this description would be clothed in white as well if they would conquer (3:5). If the believers in the church in Philadelphia likewise would conquer, they would be made a pillar in the temple of God and never go out of the city of God (3:12). The believers in the church in Laodicea were counseled to buy from the one like the Son of Man white robes to clothe themselves (3:18).

Indeed, throughout Revelation, multiple references are made to those who are considered clean and thus worthy to come into the presence of God or enter into the heavenly city (Rev 3:4–5; 7:14–15; 22:14). John's Apocalypse then ends with a description of a city—the New Jerusalem. The city is gated. Those who have their robes washed are considered clean and may enter through those very gates. By implication, those who do not have their robes washed remain outside the gates. One will note that along with the clean, the impure are mentioned in Revelation. The latter are a source of defilement for those who are pure.

In all, the themes of purity and defilement are critical underpinnings that hold together the complex fabric of John's Apocalypse. However, what did purity and defilement entail in the first-century Mediterranean setting? What were the criteria for people to be in the clean group? A brief examination of the norms and traditions of the society of John's Apocalypse is in order. Sociological methodologies of inquiry will prove helpful in providing insight in these areas.

PURITY AND DEFILEMENT

> These are the laws concerning the dead: bury the dead person as follows: in three white cloths—a spread, a shroud, and a coverlet—or in fewer, not worth more than 300 drachmas. Carry out [the body] on a wedge-footed bed and do not cover the bier with cloths. Bring not more than 3 choes of wine to the tomb and not more than one chous of olive oil, and bring back the empty jars. Carry the shrouded corpse in silence all the way to the tomb. Perform the preliminary sacrifice according to ancestral customs. Bring the bed and the covers back from the tomb inside the house. On the next day cleanse the house first with sea water, and then cleanse all the rooms with hyssop. When it has been thoroughly cleansed, the house is to be free from pollution; and sacrifices should be made on the hearth. The women who come to mourn at the funeral are not to leave the tomb before the men. There is to be no mourning for the dead person on the thirtieth day. Do not put a wine-cup beneath the bed, do not pour out the water, and do not bring the sweepings to the tomb. In the event that a person dies, when he is carried out, no women should go to the house other than those polluted [by the death]. Those polluted are the mother and wife and sisters and daughters, and in

addition to these not more than five women, the daughter's children and cousins; no one else. The polluted when washed with water poured out [from jugs] are free from pollution. . . . This law has been ratified by the council and the people. On the third day those who mourn on the anniversary of the death are to be free from pollution, but they are not to enter a temple, and the house is to be free from pollution until they come back from the tomb.[1]

In this late, fifth-century Greek funeral law a foundational sociological phenomenon is illustrated—all communities have basic structures in place that determine what is deemed clean and what is deemed unclean or defiled. A funeral is a fundamental rite of passage in any culture. In the ancient Mediterranean culture, marriages and funerals were among the two most celebrated or commemorated events in community life. Laws governing the affairs of such rites provide insight into the inner workings of culture. Note that the above funeral law cites specific cleansing procedures. At specific times, specific places were to be cleansed with specific purifying agents—seawater and hyssop. Plutarch, likewise, for example, spoke of seawater as a preferred purificatory agent.[2] Certain subgroups of the community in which the funeral law functioned, such as the women who participated in the preparation of the dead person— were considered polluted and had to undergo a cleansing procedure with a prescribed cleansing agent.

FIGURE 10. Grave Relief from Rhodes. In this grave relief from the Greek island of Rhodes, Krito mourns the loss of her mother, Timaresta. The fine artwork of the relief indicates Krito would have performed carefully all the prescribed rituals attending to her mother's funeral, including the set period of mourning, as well as attendant cleansing rituals (photograph by Gerald L. Stevens).

1. Ioulis *On Keos*, 1218.

2. Plutarch *Quaest. Graec.* 40.301a.

Such societies and communities have their own purity codes that determine what is clean or unclean. The universe, and thus the social makeup of groups, is structured orderly. This order functions by means of set rules or criteria. Impurity implies that matter is out of order and implied or set rules are broken. The idea of pollution, therefore, involves the concept that matter is out of place.[3] Both persons and inanimate objects fit in categories of clean and unclean, pure and polluted. As Jerome Neyrey summarized, "Labeling things or persons 'pure' or 'polluted' serves to establish identity and to maintain the group, which now has the power to include or exclude."[4] By exerting this power, social order is maintained. Purification, for example, creates boundaries between sacred places and non-sacred places.[5]

FIGURE 11. Temple of Apollo in Corinth. One of the oldest temples in Greece, the Temple of Apollo in Corinth goes back to the 6th cent. B.C.E. The hundreds of temples in the ancient world attest to strong beliefs about clean and unclean. Highly-ritualized purification rites communicate the grave concern entire communities had for their sense of well-being (photograph by Gerald L. Stevens).

3. Douglas, *Purity and Danger*, 41.

4. Neyrey, "The Idea and the System of Purity," 90.

5. R. Parker, *Miasma*, 23.

The concepts of purity and purification are age old. In ancient Greece, purity ideas were expressed in myths as well as in society at large. In Greek cities in the first-century B.C.E., purity concerns became an issue with regard to shrines and temples. Ancient Greek writings and inscriptions testify to the exclusion of impure people from Greek and Hellenistic temples. One inscription, found in a temple in Philadelphia in Asia Minor, prohibited those who had stolen, murdered, or had committed adultery from entering the temple.[6] This defilement was a picture of disorder and was decried greatly.[7] Already in the fifth-century B.C.E., Herodotus recorded how people copulated in sacred temples and entered shrines without washing themselves after having sex.[8] The mood in the account of Herodotus is such that the reader knows that in Greek ideology, sexual activity was incompatible with the sacred. Hence purification rites that apparently did exist were not followed by the people. However, in a massive turnaround, the people of Athens, and other cities where sacred places were polluted, purchased animals in order to perform the necessary purificatory sacrifices.[9] In this way, communities deal with disorder through purification rites. These rites shed light on purity concepts held in the minds of the audience of the Apocalypse.

The Greco-Roman individuals had two ways of canceling a pollution or impurity—cleansing rituals or confessional rites.[10] The example of sexual disgrace in the temples in Athens, recorded by Herodotus, is an instance of the first kind of impurity cancellation. A confessional rite resembles a need for compensation for purity offenses. However, in the Greco-Roman setting, cleansing rituals were most customary. Already in ancient Greece, purifications often took the form of sacrifices in an understanding that divine wrath could be washed away.[11] Sacred sites deemed unclean were cleansed by applying blood—either pigs' blood or the blood of doves—to the site.[12] People likewise were cleansed with blood. A person accused of sorcery, for example, was purified by

---

6. Such persons were considered defiled; see Regev, "Moral impurity and the temple in early Christianity," 393.

7. Fox, *Pagans and Christians*, 75.

8. *Herodotus II*, 351.

9. Stowers, "On the Comparison of Blood in Greek and Israelite Ritual," 186.

10. Douglas, *Purity and Danger*, 138.

11. R. Parker, *Miasma*, 10.

12. Aristides 48.3.

blood.[13] Cleansing rituals purified persons and restored them back to community.

LABELING AND DEVIANCE

People belonged to well-defined communities in first-century Greco-Roman society. The contours of such groups, otherwise known as group boundaries, were maintained through social processes. In different groups, people experienced the social unit, the group, differently.[14] First-century Mediterranean people were strong group-oriented persons.[15] To them, the integrity of the group—loyalty—was more important than self-reliance.[16] Purity is a socially shared map of space and time involving values held in common by members of a group and especially relevant in a strong group.[17] An unclean person, then, is a person out of place, collectively deemed a deviant. Deviant labels therefore are a matter of perspective.[18] Behavior deemed "out of place," or "out of order" by a group is labeled unacceptable in that group. In Christian groups such behavior is labeled "sin."

The labeling of deviants fulfills a social function. Fellow group members do not wish to fall subject to such labeling. As a result, group identity and group cohesion are strengthened. Group boundaries likewise are strengthened by negative labels. Values not commonly shared by the group receive labels, such as unclean. Those who are labeled unclean are thereby identified publicly as having the potential to contaminate group members with unacceptable values. Clear negative labeling helps preserve group cohesion. Transferred into the Christian arena, labeling deviant behavior as sinful can cause Christians to seek purity and to avoid certain behaviors. Therefore, in terms of behavior, purity and labeling are correlated.

13. Hippocrates *On the Sacred Disease* 148.38.

14. White, "Grid and Group in Matthew's Community," 61–90.

15. Malina, *The New Testament World* (1993), 67.

16. Hanson and Oakman, *Palestine in the Time of Jesus*, 7.

17. Malina, *Christian Origins and Cultural Anthropology*, 21.

18. Barclay, "Deviance and Apostasy," 118.

PURITY IN THE APOCALYPSE

In Revelation both linguistic terms as well as general symbols are used to express purity concepts. Purity is expressed as "in-group," the group whose members embody the ideal values of the Apocalyptic community.[19] Symbols in Revelation include clothing, locations, rites, persons and images. Behavior of in-group and out-group members is indicative of purity classification. The purity standard for the behavior of the community that ultimately dwells in the New Jerusalem is set in the inaugural vision of the Son of Man in chapter 1.

The one like the Son of Man appeared to John clothed with a long robe and with a golden sash across his chest (Rev 1:13). The Son of Man stands amidst seven lampstands (Rev 1:12). The particular dress indicates Christ in his priestly role as he tends the lampstands like a priest in the temple.[20] A priest was ceremonially clean to perform his priestly tasks. Thus the Son of Man is pictured as a pure priest. This purity is reinforced by the description of his feet. His feet were like burnished bronze, refined as in a furnace (Rev 1:15). Feet in the ancient Mediterranean world depicted the direction in life.[21] The refining of the bronze refers to moral purity.[22] Thus the direction indicated is that of moral purity. The Son of God, whose words are directed to the church in Thyatira, is described as having eyes like a flame of fire and feet like burnished bronze (Rev 2:18). The inaugural vision of the Son of Man therefore sets the tone of purity in Revelation in terms of purity. For example, by using the image of judgment, conveyed by eyes like a flame of fire, in conjunction with the purity image, a deliberate contrast is set up with the followers of Jezebel who lead an unclean lifestyle.

Purity in Clothing

From the appearance of the Son of Man dressed in a long robe, purity symbolism expressed in clothing continues throughout the Apocalypse. Robes are mentioned in the letters to the churches both to Sardis and Laodicea. A few persons in the church in Sardis are described as not hav-

---

19. Hanson, "Blood and Purity," 224.

20. Beale, *The Book of Revelation*, 208. Most scholars indeed see a priestly role here (See Beale, *The Book of Revelation*, 208–10). Few commentators attempt to deny priestly connotations, as does Aune, *Revelation 1–5*, 209.

21. Osborne, *Revelation*, 91.

22. Beale, *The Book of Revelation*, 210.

ing soiled their clothes and thus they will be dressed in white (3:4). Those who will conquer likewise will be dressed in white robes (3:5). Members of the church in Laodicea were counseled to buy white robes because they were naked (3:17–18). The next vision of heaven in Revelation shows a throne surrounded by twenty-four thrones with twenty-four elders. The elders are described as wearing white robes (4:4). Next, in chapter 6, believers are described as having white robes. Those who had been slaughtered for the word of God were each given a white robe (6:9). Likewise, the great multitude that no one could count from every nation was robed in white (7:9). On occasion clothing is described in terms of the appearance of fabric rather than the color. In chapter 15 angels are robed in pure, bright linen (14:6). The bride is clothed with linen, bright and pure, which represents the righteous deeds of the saints (19:8). The heavenly army following the divine warrior wears fine linen, white and pure, as well. All those described either robed in white or dressed in bright linen are clothed in purity and represent the community of the clean.

Spatial Purity

Beside persons representing cleanliness, places indicate purity as well. The area before the heavenly throne in Rev 4 is described as something like a sea of glass (4:6). The throne in chapter 20 is described as white (20:11). This white throne is the last appearance of "white" in the Apocalypse and sums up the themes of purity and holiness associated with this color throughout the book.[23] Those believers in the church in Laodicea who conquered would sit on the throne with the faithful and true witness (3:14, 21). The sea of glass is mentioned in chapter 15 when a vision of heaven is given and those who had conquered the beast and his image stand beside the sea of glass (15:2).

The temple was understood as the sacred dwelling place of God. Those who had washed their robes served God day and night in his temple (7:15). Believers in the church in Philadelphia, for example, were told that if they conquered they would be made a pillar in the temple (3:12), representing the eternal presence of God.[24] The holy city, the New Jerusalem, is described as the home of God (21:2–3) that displays the glory of God (21:11). The wall of the city is described as clear as glass

23. Osborne, *Revelation*, 720.
24. Beale, *The Book of Revelation*, 294.

(21:18). The city does not contain a temple for God's presence pervades everything and everyone (21:22).

Figures of Purity

Persons presented as clean often are associated with purity symbols such as the color white or clean clothing or placement in pure locales. The purity of the souls of those who had been slaughtered for the word of God (who wore white robes) located them right under the altar (6:9). This location indicates an association with the temple and hence with the presence of God. Likewise, the innumerable crowd, robed in white, stands before the throne and before the Lamb (7:9). Another large crowd, the 144,000 on Mount Zion, had not defiled themselves and is described as blameless (14:4–5). The purity of the 144,000 enabled them to stand in the presence of the Lamb (14:1).

DEFILEMENT IN THE APOCALYPSE

Those belonging to out-group members do not meet purity standards of the community and ultimately will not dwell in the New Jerusalem. From the onset of addressing the seven churches, the unclean ones are equated with "evildoers" (2:2). A typical example of a defiling influence in the church is the woman Jezebel who leads believers astray into idolatry (2:20). As in the previous examples of purity language, defilement language in the Apocalypse also contains references to clothing, spatial arrangement, and figures.

Defilement in Clothing

Whereas faithful believers are clothed in white robes, those defiled by immorality have moved outside the group boundaries and are said to have soiled their clothes (3:4). In the ancient Mediterranean religious environment, stained or unclean garments disqualified people from worship as dishonoring the gods.[25] Certain believers in Sardis likewise had disqualified themselves from worship of the Lamb. The believers in the church in Laodicea are described as naked and advised to buy garments (3:17–18).

---

25. Moffatt, *The Revelation of St. John*, 364.

Nakedness was a shameful state.[26] The image of nakedness is used here to impress the shameful realities on those who have dishonored Christ.

Clothed in purple and scarlet, the woman in Rev 17 sits on a scarlet beast and holds in her hand a golden cup full of abominations and impurities (17:3–4; 18:16). The clothing represents the luxury of Rome along with moral corruption.[27] The woman's adornment with gold and jewels and pearls represent the tricks with which she attempts to seduce a man who is not her husband.[28] The whore is said to be made naked (17:16). She will be stripped of all her luxurious clothing and left in her shame.

Spatial Defilement

Certain places in Revelation are designated as spaces of uncleanness. Revelation 9 contains a description of a bottomless pit (9:1–2). This bottomless pit is the place from which the beast arises (11:7; 17:8). The beast is an object of worship, which is idolatry in this context (13:4). The sea is presented as a place of darkness out of which the beast rises (13:1). The sea, which holds the dead, becomes like the blood of a corpse, killing every living thing in its domain (16:3; 10:13). Babylon the Great is depicted as an immoral woman (14:8) and, thus, a place of uncleanliness. Outside of the city a winepress was trodden (14:20), a place associated with impurity.[29] Defiled persons are pictured in the closing chapter of Revelation as located outside the city (22:15).

Figures of Defilement

Persons representing the unclean often are associated with immorality and idolatry. The woman Jezebel taught immorality and idolatry in the church in Thyatira (2:20). Correspondingly, the great whore in Rev 17 represents impurity and is described as a source of defilement of the nations (17:1–2, 4). Therefore, the kings of the earth are described as unclean due to their association with the great whore (18:9). That defilement spreads to those who associated themselves with immoral people is common in Revelation.

---

26. Osborne, *Revelation*, 209.

27. Ibid., 610–11.

28. Collins, *The Apocalypse*, 119.

29. A place outside the city, or outside the camp, likely refers to the place where sin offerings are burned in the Pentateuch (Exod 19:14).

PURITY AND DEFILEMENT IN THE APOCALYPSE

Most of John's audience lived in cities and were accustomed to city life.[30] The Revelation addressed believers in churches in seven cities and culminates with a contrast between two cities—Babylon the Great and the New Jerusalem. Purity and defilement themes are seen throughout the Apocalypse and present believers with a choice of allying either with the defiled city or the one pure city. The destiny of faithful believers is the New Jerusalem; those who are defiled may not enter this city:

> Blessed are those who wash their robes, so that they will have the right to the tree of life and may enter the city by the gates. Outside are the dogs and sorcerers and fornicators and murderers and idolaters, and everyone who loves and practices falsehood. (Rev 22:14–15)

"Come Out of Her, My People."

Chapter 18 of the Apocalypse opens with John seeing an angel coming down from heaven. The angel declares Babylon the Great a fallen city (18:1–2). Babylon here is identified with the ancient city of Rome.[31] The city is described as immoral and as economically corrupt (18:3). John next hears another voice from heaven command, "Come out of her, my people, so that you do not take part in her sins, and so that you do not share in her plagues; for her sins are heaped high as heaven, and God has remembered her iniquities" (18:4–5). Babylon's defilement contaminated those who lived within. The only recourse was to flee its immorality into the haven of pure Christian communion.

Throughout the Apocalypse, elements within the church and the larger society are labeled as defiled in order to exhort a return to values consistent with the ideal Christian community. Ultimately, believers will find themselves secure in the New Jerusalem community. In the letters to the seven churches, those with impure motives are labeled as deviants. False apostles are labeled as corrupted by evil (2:2), and certain members of the Ephesian and Philadelphian churches are labeled as "the synagogue of Satan" (2:9, 3:9). Such deviants are disreputable. In chapter 2 of Revelation, those adhering to the teachings of Balaam and the Nicolaitans are called out as deviants (2:14–15), as are those tolerating Jezebel (2:20).

30. Bauckham, *Theology of the Book of Revelation*, 128.
31. Talbert, *The Apocalypse*, 82–84.

Deviant believers in the church in Sardis are labeled "dead" (3:1), while deviant believers in Laodicea are "lukewarm," "wretched, pitiable, poor, blind," and "naked" (3:16–17). However, the message of Revelation is not without a word of hope; frequent calls are issued for repentance (2:4, 16; 3:3). Likewise, those who keep the commandments of God and hold fast in faithfulness to Jesus appear to avoid negative labeling (14:12).

"Blessed Are Those Who Wash Their Robes"

John communicated group boundaries for the faithful through purity language. The ultimate destination of the New Jerusalem is marked by purity, for nothing unclean ever will enter the city (21:27; 22:3). Impurities among the faithful were remedied by exiting Babylon (18:4) and experiencing cleansing. In various places in the Apocalypse the washing of robes is indicated as a way of canceling pollution. The pure ones standing before the throne and before the Lamb have the seal of the Lamb and wear white robes washed in the blood of the Lamb (7:3, 9, 14).

The use of blood as cleansing agent is introduced in the opening chapter of the Apocalypse: "To him who loves us and freed is from our sins by his blood . . ." (1:5). Likewise, blood is described as part of a confessional rite, as compensation for purity offenses: "For you were slaughtered and by your blood you ransomed for God saints from every tribe and language and people and nation; you have made them to be a kingdom and priests serving our God . . ." (5:9–10).

CONCLUSION

The audience of the Apocalypse was called to a pure life. They were called out of a defiled world and urged to wake up to reality. As Bauckham says, "Babylon must fall so that the New Jerusalem may replace her. Her satanic parody of the ideal of the city must give way to the divine reality."[32] Through the use of deviance and labeling, believers were encouraged to leave behind anti-Christian values of Greco-Roman society, as well as those compromises that allowed for room to incorporate activities and observances of the imperial cult in daily life.[33] Faithful believers likewise were encouraged to remain devoted to the values of the ideal Christian community.

32. Bauckham, *Theology of the Book of Revelation*, 130.

33. For further reading concerning the imperial cult in first-century daily life in Asia Minor see Friesen, *Imperial Cults*; and Price, *Rituals and Power*.

The reality of everyday life in Asia Minor was sobering for believers. However, the Apocalypse also provides a message of hope. Using purity language, John reminded believers of the work of Christ on the cross. Those who were faithful to that confession would be part of the Christian hope. Using the cultural understanding of the day, the atonement of Christ with its ever-flowing grace John represented by a cleansing ritual of washing robes white in the blood of the Lamb.

Understanding the sociological matrix of John's Apocalypse thus opens up a world of interpretive insight along with the challenge to apply the call to come out of the defiled city and enter the city of God in today's setting.

> For this reason they are before the throne of God, and worship him day and night within his temple, and the one who is seated on the throne will shelter them. They will hunger no more, and thirst no more; the sun will not strike them, nor any scorching heat; for the Lamb at the center of the throne will be their shepherd, and he will guide them to springs of the water of life, and God will wipe away every tear from their eyes." (Rev 7:15–17)

QUESTIONS FOR REFLECTION

- Compile a list of examples of positive and negative labeling in the letters to the seven churches in Rev 2–3. Is either more dominant over the other?

- How does the place of the martyrs in Rev 9:9; 7:9, 13–14 clarify Revelation's overall concept of sacred space in terms of purity?

- Is labeling observed as a sociological phenomenon in Christian communities today? If so, do you think such labeling is acceptable and/or effective?

- Reflecting on cleansing rituals in Revelation, can you identify activities that might be considered as cleansing rituals practiced in the modern church?

- Consider Revelation's theme of purity as expressed in clothing. Can you think of items in daily living today that might denote "purity" in a similar way?

7

Urban Persons

City and Identity in the Book of Revelation

RICHARD WARREN JOHNSON

INTRODUCTION

Deep in the mind of every Roman, as in the mind of every Greek, was the unquestioned conviction which Aristotle put into words: that what raised man above the level of barbarism . . . and enabled him to develop the higher faculties which in the barbarian are only latent, to live well instead of merely living, was his membership of an actual, physical city. Man's bodily and animal existence might be satisfied by the country; his spiritual needs could only be satisfied by the town; hence the town was at once the symptom and the symbol of all that was highest and most precious in human life, all that raises man above the beasts of the field.[1]

ROBIN GEORGE COLLINGWOOD INTRODUCES his discussion of the process by which the Romans sought to civilize the newly-conquered province of Britain with a description of the significance of the city in the Greco-Roman world. Collingwood's assessment is consistent with Tacitus's description of the tribes that inhabited the lands beyond Rome's German frontier.

It is well known that none of the German tribes live in cities, that even individually they do not permit houses to touch each other:

1. Collingwood and Myres, *Roman Britain and the English Settlements*, 186.

100

they live separated and scattered, according as spring-water, meadow, or grove appeals to each man: they lay out their villages not, after our fashion, with buildings contiguous and connected; everyone keeps a clear space round his house, whether it be a precaution against the chances of fire, or just ignorance of building.[2]

From the perspective of a cultured Roman such as Tacitus, to declare that the Germans were barbarians was synonymous with noting that the Germans had no cities.

Any attempt to understand the first-century Mediterranean world, the world in which the earliest Christians lived, that fails to address the significance of the city in Greco-Roman culture will falter. The significance of "city" in the interpretation of the book of Revelation is evident in the frequency of occurrence of the word *polis* (πόλις, "city"). With 27 occurrences of *polis* (πόλις) in the 9,851 words of the text, this word occurs more frequently in Revelation than in any other New Testament document.[3]

THE PREINDUSTRIAL *POLIS*

A major obstacle to the appreciation of the significance of the *polis* in Revelation is the vast difference between the preindustrial cities with which John and his readers were familiar and the industrial (or postindustrial) cities known to twenty-first century readers. Industrial cities were both necessary and sufficient factors in the industrial revolution. Movement of manufacturing from the home and the craftsman's shop into ever larger factories required a large population of laborers, promoting the growth of industrial cities. The growing populations of the industrial cities required ever larger quantities of manufactured products, and this growing market attracted more industries to these cities. The function of the industrial city is, therefore, to provide both the workforce and the market for industrial production. Success for a twenty-first century city is defined by the ability to attract and hold businesses and trained workers for those businesses.

2. Tacitus *Germania* 16.

3. The word *polis* (πόλις) occurs 43 times in Acts, 39 times in Luke, and 27 times in Matthew, but the greater length of these texts (18,450 words, 19,482 words, and 18,346 words, respectively) means that *polis* (πόλις) occurs in Revelation with a greater frequency than in any of these other New Testament documents. Frequency data are based on BibleWorks 7.0.012g (2006).

The preindustrial *polis* was a radically different social institution from the industrial city. Recalling Collingwood's phrase, the preindustrial Greco-Roman *polis* of the first-century Mediterranean world was the focal point of "all that raises man above the beasts of the field."[4] Drama could be found in the theater, music filled the odeon, and literature was available in the library; access to all that the muses inspired in human beings was available primarily, if not solely, in the *polis*. While danger lurked beyond the walls of the *polis*, orderly, peaceful life was possible within the *polis* because of human government.

Of course, as the situation was understood in the first century, not all of humanity was capable of reading or of appreciating drama or music, and clearly not all people were capable of governing effectively. The urban elite possessed the refinement and wisdom necessary to govern others and to grasp the value and meaning of the arts, so the *polis* existed primarily for the benefit of this elite. Citizenship was a restricted status. Access to the city was the prerogative of the elite; other populations who were of value to the elite could be granted limited, controlled access and possibly even limited residential privileges within the *polis*.

These social distinctions were evident in the correlation of urban space and society in a "typical" Greco-Roman *polis* (figure 12). The heart of the *polis* was dedicated to the temples of the patron divinities and served as a residential district for the highest level of the ruling elite. Where the terrain permitted, the elevated status of the divine and human residents of this district was evident in the geographical elevation of the center of the *polis*; i.e., the heart of the *polis* was the acropolis (upper city). Surrounding the acropolis, living in closest proximity to the seats of power, was the remainder of the urban elite. Their high status was reflected in their ready access to theaters, odeons, and libraries. Essential craftsmen (e.g., bakers, tailors, and carpenters) could be granted residential privileges in the neighborhoods that surrounded the elite core of the *polis*. The urban poor were relegated to the fringes of the *polis* or were excluded from the *polis* altogether, along with certain essential craftsmen, such as fullers and leatherworkers, whose occupations made them undesirable neighbors. Internal walls separated the various urban districts, and an external wall defined the boundary of the *polis* (distinguishing between the *polis* and the hinterland). Gates in the various

4. Collingwood and Myres, *Roman Britain and the English Settlements*, 186.

walls made access possible for those to whom the privilege was granted, but these gates were closed at night to enhance the security of the people within and to reinforce the impermeable character of the social barriers represented by the various walls. A final detail of the *polis* worth noting was the existence of markets and public squares where (during daylight hours at least) the urban residents interacted with one another.

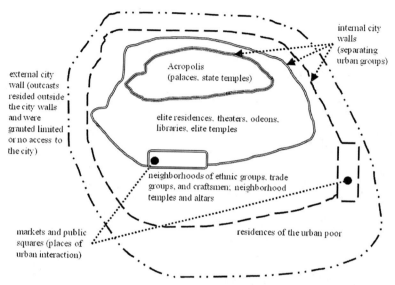

FIGURE 12. Urban Space and Society in a Greco-Roman Preindustrial *Polis*

While this model of the Greco-Roman *polis* is idealized, ancient Pergamum offers a close approximation to this portrait. The acropolis of Pergamum, as seen from the Asklepion, is shown in figure 13. Figures 14 and 15 depict a drawing and a model of the upper acropolis of Pergamum in the second century C.E. At the pinnacle of the Pergamene acropolis, looming approximately 800 feet over the valley below, were palaces of the rulers, a vast library, a sanctuary of Athena, a magnificent altar of Zeus and a (post-New Testament) temple dedicated to emperor Trajan. Clinging to the side of the upper acropolis was a theater (partially obscured by the tallest column in figure 13) and a short distance from the stage was a temple of Dionysus. At the lowest level of the upper acropolis (and depicted in the lowest portion of figure 15), just below the altar of Zeus, was the upper *agora* (ἀγορά, "marketplace"). During the pre-Roman era in Pergamum the "edifices in the citadel were under the close control of the royal family, members of the noble classes and the military dignitaries, and they gave this section of the city a sacred and austere atmosphere. The middle and lower acropolis with their own group of sanctuaries, gymnasiums, agora and other buildings of more social character were cosmopolitan places which members of the lower classes frequented without any hindrance from the ruling class in the citadel."[5] The upper *agora* was at the boundary between these socially distinct regions of the city. Ultimately the walls of the city reached the base of mountain on which the acropolis stood and, during the Roman era, the city expanded across the valley. Nevertheless, the upper acropolis was always the heart of ancient Pergamum.[6]

FIGURE 13. The Acropolis of Pergamum Viewed from the Asklepion (photograph by Richard Warren Johnson).

5. Cimak, *Pergamum*, 41

6. Gates, *Ancient Cities*, 281.

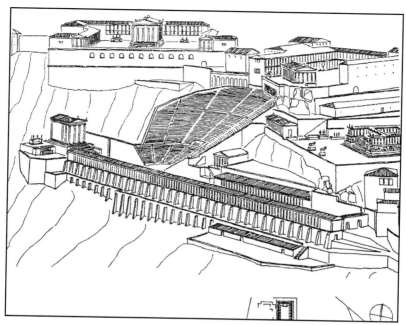

FIGURE 14. Drawing of the Upper Acropolis of Pergamum in the Second Century
C.E. (photograph by Gerald L. Stevens).

FIGURE 15. Model of the Upper Acropolis of Pergamum in the Second Century C.E.
(photograph by Gerald L. Stevens).

John addressed his message to residents of seven *poleis* (πόλεις, "cities") in Roman Asia: Ephesus, Smyrna, Pergamum, Thyatira, Sardis, Philadelphia, and Laodicea. John and the members of the churches in these *poleis* were familiar with the social dynamics of the culture in which they lived, a culture that they perceived (or once perceived) as "normal." A familiarity with this culture allows the twenty-first century reader to comprehend the book of Revelation more fully. Awareness of the importance of the *polis* in Revelation illuminates the interpretation of the vision in at least two ways: (a) John drew upon the experience of life in the particular *poleis* of Asia as he addressed his audience and (b) in the body of Revelation John presented contrasting views of two *poleis* as he described the imminent reign of God over all creation.

THE TWO *POLEIS* OF REVELATION

John described the fall of a city that he identified as great and mighty "Babylon" (18:2, 10). His description allows the reader to recognize this city as a very large and powerful, though otherwise typical, Greco-Roman *polis*. Residents of Babylon included harpists, musicians, flute players, trumpeters, and artisans (18:22), i.e., those people whose crafts enabled the elite to experience the rewards of life in a *polis*. As would be expected, the powerful lived in luxury (18:3, 7, 9), an extravagance made possible by the exploitation of others.[7] By catering to the desires of the elite, some of the merchants had themselves become wealthy (18:3, 23). Life in Babylon was much like life in any *polis* of John's world, and John's vision revealed that divine judgment was coming upon that world (18:2).

In contrast, as the conclusion of the vision neared, John described another city, New Jerusalem (21:2, 10). In very significant ways, this city differs from the *polis* identified as "Babylon." While the New Jerusalem has massive walls (21:12), the gates through these walls are never closed (21:25). This city has a majestic splendor that the ancient Mediterranean *polis* could mimic but never realize fully (21:16–21). Whereas the Greco-Roman *polis* was built around a central district that housed the state temples, New Jerusalem has no temple, "for its temple is the Lord

---

7. Exploitation is inferred in the extended description of the merchants, shipmasters, and sailors in Rev 18:11–19 and in the call to "Render to her as she herself has rendered" in Rev 18:6.

God the Almighty and the Lamb" (21:22). What the *polis* imitated with its temples (i.e., divine presence in the heart of the *polis* and divine favor upon her citizens) is a genuine reality in New Jerusalem. For most of humanity, the walls and gates of the *polis* were a reminder of their restricted access. Conversely, New Jerusalem, with its ever-open gates, is a city in which "the nations will walk" (21:24). John identifies no social class distinctions among the population within the walls of New Jerusalem. The "kings of the earth" are among those who pass through the gates of New Jerusalem (21:24), but once inside, other than "God and the Lamb," all those present are described as "his servants," and all bear the divine name (22:3–4). Again, New Jerusalem is revealed to be distinct from Babylon and its sister *poleis*; in fact, the distinctions are sufficiently great to declare that New Jerusalem stands in opposition to Babylon and its sisters.

Some people are excluded from New Jerusalem; this population is identified twice in John's account.

> But as for the cowardly, the faithless, the polluted, the murderers, the fornicators, the sorcerers, the idolaters, and all liars, their place will be in the lake that burns with fire and sulfur, which is the second death (21:8).

> But nothing unclean will enter it, nor anyone who practices abomination or falsehood, but only those who are written in the Lamb's book of life (21:27).

The difference between these outcasts and the people denied access to the *polis* is evident in the basis for the prohibition. Social status in first-century Mediterranean society was determined primarily by the stratum of society into which a person was born,[8] so the outcasts from the *polis* were largely those who were born to that status. Exclusion from New Jerusalem is based on conduct, specifically, rebellion against God. Further, admission and exclusion from the *polis* were determined and enforced by the elite class; exclusion from New Jerusalem was determined and enforced directly by God.

TO THE CHURCHES IN THE *POLEIS* OF ASIA

As noted above, John addressed his message to churches residing in seven *poleis* in Roman Asia. Extensive analyses of the ways in which

8. Malina, *The New Testament World* (2001), 109.

John's message correlates with specific aspects of life in these *poleis* have become available.[9] Consequently, a comprehensive discussion will not be attempted here. Rather, selected correlations between the content of Revelation and the lives of the believers in two of the seven *poleis* will be noted.

To the church in Pergamum Christ declares, "I know where you are living, where Satan's throne is. Yet you are holding fast to my name, and you did not deny your faith in me even in the days of Antipas my witness, my faithful one, who was killed among you, where Satan lives" (Rev 2:13). Clearly, the reference to Antipas demonstrates familiarity with the details of life in the Christian community in Pergamum. The identification of Pergamum as the location of "Satan's throne" suggests knowledge of the city in which that community resided. Recall the cluster of edifices at the pinnacle of the Pergamene acropolis described above. The altar of Zeus, the sanctuary of Athena, and the temple of Dionysus were visible throughout the city and the status of these institutions would have been impressed upon the minds of the believers in Pergamum. These qualities alone could have qualified the acropolis as "Satan's throne,"[10] but a Roman-era modification would have reinforced this identification. Pergamum was the first *polis* in Roman Asia to be granted the privilege of establishing a temple dedicated to the worship of *Roma* and the emperor.[11] The precise location of the original imperial temple has yet to be discovered, but the statue of the goddess in the sanctuary of Athena was replaced by a bronze statue of Caesar Augustus in 19 B.C.E.,[12] reflecting the devotion of the Pergamene citizens to their Roman benefactors. Colin J. Hemer concludes that the prominent imperial cult in Pergamum is the most likely explanation for the designation of Pergamum as "Satan's throne."[13] Given the paired references to Satan

9. Mounce, *The Book of Revelation* (1977), 83–130; Yamauchi, *New Testament Cities*; Aune, *Revelation 1–5*, 117–263; Beale, *The Book of Revelation*, 223–310; Reddish, *Revelation*, 49–87; Hemer, *Letters to the Seven Churches*.

10. Cf. Beale, *The Book of Revelation*, 246, who described the altar of Zeus on the acropolis as "throne-like," and Aune, *Revelation 1–5*, 182, who noted the ancient equation of "altar" and "throne."

11. Aune, *Revelation 1–5*, 182; Friesen, *Imperial Cults*, 25–32.

12. Cimak, *Pergamum*, 26.

13. Hemer, *Letters to the Seven Churches*, 87. Cf. Mounce, *The Book of Revelation*, 96–97.

in Rev 2:13, the martyrdom of Antipas probably involved conflict with the power represented by "Satan's throne."

Laodicea was located on a minor hilltop that placed the city at a strategic location with respect to the major roads through the region.[14] In terms of the availability of water, however, the location of the city was not enviable. Hemer discusses the quality of the Laodicean water supply, citing ancient and modern sources, and concludes that the water available in Laodicea was "bad."[15] Six miles north of Laodicea, and visible across a wide valley, are white cliffs formed as the hot spring-water of Hierapolis flows down the steep mountainside, allowing the dissolved minerals to solidify into impressive formations (figure 16). Since ancient times Hierapolis has been renowned for the beneficial effects of the water from its hot springs. Nine miles southeast of Laodicea is the site of Colossae, whose cold, mountain-fed water supply is described by Hemer as "pure and life-giving."[16] Between these two contrasting water sources was the water available in Laodicea. Neither hot (like Hierapolis) nor cold (like Colossae), the Laodicean water supply was tepid. The encrusting of the water pipes in Laodicea (still visible near the ancient stadium; cf. figure 17) reveals the high mineral content of the water, a character that would have given the water an unpalatable taste.[17]

14. Hemer, *Letters to the Seven Churches*, 188.
15. Ibid., 191.
16. Ibid., 188.
17. Ibid., 189.

FIGURE 16. View of Hierapolis from Laodicea (photograph by Richard Warren Johnson).

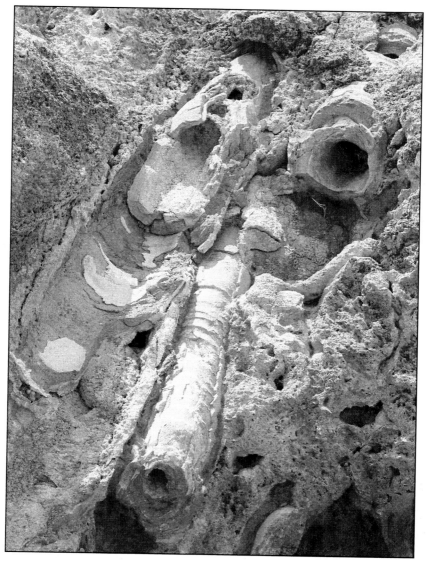

FIGURE 17. Encrusted Water Pipes in the Remains of the Water Tower of Laodicea (photograph by Richard Warren Johnson).

This contrast between Laodicea and its neighbors is probably the background against which a portion of the message of the risen Christ to the Laodiceans should be interpreted.

> I know your works; you are neither cold nor hot. I wish that you
> were either cold or hot. So, because you are lukewarm, and nei-

ther cold nor hot, I am about to spit you out of my mouth. (Rev
3:15–16)

By inference, both extremes, cold and hot, are valuable, like the waters of
Hierapolis and Colossae. Intolerable, like the emetic waters of Laodicea,
are the works of the Laodicean church.[18]

Other allusions to the contexts of the believers in the seven *poleis*
have been identified, some more plausible than others. Nevertheless, the
details highlighted here demonstrate correlations between John's vision
and the lives of believers in the seven *poleis*. These correlations are significant considerations in the interpretation of Revelation, supporting
the identification of Revelation as an occasional document. As an occasional document, Revelation was a response to events and concerns in
the lives of the first-century believers by whom it was first read.

READING REVELATION IN THE URBAN CULTURE
OF FIRST-CENTURY ROMAN ASIA

John's original audience and other first-century readers would have recognized in Revelation a critique of the social world in which they lived.
Both in the correlations between the content of Revelation and the contexts of particular *poleis* of Asia and in the contrasts between "Babylon"
and New Jerusalem, John was proclaiming divine judgment against a society operating in hostility to the God revealed in Jesus Christ. Because of
the nature of personal identity in the first century, this judgment would
have been taken personally by the citizens and residents of the *poleis*.

In a dyadic/collectivist society, such as that which existed in the first-
century Mediterranean, a person's identity was comprehended primarily
in terms of the groups of which one was a member.[19] An example of this
perception of identity is present in Paul's letter to the Philippians.

> If anyone else has reason to be confident in the flesh, I have more:
> circumcised on the eighth day, a member of the people of Israel,
> of the tribe of Benjamin, a Hebrew born of Hebrews; as to the
> law, a Pharisee; as to zeal, a persecutor of the church; as to righ-
> teousness under the law, blameless. (Phil 3:4b–6)

---

18. Emetic is from the Greek verb *emesai* [ἐμέσαι, "to vomit"]; cf. Rev 3:16. Note
Beale, *The Book of Revelation*, 303; Mounce, *The Book of Revelation*, 125–26; Reddish,
Revelation, 81–82.

19. Malina, *The New Testament World* (2001), 60–67.

Before declaring these qualifications to be worthless when contrasted with his new identity in Christ (a new group identity), Paul presents a self-portrait in terms of his various group allegiances:

1. circumcision as a ritual that demonstrated membership in the nation of Israel,

2. tribal membership in Benjamin,

3. birth status in the national group,

4. membership in a particular sectarian group within Israel (the Pharisees),

5. opposition to a sectarian group perceived as unfaithful to Israel (the church), and

6. faithfulness to the law, the defining covenant of Israel.

For those granted the status, citizenship in a *polis* was a particularly honorable and noteworthy element of group identity. Paul identifies himself as a citizen of Tarsus (Acts 21:39) and as a citizen of Rome (Acts 22:25, 27, 28).

Believers in the seven *poleis* faced pressure, implicit and overt, to conform to the standards imposed upon members of the various parties within the *poleis*. In the dyadic Greco-Roman *polis* acceptance was dependent upon and defined by membership in the groups that constituted the *polis*: citizens, worshipers of the patron divinities, participants in the trade guilds that promoted the material prosperity of the *polis*, members of the governing council of the *polis*, participants in the patron/client relationships that formed the fabric of the society, etc. Membership in these groups necessarily involved multifaceted compromises by John's audience, including sacrifices to the local gods, goddesses, and heroes revered in each *polis*.[20] In Revelation John called upon his audience to reject such compromises.

Inherent in God's impending judgment of "Babylon" was the rejection in Revelation of residence/citizenship in a Greco-Roman *polis* as

---

20. Though he was a citizen of Rome and a citizen of Tarsus, Paul would have been exempt from these compromises. Since the time of Julius Caesar, Jewish residents of the empire had been granted exemptions from activities that were inconsistent with Jewish laws and customs. While Jewish members of the churches in the seven *poleis* might have been able to avail themselves of such privileges, the Gentile members of the churches remained vulnerable to the pressure to conform to the standards of the *polis*.

the basis for an honorable personal identity. This verdict was a challenge to the communities in which John's readers lived, and was a challenge to those readers themselves. The pagan residents and citizens of the *poleis* were presented as living in opposition to the God who has the power and authority to judge all of creation. In Revelation the *poleis* in which they lived were declared to be facing divine wrath. The members of the churches in these *poleis* were challenged to establish their identity independently of the *poleis* in which they found themselves. Though John did not use Paul's characteristic phrase, John surely would have endorsed an identity established "in Christ" rather than in any earthly *polis*. John's account of New Jerusalem reinforces the call for the believers to identify themselves with Lord God the Almighty and the Lamb (Rev 21:22).

READING REVELATION IN THE URBAN CULTURE OF THE TWENTY-FIRST CENTURY

Prior to asking *how* Revelation should be read by a twenty-first century audience, another question must be asked: should a twenty-first century audience attempt to read Revelation at all? Viewed from two extremes, one could argue that Revelation has no place in the church today.

1. If Revelation is an occasional document, addressing the concerns of a first-century audience, perhaps this document is obsolete. Why read such a particular message for any reason other than to satisfy antiquarian curiosity?

2. If Revelation is primarily or solely an account of future events, perhaps the message of Revelation is for a generation yet unborn. Why treasure a document that for at least two millennia of Christianity was intended to communicate a message to someone else?

Approaching these questions in reverse order, the correlations between the content of Revelation and the lives of the believers in Laodicea and Pergamum demonstrate that the message of Revelation is not to be located solely, or even primarily, in the future. Any interpretation that grants such priority to the future may not "hear" an important message in the biblical text.

Having acknowledged the relevance of Revelation in the first-century context, the message and enduring relevance of Revelation need to be considered. How can a document rooted in the first-century be relevant today? Occasional literature is approached best from its original context, but can have relevance to the church through the centuries. The connection between 1 Corinthians and its first-century context in Greco-Roman Corinth is undeniable, yet this epistle communicates meaningfully to believers today (addressing unity in the community of believers, the role of spiritual gifts, propriety in worship, etc.). Similarly, Revelation is a first-century document that continues to communicate a message relevant to the church in every era.

Now the other question can be asked: How should Revelation be read today? This examination of Revelation in its ancient urban context, while not comprehensive or exhaustive in analyzing the message of Revelation, has exposed the issue of personal identity as a concern to John. The members of his audience were tempted to allow the criteria of the Greco-Roman *polis* to define them. In the contrast between "Babylon" and New Jerusalem, John found these criteria to be contrary to the message of the risen Christ. What criteria does twenty-first century urban society seek to impose upon the church today? Unlike John's original audience, most twenty-first-century, Western readers are primarily individualistic, not dyadic/collectivist, in their self-perception. This distinction impacts the reading and application of Revelation. Several questions, however, remain:

- By what criteria do believers today define themselves?

- Are these criteria consistent with the message of the risen Christ?

- If these criteria are in conflict with the gospel, how (specifically) should believers respond?

8

The Text of Revelation

Why neither Armageddon nor 666
May Be Exactly What You Think

JAMES JEFFREY CATE

INTRODUCTION

THE PAINSTAKING PROCESS OF copying a text is never immune to human influence. Even in the age of printing, typos sometimes occurred in Bibles with interesting and significant results. A 1547 edition of the Great Bible unintentionally omitted eleven verses (Rev. 1:9b–20a) by skipping an entire page. A 1612 copy of the King James Version accidentally printed that *Judas*, not *Jesus*, was praying in Gethsemane (Matt 26:36). A year later, a typesetter was either inattentive at best or disgruntled at worst because Ps 119:161 ended up stating *"printers"* (not *princes*) "have persecuted me without cause." A 1631 edition of the Rheims-Douai Bible accidentally omitted the word *not* in the seventh commandment and stated, "Thou shalt commit adultery" (Exod 20:14). Those Bibles were recalled and the printers heavily fined. A 1641 edition of the King James Version inadvertently omitted the word *no* and stated the opposite, "And there was . . . more sea" (Rev 21:1). In 1850, a publisher accidentally printed the "lake of *life*" rather than the "lake of *fire*" in Rev 20:15.[1] Even as recently as 1966, some initial copies of the

1. For detailed information regarding misprints, errors, and curious readings, see

Jerusalem Bible unwittingly omitted a single letter and stated, *"pay* for peace in Jerusalem" rather than *pray* (Ps 122:6).

EXISTING GREEK MANUSCRIPTS OF REVELATION

What a difference a letter or a word can make. The problem of changes in the process of copying was even more an issue before the invention of the printing press. During the first fifteen hundred years of Christianity when the New Testament text was copied by hand, the twenty-seven books that comprise the New Testament rarely were copied all together. Of the 5,567 Greek manuscripts surviving today, only 59 are copies that at one time contained all parts of the New Testament.[2] Since the Revelation of John is so distinct from the other New Testament books in terms of genre, style, and perspective, this book typically was copied individually as a separate item. Of the 313 Greek manuscripts of the Apocalypse, roughly two-thirds include no other New Testament books besides Revelation.[3] Because of this textual isolation, the Revelation of John is quite distinct from the rest of the New Testament in terms of its history of being copied. The established and well known groups of New Testament manuscripts in the Gospels and Pauline Epistles that tend to have similar readings do not transfer across consistently as the same groups or with the same importance when examining the text of Revelation.

Summary and Date

Today, 313 known Greek manuscripts of the book of Revelation are available for study.[4] These include seven papyri ($\mathfrak{P}^{18}$, $\mathfrak{P}^{24}$, $\mathfrak{P}^{43}$, $\mathfrak{P}^{47}$, $\mathfrak{P}^{85}$, $\mathfrak{P}^{98}$,

---

Herbert, *Historical Catalogue of Printed Editions of the English Bible 1525–1961.*

2. As of their latest update (Feb. 4, 2010), the Institute for New Testament Textual Research (INTF) at Münster, Germany (http://www.uni-muenster.de/INTF/) lists 125 papyri, 280 uncials, 2812 minuscules and 2350 lectionaries, even though the highest numerical designations for each category are $\mathfrak{P}^{127}$, 0320, 2903 and *l*2445 due to additions and subtractions through the years.

3. Fifty-nine manuscripts contain the Gospels, Acts, Catholic Epistles, Pauline Epistles, and Revelation. Thirty-nine more contain all sections of the New Testament except the Gospels, and one contains the entire New Testament except the Catholic Epistles. Eight contain only the Gospels and Revelation and two contain only Pauline Epistles and Revelation.

4. For a detailed summary of the Greek manuscripts of Revelation, see Aune, *Revelation 1–5*, cxxxiv-cxlviii. The numerical statistics of the manuscripts of Revelation in this essay are Aune's with supplement from the latest update of *Kurgefasste liste* from the

$\mathfrak{P}^{115}$), twelve uncials (ℵ, A, C, P, 046, 051, 052, 0163, 0169, 0207, 0229, 0308), and 294 minuscules.[5] Noticeably absent is any copy of Revelation in the lectionaries since the Greek Church never included this book in the cycle of liturgical readings. The nineteen papyri and uncials are of special significance since they come from the first ten centuries of the church, but unfortunately only three of these (ℵ, A, 046) are complete copies of the Apocalypse. Most of the papyri and some of the uncials are only small fragments.

In terms of date, the earliest fragments of Revelation are $\mathfrak{P}^{18}$, $\mathfrak{P}^{47}$, $\mathfrak{P}^{98}$, and $\mathfrak{P}^{115}$. Of these, $\mathfrak{P}^{98}$ seems to be the earliest, probably dating to the second century, but only nine verses remain (Rev 1:13—2:1). The Chester Beatty manuscript ($\mathfrak{P}^{47}$) from the late-third or early-fourth century has the most existing material on papyrus since much of nine chapters (9:10—17:2) are extant. Oxyrhynchus 4499 ($\mathfrak{P}^{115}$) from the same time period generates much attention not only because this manuscript contains fragments of twelve chapters, but also because its readings have a closeness to the readings found in the important manuscripts A and C.

Of the twelve uncials, the most significant are Codices Sinaiticus (ℵ), Alexandrinus (A), and Ephraemi Syri Rescriptus (C). Unlike the other uncials, these three are early and contain extensive amounts of text. Sinaiticus from the fourth century is the earliest complete copy of Revelation available today; however, Alexandrinus and Ephraemi, both from the fifth century, are considered to contain a superior form of the Alexandrian text. Unfortunately, the famous uncial Vaticanus (B) has no extant portion of Revelation, other than a fifteenth-century hand known as minuscule 1957 that supplied the missing leaves at the end at a much later date.

INTF. Since Aune's publication, the INTF has included three additional manuscripts of Revelation into their catalogue: $\mathfrak{P}^{115}$, 0308, and 2864. Additionally, 205^{copy} and 2036^{copy} are now known as Gregory-Aland 2886 and 2891, respectively.

5. Specialists who study manuscripts typically divide New Testament manuscripts into four categories based on material, handwriting, and format: (1) papyrus manuscripts, which tend to be early, were written on plant fiber instead of animal skin; (2) uncial manuscripts were written on animal skin known as parchment and in all capital letters; (3) minuscules were also written on parchment but in a cursive Greek handwriting that began to be used in the ninth century; and (4) lectionaries were used for reading in worship and did not contain continuous text but groups of passages from different New Testament books.

The 294 minuscules of Revelation form a cache of evidence of varying quality. Unfortunately, sixty of these (over 20 percent) were hand-copied in the age of printing. Furthermore, at least a half dozen of these are hand-written copies of the Textus Receptus.[6] Nevertheless, three of the minuscules (2053, 2062, and 2344) are of special significance because they record an early form of the Alexandrian type of text and are considered equals in superiority with the great uncials A and C, even though these three minuscules originate between the eleventh and thirteenth centuries.[7]

Evidence from the Church Fathers

The witness of the church fathers as they quoted or referred to the text of Revelation is also deficient compared to the rest of the New Testament. Irenaeus and Tertullian, among a few scattered others, offer occasional evidence on variant readings. In the third century, despite his stated intentions, no evidence indicates that Origen ever made a systematic treatment of the Apocalypse.[8] The main patristic witnesses to the text of Revelation are from Andreas, Arethas, and Oecumenius, but these commentaries come from the seventh to tenth centuries and therefore are less helpful as textual witnesses. Roughly one-third of the extant manuscripts of Revelation are simply copies of these commentaries with their text imbedded in between comments.

6. The Textus Receptus was a sixteenth-century print edition of the Greek New Testament based on medieval manuscripts with a Byzantine type of text.

7. The "Alexandrian" type of text is generally recognized as the most important group of early manuscripts in all parts of the New Testament. This type of text gets its name from church fathers in Alexandria, Egypt (such as Clement, Origen, and Didymus) who exhibit similar readings to these types of manuscripts.

8. Regarding Origen's intentions to write a commentary on Revelation, see Klostermann and Benz, *Origenes: Matthäuserklärung*. Unfortunately, Origen's comment only survives currently in Latin, not in Origen's language of Greek, nor in translation for English readers. Adolf Harnack argued that 39 anonymous scholia in minuscule 2351 were Origen's long lost comments on Revelation (Diobouniotis and Harnack, *Der Scholien-Kommentar*, 1–88), but further studies show these scholia are simply a collection of early comments from multiple church fathers since two are from Irenaeus and one is from Clement. Unfortunately, the fourth edition of the United Bible Society's *The Greek New Testament* (UBS4) still cites the scholia in its critical apparatus as Origen[dub] instead of more accurately as 2351[schol].

Limited Nature of the Evidence

The limited nature of the manuscript evidence for the Apocalypse is well illustrated when the first published edition of the Greek New Testament was produced. Desiderius Erasmus of Rotterdam accomplished this task in a matter of months in 1516. But when he came to the book of Revelation, he had only one manuscript available for his use, which unfortunately was late, difficult to use, and incomplete. The manuscript was Codex Johannis Reuchlini, known today as 2814. This twelfth-century manuscript of Revelation is in the form of a commentary of Andreas of Caesarea and is missing its final leaf.[9] With no further options and trying to meet a publishing deadline, Erasmus himself hastily composed the missing last six verses (22:16–21) by translating from the Latin Bible back into Greek. Considering the circumstances, he did an admirable job, but in the process he unintentionally introduced variant readings in Greek that have no prior manuscript evidence.

An example of a variant accidentally created by Erasmus is his "book of life" reading in 22:19. Are the disobedient to be punished by their exclusion from the "tree of life" (as in Greek manuscripts before Erasmus) or from the "book of life" (as Erasmus printed)? No evidence shows that the reading "book of life" in that verse existed in Greek prior to the printed text of Erasmus. Two Greek manuscripts have this reading (minuscules 296 and 2049), but both of these are sixteenth-century, hand-written copies of the Textus Receptus based on Erasmus's publication. The variant probably arose as a confusion in Latin between *ligno* ("tree") and *libro* ("book") since the term "book of life" is used elsewhere in Revelation.[10]

THE PROBLEM FOR ENGLISH READERS

In light of this situation with the manuscript history, an English reader of the book of Revelation might not be aware of the uncertain wording of some passages due to variations among the surviving manuscripts. Fortunately, the current trend with English translations is to note variant

9. Manuscript 2814 was not included in Herman Hoskier's exhaustive collation of all known manuscripts of Revelation (1929). The location of 2814 was unknown until Franz Delitzsch rediscovered this manuscript in 1861. See Scrivener, *A Plain Introduction*, p. 320.

10. Rev 3:5; 13:8; 17:8; 20:12, 15; 21:27.

readings in marginal notes. For example, in Revelation alone, the NIV lists two variations in the Greek manuscripts, the NLT six, the ESV eleven, the NJB thirteen, the NRSV seventeen, the NET Bible thirty-nine, and the HCSB eighty-two. In comparison, the main critical editions of the Greek New Testament in print today list as many as two hundred.[11] In comparison to the rest of the New Testament, only Mark, John, and 2 Peter have a higher proportion of variant readings in their texts, which is ironic in light of the stern warning at the end of Revelation not to alter the text (22:18–19).

Sometimes careful readers notice differences in the text between modern English translations based primarily on Alexandrian manuscripts in comparison to translations such as the KJV or NKJV that are based on Byzantine manuscripts.[12] Based on the studies of Josef Schmid and others,[13] generally the major superior manuscripts of Revelation seem to be the Alexandrian witnesses Codices Alexandrinus (A) and Ephraemi Syri Rescriptus (C) and minuscules 2053, 2062, and 2344. The Alexandrian manuscripts of secondary importance include Codex Sinaiticus (ℵ), 𝔓⁴⁷, and the occasional testimony of Origen. The Byzantine manuscripts of Revelation divide into two distinct groups, a "Koine" main group and an "Andreas" group found distinctly in that patristic commentary, both of which are considered inferior to all the Alexandrian witnesses. Nevertheless, whenever a difference in readings occurs between manuscripts, external evidence must be balanced with internal evidence for determining the best reading. External evidence includes data such as which reading is earlier, more widespread, and found in

11. The UBS4 lists 71 variant readings while the 27th edition of the Nestle-Aland *Novum Testamentum Graece* (Stuttgart, 1993) lists over 200.

12. The Byzantine manuscripts comprise the vast majority of Greek manuscripts in existence today and most date from the 11th to 15th centuries. Since no evidence of this type of text exists before the fourth century, the Byzantine type of text generally is considered to be inferior to the Alexandrian type of manuscripts. Nevertheless, when print editions of the Greek New Testament and English translations (such as the KJV) began to be made in the 16th, 17th, and 18th centuries, these were based on the Textus Receptus and Byzantine manuscripts. As Alexandrian manuscripts began to be discovered in the 19th and 20th centuries and their importance increasingly recognized, virtually all modern English translations (except for the NKJV) have been based upon an Alexandrian type of text.

13. Schmid, *Studien zur Geschichte des griechischen Apokalypse-Textes*; Kilpatrick, "Professor J. Schmid," 1–13; Birdsall, "The Text of the Revelation," 228–37; D. Parker, "A New Oxyrhynchus Papyrus," 159–74.

different textual groups. Internal evidence includes factors such as which reading is shorter, more difficult, and more likely to have caused the origination of the other readings.

EXAMPLES OF ALTERNATE READINGS

Readers of the text in English now may be wondering what passages in Revelation contain variations in the manuscripts. The purpose here is not to cover all the variants. However, enough examples can be given to raise some thought-provoking questions.

Sampling Some Variants

Sometimes the spelling of a word in Greek that is similar to another word that also could fit the context caused variant readings. In Rev 1:5, are God's people "freed" (*lysanti*) or "washed" (*lousanti*) from their sins? Both verbs sounded and looked alike.[14] In 8:13, what flies through mid-heaven, an "eagle/vulture" (*aetou*) or an "angel" (*aggelou*)? In 18:3, have the nations "fallen" (*peptōkasin* or *peptōkan* or *peptōken*) or "drunk" (*pepōkasin* or *pepōkan* or *pepōken*) or even "given drink" (*pepōtiken*)? In 19:13, was the Horseman's robe "dipped" (*bebammenon*) in blood or "dyed" (*rerammenon* or *errammenon* or *errantismenon* or *perireram-menon*) with blood?

Sometimes confusion of words involved an entire phrase and not merely a single word. In Rev 22:14, is the seventh and last beatitude in the book directed towards those who "wash their robes" or those who "do his commandments"? The earlier manuscripts (ℵ, A) have the first reading even though the second reading has early patristic testimony from Tertullian and Cyprian. The first reading would be an allusion back to 7:14 where the martyrs have washed their robes, but the second reading would be an allusion to those who keep the commandments of God in 12:17 and 14:12, even though a different Greek verb is used. In English, the two readings do not appear similar, but in Greek the verbs (*plynontes/poiountes* for "wash"/"do"), nouns (*stolas/ entolas* for "robes"/"commandments"), and pronouns (*autōn/autou* for

---

14. In Greek, the difference between *lysanti* and *lousanti* is only a single letter, omicron, which, unfortunately, is not as clear in the English transliteration. The Greek vowel upsilon transliterates into English as "y" when standing alone but as "u" when combined with another vowel.

"their"/ "his") resemble each other in both sight and sound. The substitution of the second reading for the first possibly could go unnoticed, even by correctors checking a finished manuscript.

With some variants, what initially looks like an insignificant spelling error can have extensive implications. In Rev 15:6, were the seven angels dressed in "linen" (*linon*) or "stone" (*lithon*)? Based on a superficial reading of Revelation, one might expect "linen" in this context since linen seems to be mentioned elsewhere throughout the book. But on closer examination, "linen" (*linon*) is never used; instead, a completely different Greek word, "fine linen" (*byssinos*), is used (18:12, 16; 19:8, 14). The external evidence is somewhat split but leans slightly towards "stone" (A, C, 2053, 2062) more than "linen" ($\mathfrak{P}^{47}$, ℵ, 046, *Byz*). "Stone" seems to be the more difficult reading since the thought of an angel wearing designer stoneware initially appears as nonsense even in apocalyptic literature. Nevertheless, the symbolism of wearing stone is probably rooted in Old Testament precedent. In Ezek 28:13, a book repeatedly mined for allusions throughout Revelation, the king of Tyre is lamented as having been in Eden and clothed with every kind of precious stone (*lithon*). So, were the angels in 15:6 appearing splendid like a leader from the idyllic world of Eden, or were they appearing splendid with fine clothing? The manuscripts differ.

Other times in the manuscripts, an adjective or noun was added to clarify the meaning or sometimes removed to avoid a redundancy. In 4:8, did the four living creatures proclaim "holy" three times as in Isa 6:3, or eight times (ℵ), or even nine times (*Byz-Koine*)? In 9:16, is the army 100 million or 200 million strong? In 11:19, was an "earthquake" also part of the cosmic signs in the theophany? In 18:13, is "spice" included in the cargo list of abandoned merchandise? In 19:15, is the sword simply "sharp" or "double-edged" and sharp (as in 1:16; 2:12)? In 22:1, is the river that is described as "clear as crystal" also "pure"?

Several times in Revelation, the text is ambiguous regarding who said, did, or received something, and variants arose at these places. In Rev 5:9, who or what was ransomed to God by the Lamb's blood? Many Greek manuscripts include the pronoun "us" for clarification. English translations often add "people," "persons," or "men" in italics for the same reason, even though none of those words are stated in any of the Greek manuscripts. In 11:1, who does the speaking is unclear, whether John or possibly an angel, and manuscripts differ. In 11:12, variations exist among the manuscripts regarding who heard the loud voice from heaven. Was this voice heard by John, the two witnesses, or even the scared spectators? At the transition between chapters 12 and 13, manuscripts differ regarding who stood on the beach. Was this John or the beast? This variant has further uncertainty simply because the spelling of the verb in question differs only by a letter at the end that was sometimes optional on other forms of Greek verbs. In 13:10, who is supposed to kill or be killed by the sword is unclear since several different readings are found in the manuscripts. In 15:3, some manuscripts have "king of the nations," others "king of the ages," and still others "king of the saints." All of these represent variations among the manuscripts, some with evidence that is more straightforward to handle and others with issues that are still uncertain.

Some variant readings might not seem too important at first glance, but on closer examination they end up affecting the text in interesting ways. In both 1:6 and 5:10, manuscripts differ regarding God's people being called a "kingdom" or "kings" along with priests. The external evidence alone in both passages heavily favors "kingdom" as the preferred reading. The difference between "kingdom" and "kings" might seem insignificant initially. "Kingdom" along with "priests," however, is a reading that makes a strong connection of both passages in Revelation as the fulfillment of Exod 19:6, in which God's people are called a "kingdom of priests." Such background is important in Revelation since seventy percent of its verses have allusions to the Old Testament. Furthermore, nowhere in Revelation are God's people ever called "kings" even though they reign with God according to 20:6. Throughout Revelation, "kings" (or usually "kings of the earth") is a term referring to worldly leaders opposing God's rule, and never to God's people. The repeated use of the term "king" in this negative way alone sets up the ultimate description of the Lamb/Horseman as the actual ruler of all apparent autocrats with the distinct title, "King of kings" (17:14; 19:16).

Sometimes an accidental variant can have important implications. In Rev 13:7, an eyesight error seems to have caused a rather large omission in many of the early and important manuscripts. The first half of the verse is omitted in $\mathfrak{P}^{47}$ A C 2053 and even the Latin copies of the second-century father, Irenaeus. The variant must have originated early in the copy process. In Greek, the opening three words of the first half of the verse (*kai edothē autō*) are identical to the opening three words of the second half of the verse. Similar wording often created an accidental error called haplography in which a scribe's eyes jumped from one phrase to the next resulting in an omission. In 13:7, the omitted phrase is, "And [permission] was given to him [the beast] to wage war against the saints and to conquer them." The sentence is difficult theologically because its thought easily provokes questions of theodicy. Why would God allow his faithful ones to be embattled and conquered? Nevertheless, the omission seems to be accidental, and, significantly, $\mathfrak{P}^{115}$ has evidence for the longer reading without the omission at an early date.

Sometimes a simple variant reading in the manuscripts intensifies the meaning of a passage. For example, in Rev 2:20, just how well did the church in Thyatira know "Jezebel"? This church is rebuked for tolerating a false teacher labeled as "Jezebel," and she is identified as "that woman" (*tēn gynaikēn*). But in Greek, the noun *gynē* can mean either a woman in general or a wife in particular. A few manuscripts, including A and 046 among others, add the personal pronoun "your" (*sou*) so that she is called "your wife Jezebel." This secondary reading makes the charge more personal as if the church metaphorically, or possibly even the church leader literally, is married to this woman. But on the other hand, this variant reading might simply be accidental (whether by addition or omission) since the same pronoun (*sou*) is used four other times in the immediate context.

Other times, a variant reading, even an obscure one, can shed light on how the text could be misunderstood. Two verses later in Rev 2:22, an interesting variant occurs regarding Jezebel's punishment. Virtually all manuscripts have the reading that she will be thrown onto a "bed" (*klinē*) with the implication that this judgment is a "sickbed" from which the English word "clinic" originates. Nevertheless, at least four singular readings serve as substitutions: "prison" (*phylakēn* as in A), "oven/furnace" (as in the Armenian version), "sickness" (as in the Coptic Sahidic version), or "grief/sorrow" (according to Primasius).[15] Obviously, scribes and translators consulted their theological thesaurus to come up with different means of discipline. These singular readings probably represent scribal attempts to prevent an unwanted misreading

---

15. "Singular readings" are readings that are found in only one witness, whether a manuscript, a version, or a church father. Generally, a singular reading is not given much consideration as a significant reading, but often singular readings provide important information about how texts were interpreted by at least one scribe or translator.

of Jezebel's punishment. Evidently, later scribes were simply trying to prevent the misunderstanding that Jezebel would be the recipient of a bed or couch as if for her immoral activities.

Sometimes, a variant reflects the history of interpretation. In Rev 6:17, is the day of wrath "their" (*autōn*) wrath or "his" (*autou*) wrath? In the preceding verse, the antecedent of the pronoun is *either* "the One who sits on the throne" *or* "the Lamb" *or* possibly both. Despite the reading in A, the external and internal evidence weighs heavily towards the plural pronoun ("their"), not the singular ("his"), as being the earlier and preferred reading. That scribes changed the singular pronoun to the plural for grammatical reasons is less likely than the thought that scribes changed the plural pronoun to the singular for theological reasons. Certainly as Christian expression progressed through the centuries, plural pronouns were used less and less for what would later be called the First and Second Persons of the Trinity.

Another variant of theological interpretation is found in Rev 21:3. A loud voice makes the climactic announcement, "God's dwelling is with men, and he will dwell with them, and they will be his people." After these words, the next part of the announcement, however, was the source of much confusion among scribes because five different arrangements of the words exist in the manuscripts. Based on external evidence such as A and other witnesses, most likely the earliest reading stated literally, "And God himself with them will be their God," but with the implied meaning that "God himself will be with them [as] their God." That word arrangement, however, could also be misunderstood as if God reigned as God with the help of his people. Attempts to avoid such a theological misunderstanding are probably what motivated the alternative readings in other manuscripts by either shortening ("and God himself will be them") or by rearranging the wording ("and God himself will be with them [as] their God"). Elsewhere Revelation emphasizes that God's people will reign with him (5:10; 20:4–6; 22:5), but the alternative readings probably arose to avoid a potential misreading as if God's people would eventually share in God's sovereignty.

What about Armageddon?

Sometimes scribes of the New Testament had trouble spelling, locating, or understanding certain geographical references. In Rev 16:16, one of the most famous place names in all of the Bible—Armageddon—ends up with considerable variation in the manuscripts because the word is a Hebrew spelling indirectly referring to a place in Palestine unfamiliar to many in the early church. Furthermore, the term "Armageddon" occurs only in 16:16, and never elsewhere in the entire Bible, not even in other passages of Revelation describing a climatic eschatological battle (17:14; 19:14–21; 20:7–10). *As a result of this overwhelming geographical and historical obscurity of the term "Armageddon" in 16:16, the manuscripts and versions record over a dozen different spellings of basically two different words, Armageddon and Megiddo.* Much of the confusion arose since the term Armageddon has no known prior usage in Greek before its occurrence in this verse. The meaning of Armageddon in Hebrew is not certain, but most likely meant "Mount(ain) of Megiddo," which only furthered the confusion because Megiddo is located in a valley, not on a mountain. As an apocalypse, most likely the author intended Armageddon as another symbolic reference similar to others such as Sodom, Egypt, Babylon, or the Euphrates used elsewhere in the book. Later scribes tried to relieve this term of its difficulty by simplifying the expression to Megiddo; however, in doing so, readers could end up missing the intended meaning of the difficult term as if the reference was a literal location on a Palestinian map and not simply a symbolic reference to a final eschatological battle.

FIGURE 18. Papyrus Manuscript 𝔓¹¹⁵ Fragment. This fragment of 𝔓¹¹⁵ shows the number of the beast as 616 (the letters XIC in the third line with a stroke on top; X = 600, I = 10, and C = 6).

What about 666?

Not only is a famous term such as Armageddon the subject of variant readings in the manuscripts of Revelation, but also the most famous number in the Bible, 666. In Rev 13:18, the author encouraged the readers to decipher the symbolic number of the beast. Most likely, the ancient practice of gematria was being utilized in which the numeric values of the letters in a word were added up into a single number cryptically representing the word. Since Greek and Hebrew letters also functioned as the character set for numbers, every Greek or Hebrew word had a numeric value. But conversely, any number, especially large ones, could represent innumerable combinations of letters in words or abbreviations.

Ancient and modern minds have considered numerous possibilities for 666 without any consensus. Possible scenarios include "Latins" or "Titan" (i.e., the Roman Empire), "Caesar Nero," "beast," or abbreviations for one or more of the Roman emperors, among many other conjectures (some involving different combination of Hebrew, Aramaic, Greek, and Latin). *The number puzzled not only early interpreters such as Irenaeus who discussed various possibilities at length,*[16] *but also seems to have puzzled scribes since at least four different numbers are used in manuscripts and versions.* Minuscule 2344 has the number 665, while one Old Latin manuscript (Beuron 61) has 646. More significantly, the important manuscripts 𝔓[115] and C have the number 616, a reading that Irenaeus mentioned in the second century even though he did not consider the reading original.[17] The combination of these three early and important witnesses to the reading 616 cannot be dismissed quickly. The number of the beast very well may have been 616, not 666.

CONCLUSION

In light of these and other differences, the surviving manuscripts of Revelation provide a fascinating collection of various readings and interpretations. Even though in some passages the earliest and best reading is difficult to determine based on the available data, nevertheless, all the readings are important because they provide material evidence as to how the text was read and understood at different times and places in history. Further, even though Revelation has less surviving manuscript evidence

16. Irenaeus *Against Heresies* 5.30.1–4.
17. Ibid., 5.30.1

than the other books of the New Testament, what is available today is sometimes remarkable. As with the number of the beast in 13:18, two of the most important manuscripts of Revelation are $\mathfrak{P}^{115}$ and C, both of which were nearly lost to later generations. All that remains of $\mathfrak{P}^{115}$ are 26 fragments that were found in the trash heaps near Oxyrhynchus, Egypt and published in 1999.[18] Codex Ephraemi Syri Rescriptus (C) also narrowly escaped an ignominious fate. This fifth-century copy of the Old and New Testaments was erased in the twelfth century and written over with the works of Ephraem of Syria so that the biblical text that the parchment originally recorded has to be meticulously extracted from under a layer of later writing. One can only hope that further manuscripts will continue to be discovered in the years ahead to shed additional light on the text and history of interpretation of the Apocalypse.

QUESTIONS FOR REFLECTION

- How often have you heard or read discussions about the differences in wording between manuscripts when studying a passage of the New Testament? Have you noticed or read the marginal notes in English translations of the Bible about manuscript issues before reading this chapter?

- Which difference in wording in Revelation affects your understanding of a passage the most? Why?

- How do the differences in wording on Armageddon (16:16) and 666 (13:18) affect your understanding of how those passages were understood by scribes copying the text?

18. Gonis, *The Oxyrhynchus Papyri*, vol. 66. Besides $\mathfrak{P}^{115}$, five other fragments of Revelation have also been found at Oxyrhynchus: $\mathfrak{P}^{18}$, $\mathfrak{P}^{24}$, 0163, 0169, and 0308.

9

Confronting the Beast

The Imperial Cult and the Book of Revelation

RICHARD WARREN JOHNSON

INTRODUCTION

Among these I considered that I should dismiss any who denied that they were or ever had been Christians when they had repeated after me a formula of invocation to the gods and had made offerings of wine and incense to your statue (which I had ordered to be brought into court for this purpose along with the images of the gods), and furthermore had reviled the name of Christ: none of which things, I understand, any genuine Christian can be induced to do.[1]

A STONE IN THE EPHESUS Museum in Selçuk, Turkey bears an inscription that includes the words ΘΕΩΙ ΚΑΙΣΑΡΙ (*theōi kaisari*; "to the god Caesar"). Ephesus was the home of a temple dedicated to the Flavian emperors (Vespasian, Titus, and Domitian), another to Hadrian, one to Augustus Caesar, and a sanctuary dedicated jointly to *Dea Roma* (the goddess Roma) and the Divine Julius Caesar. Traveling north, atop the acropolis of Pergamum lie the remains of the Sanctuary of Athena where the goddess's statue looked out over the lower city. In 19 B.C.E., after Pergamum had been incorporated into the Roman Empire, that

---

1. Pliny the Younger *Letter* 10.96.5.

sculpture was replaced by a bronze image of Augustus Caesar.[2] Turning south and journeying inland, in Sardis the reconstructed city gymnasium bears an inscription boasting of Sardis's status as ΔΙΣ ΝΕΩΚΟΡΟΣ ΤΩΝ ΣΕΒΑΣΤΩΝ (dis neōkoros tōn sebastōn; "Twice Temple Warden of the Augustans"). These three cities shared more than a common heritage of emperor worship; together with Smyrna, Thyatira, Philadelphia, and Laodicea they were home to the early Christian communities to whom Revelation was addressed.

In his study of the imperial cult S. R. F. Price identifies three categories of evidence of emperor worship in Roman Asia Minor: the presence of imperial altars, the establishment of imperial temples, and the appointment of imperial priests. For each of the seven cities of Revelation Price confirms at least one of these categories as present, with all three classes identified in four of the cities (Ephesus, Smyrna, Pergamum, and Sardis).[3] Despite abundant evidence for the existence of the imperial cult, readers separated by two millennia from the Greco-Roman culture of first-century C.E. Asia Minor struggle to grasp how, despite their evident mortality, the men who ruled the Mediterranean world could be worshiped as transcendent, divine, omniscient, omnipotent, omnipresent beings. This struggle is rooted in a misconception that Price describes as making "Christianizing" assumptions about the imperial cult. To attempt to comprehend the worship of the Roman emperors in terms derived from Christian theology and experience is to impose alien criteria to the neglect of "indigenous standards."[4]

To equate the status attributed to the "divine" Roman emperors with the Christian perception of God is to fail to appreciate the role of the gods in ancient Mediterranean pagan culture. Worship of the pagan gods functioned as an integral component of a complex society that differed in many ways from the culture inhabited by twenty-first century western Christians. A useful basis for comprehending ancient Mediterranean paganism in general and the imperial cult in particular is to recognize the Greco-Roman world as an honor/shame culture and a limited-goods society.[5]

2. Cimak, *Pergamum*, 26.

3. Price, *Rituals and Power*, 252–60, 264–65.

4. Ibid., 10.

5. For a more thorough discussion of the dynamics of honor/shame cultures and limited-goods societies, see Malina, *The New Testament World*, 27–57, 81–107.

AN "INDIGENOUS STANDARD" FOR
GRECO-ROMAN PAGANISM

In a limited-goods society all necessary commodities (water, land, food, fuel, building materials, fabric, housing, employment, etc.) are perceived to exist in finite, limited quantities. Survival is dependent upon gaining access to these vital wares. Among the ancient Greeks and Romans a common solution to this problem was to establish a patron/client relationship. The superior (patron) in this relationship had access to commodities that were otherwise unavailable to his or her subordinates (clients). In exchange for access to the goods mediated by the patron, clients were expected to support the patron's political aspirations, to provide labor for "public works" projects carried out by the patron, and to perform other deeds designed to enhance the patron's honor (honor being another "limited good").

Honor was a vital matter in the New Testament world and concern for honor was present in every public exchange between adults. As a sociological category, "honor" is defined as "the *public* recognition of one's social standing,"[6] as "a claim to worth that is publicly acknowledged."[7] The honor of a patron was proportional to the number of clients whose requirements he or she could satisfy.

A "local" patron could be expected to provide resources for his or her clients on a local scale. Representation of a client before the city council was a reasonable expectation; however, some needs exceeded the capacity of the "local" patron. When the necessary limited good was mediated at the provincial level a higher-level patron was required. The "local" patron could seek the mediation of an official in the city government, entering into a relationship in which the "local" patron became a client to a "city" patron. That "city" patron was, in turn, a client to a "provincial" patron, from whom the needed commodity could be requested. If the limited good was beyond the scope of the "provincial" patron, this person would approach a still-higher level patron, perhaps an aristocrat in Rome. Eventually this interlocking chain of patron/client relationships would lead to the emperor himself, the highest-level, most honorable of human patrons.

6. Moxnes, "Honor and Shame," 20.
7. Plevnik, "Honor/Shame," 106.

Some commodities exceeded the capacity of any human patron: rain to water crops, protection from earthquakes, and favorable winds for a merchant ship. In these situations a "cosmic" patron beyond the human realm was needed. Athena gave the olive tree to the people of Attica, so they honored her as the patron goddess of Athens and provided her with a majestic temple on the Athenian acropolis. Poseidon could protect the maritime commerce upon which Corinth depended, so this city dedicated the Isthmian Games to the god of the sea. Worship of the pagan gods was, in part, a component of the patron/client relationship that existed between the divinity and mortals.

A significant element of Greco-Roman paganism was the perceived need to honor the gods and goddesses who were recognized as patrons able to provide the necessary, limited, cosmic quantities. A clear example of this perception is present in the conflict that confronted Paul during his sojourn in Ephesus. After the apostle had labored there for an extended period a disturbance arose because of the perceived impact of his activity.

> A man named Demetrius, a silversmith who made silver shrines of Artemis, brought no little business to the artisans. These he gathered together, with the workers of the same trade, and said, "Men, you know that we get our wealth from this business. You also see and hear that not only in Ephesus but in almost the whole of Asia this Paul has persuaded and drawn away a considerable number of people by saying that gods made with hands are not gods. And there is danger not only that this trade of ours may come into disrepute but also that the temple of the great goddess Artemis will be scorned, and she will be deprived of her majesty that brought all Asia and the world to worship her." (Acts 19:24–27)

The concerns expressed by Demetrius were two-fold: peril to the silversmiths' source of income and loss of honor by the goddess. In the mind of the Ephesian mob these two aspects of the problem were inseparable; Artemis's loss of honor would call into question the loyalty of her clients and endanger the supply of goods (i.e., income) mediated by her. Defending the honor of Artemis and protecting their livelihoods were unified objectives of the Ephesians's response to Paul.

Comprehending the Roman imperial cult is a matter of comprehending the status and role of the emperors according to these "indigenous standards." Though mortal, the "divine" emperors were recognized as controlling and mediating the most limited of worldly goods, and, thus, as occupying a status that exceeded (even transcended) the realm of common human beings and could be related most appropriately to the realm of the gods. An inscription from Roman Asia dated to ca. 9 B.C.E. describes Augustus Caesar as "a savior who put an end to war and brought order to all things." He was credited with "surpassing those benefactors who had come before" and with "leaving to those who shall come no hope of surpassing (him)."[8] Surely a being who can provide such rewards to his clients is more than human; no human category of honor is adequate to describe him. The inscription describes Augustus's advent as "the birth of the god."

THE EMPEROR'S ASCENT TO DIVINITY

Prior to the rise of the Mediterranean empires, the city was the defining political entity of the Greek world. The autonomous city in a well-ordered relationship with the gods expected to survive all perils. Eventually empires emerged in which one ruler was able to exert authority over multiple cities (e.g., the empire of Alexander the Great), and the citizens of the subject communities adjusted their cosmologies to accommodate the new situation. Price suggests that the rise of ruler cults in the Hellenistic world was "an attempt to come to terms with this new kind of power. . . . The cults of the gods were the one model that was available to them for the representation of a power on whom the city was dependent which was external and yet still Greek."[9] Mary Beard describes the dynamic of pagan religion by noting that "the range of divinities, their different characteristics, responsibilities and family relationships represented an ambitious attempt to classify the world, to explain (and dispute) the nature of power and social relations, to understand the universe and humanity's place in it."[10] In this context the elevation of the geographically remote ruler to divine status was intelligible. With a power and dominion that exceeded the human scale to which residents of the Greek cities were accustomed, the status of the emperor could be comprehended as more nearly divine than human, and the imperial cult was born.

8. Friesen, *Imperial Cults*, 34.

9. Price, *Rituals and Power*, 29–30.

10. Beard, *The Parthenon*, 145.

Ultimately the Roman emperor was accorded an intermediate place between human beings and the immortal gods. "Standing at the apex of the hierarchy of the Roman empire the emperor offered the hope of order and stability and was assimilated to the traditional Olympian deities. But he also needed the divine protection which came from sacrifices made to the gods on his behalf. The emperor stood at the focal point between human and divine."[11] Two aspects of this explanation for the origins of the imperial cult are worth noting.

1. The innovation involved in the worship of the ruler/empire was perceived to fit into the order of the cosmos. Steven J. Friesen comments that "the exercise of imperial power is accomplished with a more or less successful effort to define society in terms that make this power seem normal, or at least inevitable. In the Roman province of Asia, imperial cults were a crucial part of this discourse."[12]

2. The elites in the subject cities were active agents in the promotion of the imperial cult; the imperial cult was not forced upon them by an external power. "The elite families . . . led sacrifices, underwrote festivals, built temples, voted honors, and so forth as part of their full range of civic duties. The elite families mobilized the masses in support of the emperor and enhanced their own standing in the process."[13]

Leonard Thompson notes correctly the lack of evidence for widespread official imposition of the imperial cult in Roman Asia during the reign of Domitian.[14] Pressure to conform to the will of Rome did not necessarily come directly from the Romans themselves. Rather, the empire allowed its provincial agents to impose order.[15] Through the imperial cult the elites simultaneously ingratiated themselves to their Roman masters and exalted themselves in their home communities. "Through this imperial cult priesthood, the Demetriastai were able to contribute to

11. Price, *Rituals and Power*, 233.

12. Friesen, *Imperial Cults*, 19.

13. Ibid., 203.

14. Though, note the official compulsion under a later emperor described in Pliny's letter to Trajan (quoted at the beginning of this chapter).

15. Thompson notes the probability that "potential beneficiaries approaching power from below" would be "eager to display their zeal for Domitian." Thompson, *The Book of Revelation*, 106.

the functioning of the city [of Ephesus] and to increase their own status within the city."[16]

The active involvement of provincial elites in the promotion of the imperial cult and the mediating position of the divine emperor (between mere humans and the other gods) are related directly to the seemingly enigmatic declaration by prominent scholars that "there is no such thing as *'the* imperial cult.'"[17] The key to understanding the point made by Beard, North, and Price is their emphasis on the definite article "*the.*" Local circumstances influenced significantly the form of emperor worship in the various communities. How the local elites negotiated the appointment of priests, where the imperial cult was housed, and how imperial festivals were coordinated with festivals of the other gods varied from one city to another. The operation of the imperial cult lacked uniformity, but "there was a series of different cults sharing a common focus in the worship of the emperor, his family or predecessors, but . . . operating quite differently according to a variety of different local circumstances."[18]

While Romans and provincial elites benefited from the hegemony of Rome, the relationship between the imperial power and the subject peoples was profoundly asymmetrical. Writing during Nero's reign (54–68 C.E.) Petronius offered a negative portrait of the routine exercise of Roman supremacy.

> The conquering Roman now held the whole world, sea and land and the course of sun and moon. But he was not satisfied. Now the waters were stirred and troubled by his loaded ships; if there were any hidden bay beyond, or any land that promised a yield of yellow gold, that place was Rome's enemy, fate stood ready for the sorrows of war, and the quest for wealth went on. There was no happiness in familiar joys, or in the pleasures dulled by the common man's use. The soldier out at sea would praise the bronze of Corinth; bright colours dug from earth rivaled the purple; from this side the African . . . from that side the Chinaman had plundered his marvelous silks, and the Arabian people had stripped their own fields bare.[19]

---

16. Friesen, *Imperial Cults*, 65.

17. Beard *et al.*, *Religions of Rome*, vol. 1, 348.

18. Ibid., 318.

19. Petronius *Satyricon* 119.1–12.

The imperial cult coerced non-Romans into cooperating with such exploitation. Repeating Friesen's statement, "imperial cults were a crucial part" of a discourse that defined "society in terms that make this power seem normal, or at least inevitable."[20]

How Rome benefited from this commercial arrangement is clear; how provincial proponents of imperial power benefited is also comprehensible. The materials that filled the ships described by Petronius were mined, harvested, and manufactured in provincial cities and loaded in provincial harbors, often onto ships owned by non-Romans. Wealth was available to those who served as agents in this commerce. Gaining the confidence of Rome through participation in the imperial cult was a useful means to ensure continued rewards from this mercantile system; loyal subjects of the emperor would be perceived as more trustworthy and more deserving business partners. The common people in the provinces (who comprised more than ninety percent of the population) had less to gain from worshipping the emperor, but they were dependent upon elite patrons who could persuade them to bow before the imperial altar. This seemingly irresistible veneration of the emperor was one of the more insidious aspects of the imperial cult that allowed Roman imperial priorities to control people at all levels of society.

RESISTANCE TO THE IMPERIAL CULT

Rome's will was resisted at great peril, but John called for resistance. After noting that "the merchants of the earth have grown rich from the power of her luxury" (Rev 18:3), John reports a summons: "Come out of her, my people, so that you do not take part in her sins, and so that you do not share in her plagues; for her sins are heaped high as heaven, and God has remembered her iniquities" (Rev 18:4–5). The basis for the condemnation of "Babylon" (a metaphorical reference to Rome) is reminiscent of Petronius's critique of Roman luxury: "she glorified herself and lived luxuriously," and again, "she says, 'I rule as a queen; I am no widow, and I will never see grief'" (Rev 18:7).

The collaborators would share a similar fate. Observe the following dramatic description.

> And the kings of the earth, who committed fornication and lived
> in luxury with her, will weep and wail over her when they see

20. Friesen, *Imperial Cults*, 19.

the smoke of her burning; they will stand far off, in fear of her torment, and say,

"Alas, alas, the great city,
    Babylon, the mighty city!
For in one hour your judgment has come."

And the merchants of the earth weep and mourn for her, since no one buys their cargo anymore, cargo of gold, silver, jewels and pearls, fine linen, purple, silk and scarlet, all kinds of scented wood, all articles of ivory, all articles of costly wood, bronze, iron, and marble, cinnamon, spice, incense, myrrh, frankincense, wine, olive oil, choice flour and wheat, cattle and sheep, horses and chariots, slaves—and human lives.

"The fruit for which your soul longed
    has gone from you,
and all your dainties and your splendor
    are lost to you,
        never to be found again!"

The merchants of these wares, who gained wealth from her, will stand far off, in fear of her torment, weeping and mourning aloud,

"Alas, alas, the great city,
    clothed in fine linen,
        in purple and scarlet,
    adorned with gold,
        with jewels, and with pearls!
For in one hour all this wealth has been laid waste!"

And all shipmasters and seafarers, sailors and all whose trade is on the sea, stood far off and cried out as they saw the smoke of her burning,

"What city was like the great city?"

And they threw dust on their heads, as they wept and mourned, crying out,

"Alas, alas, the great city,
    where all who had ships at sea
    grew rich by her wealth!
For in one hour she has been laid waste." (Rev 18:9–19)

The "kings of the earth" to whom John referred bear a striking resemblance to the wealthy provincial elites who promoted the imperial cult and benefited from commerce with Rome.

An obedient response to John's call to "come out" would impact all aspects of the believers' lives. The departure would separate them from the obvious idolatry involved in offering prayers and sacrifices to the emperor, but also would impair relationships with patrons who were active in the imperial cult. Whether explicit or implicit, denunciation of the patron's role in the cult would imperil access to the limited goods necessary for survival. Despite the cost, John's summons was absolute: "Come out."

John's description of the beast from the sea is recognized as an image of Roman imperial power.[21] Reacting to the rise of the beast, people offered what seemed to be the inevitable response: "They worshiped the dragon, for he had given his authority to the beast, and they worshiped the beast, saying, 'Who is like the beast, and who can fight against it?'" (Rev 13:4).

The first beast was not alone. "Then I saw another beast that rose out of the earth; it had two horns like a lamb and it spoke like a dragon. It exercises all the authority of the first beast on its behalf, and it makes the earth and its inhabitants worship the first beast, whose mortal wound had been healed" (Rev 13:11–12). Considering the context of John's audience, the beast that rose out of the earth is identifiable readily as a representation of the provincial elites who promoted and benefited from the imperial cult.[22] The Ephesian leaders who erected the temple dedicated to Domitian, his brother Titus, and his father Vespasian were fully aware of the seemingly irresistible power of the beast. The altar in that temple was decorated with an abundance of military images, including swords, shields, armor, and a figure that may represent a conquered foe (figure 19).

21. Aune, *Revelation 6–16*, 733; Beale, *The Book of Revelation*, 684; Beasley-Murray, *Revelation*, 209; Boxall, *The Revelation of Saint John*, 187; Mounce, *The Book of Revelation* (1977), 251; Reddish, *Revelation*, 250.

22. Aune, *Revelation 6–16*, 756; Beasley-Murray, *Revelation*, 216; Boxall, *The Revelation of Saint John*, 194; Mounce, *The Book of Revelation* (1977), 259; Reddish, *Revelation*, 258. Beale's interpretation is subtly different; he identifies the second beast with false teachers who were "encouraging compromise with the culture's idolatrous institutions, which are all associated in some way with the Roman cult" (*The Book of Revelation*, 708).

FIGURE 19. Detail from the Altar of the Temple of the Flavian Emperors in Ephesus (photograph by Richard Warren Johnson).

John rejected the ultimate dominion of Rome and the pressure to conform to the imperial cult. An explicitly stated principle in Revelation is the demand that God alone be worshiped. Twice John fell at the feet of an angel in worship; each time he received a similar rebuke.

> You must not do that! I am a fellow servant with you and your comrades who hold the testimony of Jesus. Worship God! (Rev 19:10)

> You must not do that! I am a fellow servant with you and your comrades the prophets, and with those who keep the words of this book. Worship God! (Rev 22:9)

Though cooperation with the elite functionaries of the imperial cult would have enhanced the honor of the city and offered an avenue for personal advancement, John rejected this compromise. The imperial cult demanded an allegiance that belonged only to God and validated actions that reduced human beings to the status of commodities to be exploited. John insisted that the faithful members of the seven churches could neither acquiesce to this mandate nor participate in this exploitation. Both beasts must be resisted; those who worship the beast are destined to face divine judgment.

> Then another angel, a third, followed them, crying with a loud voice, "Those who worship the beast and its image, and receive a mark on their foreheads or on their hands, they will also drink

the wine of God's wrath, poured unmixed into the cup of his anger, and they will be tormented with fire and sulfur in the presence of the holy angels and in the presence of the Lamb. And the
smoke of their torment goes up forever and ever. There is no rest
day or night for those who worship the beast and its image and
for anyone who receives the mark of its name." (Rev 14:9–11)

Though the beast appeared invincible, it was doomed to destruction.
"The fifth angel poured his bowl on the throne of the beast, and its kingdom was plunged into darkness" (Rev 16:10).

CONFRONTING THE BEAST TODAY

The Parthenon in Athens is oriented toward the east, and ancient worshippers of Athena would have gathered before the east face of the temple.
A short distance east of the Parthenon, in the area where worshippers
congregated, are the remains of a small circular structure. This edifice
has been identified as either a temple or an altar, and an inscription notes
the dedication of the site to ΘΕΑΙ ΡΩΜΗΙ ΚΑΙ Σ[ΕΒΑΣΤ]ΩΙ ΚΑΙΣΑΡΙ
(*theai rōmēi kai s[ebast]ōi kaisari*; "to *Dea Roma* and to A[ugust]us
Caesar") on behalf of the ΔΗΜΟΣ (*dēmos*; "People") of Athens (figure
20).[23] Through this architectural arrangement and symbolism, Roman
conquerors insured that the Athenians in the very act of worship of their
patron goddess Athena always confronted a public reminder of ultimate
Roman supremacy and patronage.

23. Brouskari, *The Monuments of the Acropolis*, 158–62; Camp, *The Archaeology of
Athens*, 187–88. This altar/temple is visible on Google Earth imagery of the Athenian
Acropolis as a circle a short distance east of the Parthenon.

FIGURE 20. Altar/Temple of *Dea Roma* and Augustus Caesar at the Parthenon. These remains of the altar/temple of *Dea Roma* and of Augustus Caesar are seen before the East Façade of the Parthenon in Athens (photograph by Richard Warren Johnson).

Nineteen centuries later a similar reminder was placed near that same location on the Athenian acropolis. A large Greek flag flies at the eastern extreme of the Acropolis platform. During World War II, after the German army occupied Athens on April 27, 1941 the victors ordered Konstantinos Koukidis, the guardian of the banner, to replace the Greek flag with a Nazi flag.[24] Like the Romans before them, the Third Reich wanted to ensure that the subject people were aware of the identity of their masters, and wanted their exercise of power to appear "normal, or at least inevitable" (to appropriate Friesen's phrase). The Greeks resisted. On May 30, 1941 Apostolos Santas and Manolis Glezos evaded the German guards and removed the Nazi banner.

Most manifestations of beastly power are less blatant, but their subtlety makes them more dangerous. Proper care for the environment is both wise public policy and a valid interpretation of the stewardship

24. Koukidis complied, then wrapped himself in the Greek flag and leaped to his death. The flagpole from which the flags flew was in the middle of the octagonal structure visible in Google Earth imagery at the eastern extreme of the Athenian Acropolis. A photograph of the Nazi flag flying on the Acropolis can be found at http://en.wikipedia .org/wiki/Axis_occupation_of_Greece_during_World_War_II.

to which humanity was appointed in the Genesis creation narratives. However, consider the following scenario. A wealthy nation enacts and enforces stringent environmental regulations that result unintentionally in the relocation of industrial production to a poorer nation. The lure of economic development convinces the government of the poorer nation to ignore the environmental damage and the consequent impact on the health of their citizens. Because of the significantly lower labor costs in the poorer nation, the product once produced domestically now can be imported into the wealthy nation at no increase in cost to the consumer.

What are the consequences of these acts? The following list is only a sampling.

- Citizens of the wealthy nation have the product they desire and have "exported" the pollution.

- Poorer, less-skilled workers in the wealthy nation are displaced from their jobs and are forced to seek other (probably lower-paying) employment.

- Corporations have leverage over the poorer nation; if the "client" nation will not cooperate, production can be shifted to a country with a more compliant government and population.

- The wealthy nation itself could become a "patron" to the poorer nation, offering military protection in exchange for cooperation (but threatening military intervention in case of any threat to corporate property and financial security).

Who is responsible for the negative consequences? Consider the possibilities in the following probing questions.

- Should the government of the wealthy nation be held accountable for the consequences of the regulations?

- Were the corporations' actions immoral; are they morally culpable for their exploitation of a geo-political loophole?

- Are the consumers in the wealthy nation responsible for their willingness to overlook the pollution of another country and the exploitation of another population?

- Is the economic philosophy implicit in a consumer-based economy the true culprit?

How do the citizens of the poorer nation perceive the situation? In 1989 J. Nelson Kraybill, an American Mennonite, was teaching the book of Revelation to Christian students in Uruguay. He asked them: "Who is like the Beast today?" Because of what they perceived as patronizing, imperialist policies, the students readily identified the United States as the Beast.[25]

The "religious" or "spiritual" implications of the above scenario may seem unclear, but consider the following situation. At a meeting of a civic club in Indiana the people around Kraybill noticed his abstention from the recitation of the pledge of allegiance to the U. S. flag. Explaining his action, he stated: "I love this country, and I'm grateful for opportunities and freedoms I have here. But I am first of all a Christian, and I have Christian brothers and sisters around the world. My citizenship is with anyone who follows Jesus, and it's hard for me to pledge allegiance to anything else." Confronting the Beast requires us to consider (and sometimes reconsider) all our allegiances and their consequences.

As portrayed by John the characteristics of the Beast are (a) the demand for allegiance that belongs only to God, and (b) the exploitation of the weak for the benefit of the powerful. When such conditions prevail, John's call to the church is "Come out!" Scenarios other than the one described above can be imagined: a patronizing government that, in the interests of "the public good" or "patriotism," restricts the freedom to criticize certain policies or actions; a health program, whether corporate or governmental, that promotes abortion and euthanasia in the interests of cost control. In your experience, who is the Beast (or, who are the Beasts)? How do you recognize the beastly nature? How will you respond? The answers to the first two questions are not always obvious. The responses to the last question are not always simple or comfortable.[26]

---

25. Kraybill, "Apocalypse Now."

26. Acknowledging the "unprecedented complexity" of the world in which we live, Neal Elliott observes that in such contexts we find ourselves able to offer only "maddeningly vague counsels." Quoting Göran Therborn, Elliott suggests "defiant humility" as "the most adequate intellectual stance" (Elliot, *The Arrogance of Nations*, 165–66).

10

How Green Was John's World?

Ecology and Revelation

JAMES JEFFREY CATE

INTRODUCTION

WHEN ONE THINKS ABOUT care and stewardship of the earth and its environment, the book of Revelation is usually the last place a Christian seemingly would turn.[1] The book seems to emphasize the destruction of the earth, not its preservation. In quick successive scenes, large portions of water, land, and sky end up polluted or destroyed. The images in Revelation appear so grim that the deforestation of Truffula trees at the end of *The Lorax* seems minor in comparison.[2]

1. One noteworthy connection between the book of Revelation and environmental concern was a symposium of over two hundred scientists, theologians, philosophers, economists, and policy makers in 1995 on a ferry in the Aegean Sea (not far from Patmos) to mark the 1900th anniversary of the writing of the Revelation of John. The weeklong symposium was called by Bartholomew I, head of the Orthodox Church, and met to address environmental degeneration, specifically the oceans. Outcomes from the symposium were published as Hobson and Lubenco, *Revelation and the Environment AD 95–1995*.

2. In 1971 as concern about pollution grew, Theodor Seuss Geisel (commonly known as "Dr. Seuss") wrote a children's book entitled, *The Lorax*. In the story, the loveable Lorax railed unsuccessfully as an environmental prophet against the greed-driven industrialization of the "Once-ler" whose factories polluted the water and air and killed off trees and animals. The book became one of the most popular stories of Dr. Seuss, and a generation of children learned the importance of environmental issues.

Unfortunately, these perceptions have led modern readers of Revelation to neglect concern for ecological issues related to the earth and the natural environment. Assumptions are then quickly made based on faulty presuppositions. Misguided apocalyptic expectations cause some to question, "Why worry about the environment if it's all going to be destroyed anyway?" Or based on radical dualistic perspectives that denigrate anything perceived to be non-spiritual, others ask, "Isn't heaven more important than the earth after all?" Or fueled by suspicions of hidden political, religious, or scientific agendas, others declare, "We were called to love God and people, not the trees." Or based on rabid anthropocentrism and extreme dominionism, still others assert, "God gave the planet to us and we can do with it just as we please." Because of such faulty logic and misperceptions, environmental issues often go largely ignored by those today who tend to treasure the book of Revelation the most. Even though John of Patmos was no ancient Lorax, he was no Once-ler either. So just how green was John's world?

UNDERSTANDING JOHN'S MESSAGE OF JUDGMENT

John's Use of Apocalyptic Images

Images of destruction abound throughout Revelation, but these images should be understood in their proper context. The book depicts such scenes not out of disregard for the earth but because such epoch-ending calamities are characteristic of apocalyptic writing. This peculiar genre of literature, which originated among Jewish writers and was also utilized by early Christians such as John of Patmos, has many distinct features. Primarily, apocalypses, for which the New Testament book of Revelation is the namesake (Greek, *apokalypsis*, ἀποκάλυψις, in 1:1), arose as a literary vehicle to encourage a beleaguered community of faith to remain loyal and obedient to God in the face of fierce opposition from outside oppressive powers. The message in apocalypses typically is conveyed in repetitive symbolic visions, which feature bizarre and exaggerated details to convey simple truths. The details are often extreme because the apocalyptic writer in the face of severe persecution felt hopelessness towards this present world seemingly ruled by unconquerable tyrants. Instead, the Apocalypticist expressed vivid hope for God to break into the present world cataclysmically and establish a new world in which peace, justice, and righteousness prevailed. So the target enemy in apocalypses was never the natural world, but the oppressive autocrats who suppressed the community of faith.

The scenes of devastation pile up as the narrative of Revelation unfolds. Initially, the world appears as if coming apart at the seams as calamities occur quickly and repetitively. These destructive scenes, however, are neither random nor haphazard. They are presented as the outlet of divine justice against human injustice and based on biblical precedent such as the plagues in Egypt. At first glance, things seem chaotic, but God has matters in hand as the judgments originate in heaven with a sovereign purpose, as seals are broken, trumpets blown, or bowls emptied. Even the destructive judgment of hail in 8:7 is described as being "thrown" upon the earth.

The earth itself, however, is not the target of God's wrath, even though initially the visions might be misunderstood that way. The natural world is not the enemy but ends up suffering the collateral damage caused by human injustice and rebellion against God's rule. For example, when a swarm of diabolical locusts emerge in 9:3–11, unlike the normal variety, these voracious eaters were instructed not to harm plants, grass, or trees. Or, in 16:4–7, when the fresh waters become polluted as blood, the judgment is explained as divine justice against the persecutors of God's people, not as disregard for the earth. In a manner similar to Dante's judgments of reciprocity in the *Divine Comedy*, since they had shed innocent blood, they are now given blood to drink (16:6).

FIGURE 21. Early Morning Mist on a Serene Lake. An early morning mist rises from a peaceful moment on a serene lake. Such idyllic scenes caused the ancient Greeks to reflect on the order and beauty of the world, an order and beauty emphasized in the Greek word *kosmos* (photograph by Gerald L. Stevens).

John's Regard for Creation

Despite the presence of disturbing and violent imagery throughout Revelation, the author clearly thought of the natural world as an amazing and beautiful place. The ancient Greeks used the word *kosmos* (11:15; 13:8; 17:8) to refer to the world because of its orderly arrangement and adornment. Diverse aspects of this adorned world are used extensively as symbolism throughout Revelation. Forces of weather are mentioned frequently. The sight and sound of lightning and thunder serve as signs of majesty and power (4:5; 6:1; 8:5; 10:3–4; 11:19; 14:2; 16:8; 19:6). The elegance of snow is used to depict whiteness and purity (1:14). Rainbows (4:3; 10:1) convey greatness and beauty. Clouds (1:7; 10:1; 11:12; 14:14–16) and their whiteness symbolize transcendence above the mundane activities of mortals. Depending on the context, winds could be considered beneficial for bringing rainclouds or a destructive act of judgment (7:1). Hail (8:7; 11:19; 16:21) represented a terrifying omen, and earthquakes (6:12; 8:5; 11:13, 19; 16:18) shook the pillars of the earth to the core.

First-century readers like John were also in awe of the broader cosmic tapestry in the skies above. In Revelation, celestial objects figure prominently as positive but sometimes negative imagery. At times, brightness or greatness are symbolized with the sun (1:16; 10:1; 12:1) or even the moon (12:1), the planet Venus (2:28; 22:16),[3] or the stars. More noticeably like other examples of apocalyptic literature, Revelation repeatedly describes astronomical disturbances as signs of divine judgment. The sun is darkened (6:12; 8:12; 9:2) or becomes intensely scorching (16:8). The moon turns red (6:12). Stars fall from the sky (6:13; 12:4). In a world without telescopes, much of this imagery arose from the occasional occurrence of meteors, eclipses, and other anomalies in the skies, which would have been interpreted as supernatural acts with divine intent. Nevertheless, the objects in the celestial sphere were viewed with wonder and respect.

Geographical features of the natural world also appear prominently in Revelation. The wilderness serves as a place of refuge and safety (12:6). The sand of the seashore is used as imagery for the scenes in chapters 12 and 20. The sight and sound of "many waters" (1:15; 14:2; 17:1; 19:6) recall the explosive power of crashing waves or cascading falls. The seas are mentioned dozens of times, and the importance of fresh-water sources such as springs and rivers are recalled repeatedly as well. One of the most prominent images of eternal life in the final vision is the river of the water of life (22:1–2). Notably, John saw this final vision from an alpine vantage point on a "great high mountain" (21:10).

A significant amount of flora adorns these geographical features in John's world. Eternal life is symbolized in the new earth by the reappearance of the tree of life (22:2–19) from the idyllic world of Eden. Its fruit and leaves are depicted as lush and beneficial for all peoples. Trees are mentioned in general (7:1, 3; 9:4) and the fig (6:13), palm (7:9), and olive (11:4) garnish specific references. The loss of trees and green grass is considered a devastating judgment (8:7), but these and other forms of

---

3. Venus is referred to as the "morning star" due to its brightness when appearing on the horizon at dawn or dusk. The planet was called "Ishtar" by the Babylonians, which is the basis for the planet's modern name of "Venus" in western civilization. Most Jews and early Christians refrained from using astrological names based on foreign pantheons to refer to objects in the sky or even days of the week (Rev 1:10) or months of the year.

vegetation are spared from the destructive locusts that emerge in chapter 9. Clearly, the devastating judgments are not targeting the natural environment but the perpetrators of oppression and injustice.

A remarkable amount of fauna also features in the cast list of Revelation. Some play negative roles, such as snakes (Greek, *ophis* in 9:19; 12:9–15; 20:2), serpents (Greek, *drakōn* in 12:1—13:11; 16:13; 20:2), locusts (9:3), scorpions (9:10), dogs (22:15),[4] unclean birds, and detestable beasts (18:2). On the other hand, positive aspects of fauna are found in Revelation as well. Domesticated animals such as horses (6:2–8; 9:7–19; 19:11–19), cattle (4:7) and sheep (18:13) are mentioned. The most prominent symbol for the heroic protagonist is "the Lamb." Wild animals (6:8) are referenced, including the leopard, bear, and lion (13:2) and even fearsome features such as horns, feet, eyes, mouth, and teeth. Birds (19:17, 21) and specifically an eagle (8:13) appear in the visions. Four living creatures, based on Ezek 1:10, are introduced as a lion, ox, human, and eagle (4:7). These four creatures make appearances throughout the book, and individually they most likely symbolize the strongest representatives of the wild animals, the domesticated animals, avian creatures, and sentient life. Collectively, however, they represent all animate life, "every creature in heaven and on earth and under the earth and in the sea, and all that is in them" (5:13).

John's Regard for the Creator

Throughout Revelation, God is worshipped as Creator. The twenty-four elders proclaim, "Worthy are you, our Lord and God, to receive glory and honor and power, for you created all things, and by your will they existed and were created." The angel who stood on the sea identified God as the one "who created heaven and what is in it, the earth and what is in it, and the sea and what is in it" (10:6). The first of three angels in the vision in chapter 14 instructs those on earth to "worship him who made heaven and earth, the sea and the springs of water" (14:7). God is called the "Lord of the earth" (11:4) and described as the one who judges "those who destroy the earth" (11:18). Instead, the destroyer is identified

---

4. The negative depiction of dogs in Rev 22:15 should be understood in the historical context of the ancient world. Dogs were not household pets but were considered scavengers and a nuisance not unlike rats or crows today. The term "dog" often was used insultingly as a metaphor for the undesirable elements of society (see Matt 7:6; Mark 7:27; Luke 16:21; Phil 3:2; 2 Pet 2:22).

spiritually as the same adversary who sparked the original chaos at the beginning in the opening chapters of Genesis (Rev 12:7; 20:2). And this destroyer empowers Babylon the Great politically as the one who corrupts the earth (19:2). Clearly, throughout Revelation, God is described as the *creator* of the earth and opposed to its *destroyer*.

UNDERSTANDING JOHN'S MESSAGE OF THE END

The final vision (21:1—22:5) of the book of Revelation is the climactic scene in which the earth plays a prominent role in the expression of Christian eschatological hope. This passage expresses that hope more vividly and extensively than any other passage in the New Testament. Too often assumptions are read into this scene, and the picture ends up distorted and misunderstood. The final scene is not eternal reward in some kind of nebulous celestial sphere apart from the earth and its environment. On the contrary, the thirty-two verses of the final vision depict the terrestrial sphere as the locus of doing God's will on earth as in heaven.

The End Is Not the End of the Earth

Surprising to some, despite scenes of devastating judgment earlier in Revelation, when the end finally does come and the new world is ushered in, the final vision never describes any kind of climactic destruction of this present world. The text simply reads, "Then I saw a new heaven and a new earth for the first heaven and the first earth had passed away" (21:1). This image has no fiery meltdown of all things earthly as in 2 Pet 3:10–12. Even the depiction five verses earlier of earth and sky fleeing from the presence of the One on the throne (20:11) seems to be a metaphorical emphasis on the transcendence of God, not the annihilation of the planet or the cosmos. The description is not of extinction, but transition. The world does not die. Instead, the world continues.

Revelation does describe a catastrophic moment that ushers in the transition of the ages. That moment, however, is not the destruction of the earth; that transition is described as the fall of the bloated urban monstrosity of ancient Rome symbolized as Babylon (18:1–24). The scattered debris are not the skeletal remains of all creatures great and small, but the smoldering trash of a city's once treasured merchandise, the broken pieces of its crass consumerism now a desolate wasteland (18:11–13).

The lack of a destructive end to the earth appears somewhat unexpected in Revelation. The preceding judgments of seals, trumpets, and bowls seem to increase in intensity. A reader might naturally assume a climactic crescendo ending in obliteration. But such a fate does not happen. Further, while John makes extensive use of Old Testament imagery, even from the opening chapters of Genesis, he makes no comparison or allusion to either Noah or a destructive flood like other writings with an apocalyptic perspective.[5] Instead, in Revelation, when the end does come and the new emerges, the transition is rather benign in comparison.

Furthermore, in Revelation, the eschatological hope is not to leave this world and "go to heaven when you die." Instead, the consummation of the ages is when God's presence comes to earth (21:3, 22; 22:4–5). In the New Testament, the Christian hope was the bodily resurrection of the dead at the end of the ages (1 Cor 15:20–58) and the recreation of all things (Rom 8:18–25). The final scene of Christian eschatology in Revelation is not the removal of God's people from this world. John never describes this new reality as "heaven"; instead, this new existence comes down "out of heaven" (21:2, 10) to earth. The earth is not "left behind"; instead heaven comes to earth. John depicts no bumper stickers proclaiming "not of this world"; instead, God's presence invades the terrestrial sphere (21:3, 22; 22:4) as heaven and earth are joined as one and the same. John does not describe the Christian hope as a "pie-in-the-sky" gloryland "way beyond the blue," because John succinctly states, "and they shall reign *on earth*" (5:10). The expression of Christian hope in the New Testament has never been about "life after death in heaven." That hope is about bodily resurrection and the recreation of all things on earth.[6]

The Scriptural Background for the End Includes the Earth

The imagery of the final vision in 21:1—22:5 is deeply rooted in Genesis, Ezekiel, and Isaiah, and that imagery is vested with earthly reality.[7] These

---

5. Matt 24:37–38; paralleled in Luke 17:26–27; 2 Pet 2:5.

6. For a detailed reexamination of the Christian eschatological hope as described in the New Testament, see Wright, *Surprised by Hope*. Also, see Wittmer, *Heaven Is a Place on Earth*.

7. Isa 4:3; 8:8; 25:8; 35:8, 10; 43:18; 51:11; 52:1; 54:11–12; 55:1; 58:8; 60:1–3, 5, 11,

Hebrew writings convey no concept of a non-earthly existence, especially as a divine reward for the righteous. The opening words of John's final scene, "a new heaven and a new earth," are a direct adaptation from the opening words of Isaiah's grand vision of a new creation (Isa 65:17–25). Isaiah's description of hope and reward in that vision most certainly served as the foundation for John's.[8] In Isaiah 65 the description of hope is a scene of a peaceful earthly existence. Houses are built and inhabited (Isa 65:21a, 22a). Vineyards are planted and harvested (Isa 65:21b–22a). Children are born and raised (Isa 65:23). Even though human life is not described as endless, longevity becomes the norm (Isa 65:20, 22b). The hunter and the hunted live in a peaceful co-existence, "The wolf and the lamb shall feed together, the lion shall eat straw like the ox . . . they shall not hurt or destroy on all my holy mountain, says the Lord" (Isa 65:25). Clearly, Isaiah's vision upon which John's is based is not describing the absence of the earth nor its environment.

Not only is Revelation's final scene heavily dependent on Isa 65, but also on Ezekiel's vision of the restored Temple and land (especially, Ezek 47:1–12).[9] In that passage, the priestly prophet of the exile emphasized a life-generating river of water flowing out of the temple with trees abounding on both sides of its banks just as in Rev 22:1–2. Ezekiel's vision is one of greenness and vitality. Wherever the water flows, life thrives. The salt sea and its barren surroundings becomes fresh water and teem with life. Fish swarm. Trees flourish. And for John, like Ezekiel, their fruit is not seasonal, but monthly, and their leaves are for healing, not shade.[10]

John's emphasis on river and tree also is based on the lush depiction of Eden in the second chapter of Genesis.[11] There a river flows to water the garden. Trees spring from the ground. A tree of life provides immortality. Animals and birds inhabit the verdant environs. Once again,

---

19–20; 61:10; 62:6; 65:17, 19; 66:22; Ezek 11:20; 28:13; 33:29; 37:27; 40:1–3, 5; 43:2, 16; 47:12; 48:16–17, 30–35; Gen 2:9–10.

8. Not only do Rev 21:1 and Isa 65:17 use the same wording to introduce the visions, but in Rev 21:4, John borrowed from Isa 65:19 to mention the absence of crying (Greek, *kraugē*) in the new creation.

9. No other book of the New Testament is more heavily dependent on Ezekiel than Revelation. Revelation has allusions to 31 of the 48 chapters in Ezekiel.

10. Rev 22:1–2; Ezek 47:12.

11. Not only does the Revelation of John mention the tree of life (2:7; 22:2, 14, 19) from Genesis (2:9; 3:22, 24), but also direct reference is made to "that ancient serpent" (Gen 3:1–24; Rev 12:9; 20:2).

in Genesis, like Isaiah and Ezekiel, the picture is of an earthly existence. The ideal world of these Old Testament writers was planted in the terrestrial sphere, not the celestial, and so is John's picture of the Christian hope in the final scene of Revelation. Essentially, the last two chapters of Revelation describe Eden restored and transcended. In Eden, care and stewardship of the garden was the norm (Gen 2:15), not the curse. The consistent biblical perspective is that God as "Lord of the earth" (Rev 11:4) holds the title deed to all land, and his people are merely servants and stewards to do his will.[12]

In light of God's lordship over creation, that the two most prominent symbols of eternal life in Revelation are the river of the water of life and the tree of life is not surprising. The ultimate message of Revelation is not doom and destruction but life and hope. The main symbols of the new creation are the river and the tree, key elements for a green world. The image of a tree is so prominent that this image is mentioned as the first example of divine reward in the letters to the seven churches in the opening chapters of the book (2:7). The quality of these symbols is noticeable in that the water is described as "clear as crystal" (22:1) and being *gratis* (21:6; 22:17), a world without water pollution, shortages, restrictions, or disputes.[13] This mysterious river appears never-ending since the sea no longer exists where rivers normally terminate.

Some readers of Revelation are surprised and disappointed to read in the final vision that the sea is no more (21:1). This statement, however, must be understood contextually in the conceptual world of the original readers. For them, the oceans and great seas such as the Mediterranean or the Aegean were more than just a water source unfit for drinking or a dangerous environment for their sailing vessels. The sea was considered a hostile enemy and often personified as such (20:13). The absence of the sea in the final vision of Revelation would be considered the removal

12. See Lev 25:23; Ps 24:1. Even though Revelation never has the term "steward" (*oikonomos*) or "stewardship" regarding the natural world, God's people in Revelation are repeatedly described as God's "servants" to do God's will (Rev 1:1; 2:20; 6:15; 7:3; 10:7; 11:18; 13:16; 15:3; 19:2, 5, 18; 22:3, 6). Revelation is indebted deeply to the Old Testament perspective. Seventy percent of the verses in the Revelation of John have allusions to Old Testament passages.

13. New Testament manuscripts 051, 2030, 2377 and the text embedded in the commentary of Andreas of Caesarea even add the word "pure" (*katharon*) to describe the water in 22:1. Certainly, clean drinking water was important in the ancient world even as today. Ezekiel 34:18, for example, criticizes those who would drink clean water but then muddy the rest for everyone else.

of an antagonist that periodically rose up to seize life and property. Furthermore, the absence of the sea represented the removal of another barrier in the final vision. From the Jewish perspective, the seas restricted travel, the temple restricted people, and the night restricted activity. In the final vision, John describes all these obstacles being removed, as even the sun and moon become unnecessary (21:1, 22–23; 22:5).

CONCLUSION

John's world was a green world and so is the Christian eschatological hope. From an island in the Aegean, John saw the natural world of his day full of wonder and mystery and used such imagery to convey his message. In his visions, water, land, and sky suffer as the unintended by-product of judgments targeting the perpetrators of injustice and oppression, but the earth is never the enemy. God is worshipped as creator of the earth, not its destroyer. The judgments do not climax in a cataclysmic destruction of the planet. Instead, a new world emerges in which God's presence invades the terrestrial sphere. In the end, John's expression of the great eschatological hope is a green world in which an unending river sustains life and trees promote vitality. John's world was a green world and so should be ours.

QUESTIONS FOR REFLECTION

- Why do you think environmental and ecological issues are not discussed more often in evangelical circles?

- What new insight(s) did you gain by the discussion of the role of the earth in John's final vision in Revelation (21:1—22:5)?

- What do you think early Christians would say about the earth and the environment if they could see the condition of our world today?

11

Revelation as Drama

A Staging of the Apocalypse

Sylvie T. Raquel

INTRODUCTION

THE BREADTH OF THE Apocalypse's influence is immeasurable. John's vision has touched art, literature, poetry, filmmaking, drama, and even psychology and sociology.[1] But the book has been dissected in so many ways that infusing any fresh outlook on the narrative seems impossible. The most popular ways of interpreting the book have appealed to its strong apocalyptic genre and Old Testament references. No doubt, John bathed his vision in Jewish Scriptures, imageries, and symbolism. Yet, the seven churches to whom the message was addressed were not uniquely Jewish but quite diverse. Although the Septuagint circulated in early Christian communities, most members were not so acquainted with its content that they were able to grasp all of Revelation's scriptural allusions.[2] As a matter of fact, John drew the matrix of his visions from Jewish and Gentile heritages.[3] Most of the imagery, symbolism, parallels, and contrasts he used fit both cultural traditions.

---

1. Wainwright, *Mysterious Apocalypse*, 189–201.

2. By the time of the Seer's writing, the congregations accepted the concept and importance of Scriptures. This acceptance, however, does not mean they were well known.

3. Bowman, "Revelation," IDB, 4:62.

Most scholars agree that the book of Revelation combines prophetic, epistolary, and apocalyptic genres. This hybrid design rests heavily on John's Semitic background. At the same time, John's first-century, Greco-Roman audience also would be sensitive to another class of writing not often emphasized in an approach to his work: drama. The Apocalypse exhibits some of drama's characteristics: the story evolves in a clear pattern that includes plot, characters, action, thought, and spectacle.[4] John even supplied interludes and moments of silence to offer rest to his audience. Did John methodically craft his work to fit the structure of Greek or Roman drama? John Wick Bowman believes so and classifies the book as "a drama quite artificially constructed of seven acts in each of which occur seven scenes."[5] Whether John received his visions in such a format or just borrowed this particular paradigm, he claimed the divine inspiration of his message. Even if drama were not John's primary intention, its pattern influenced the book's literary structure and character. Drama provided an innovative medium for the setting of his writing.

The Apocalypse displays the characteristics of Roman productions with the content of Greek compositions. The Greek theatrical productions originally constituted a major event that united the community "in an expression of its civic pride and sacred convictions."[6] Greek theater evolved from Greek rituals and ceremonies that sought to bring propitious relationships between the gods and humankind. Greek drama attempted to explain the factors that contributed to divine favor or disfavor and their consequences for the life of the community. Therefore "drama for the Greeks was not mere escapism or entertainment, not a frill or a luxury. Connected as it was with religious festivals, it was a cultural necessity."[7]

Although drama was not the most popular means of entertainment for the Romans, the genre still was a prominent cultural medium. Plays served as one of the primary avenues to promote philosophical, religious, and political ideas. In the same way, John tried to promote and propagate

4. The plot develops around the following elements: an introduction, the letters to the seven churches, the two visions of heaven, the three cycles of calamities (seals, trumpets, and bowls), the visions of victory, and a conclusion.

5. Bowman, *The Drama of the Book of Revelation*, 7.

6. Klaus, Gilbert, and Field Jr., *Stages of Drama*, 13.

7. Jacobus, *Bedford Introduction to Drama*, 7.

certain theological convictions.[8] He sought not only to set forth the divine theology of history but also to encourage the persecuted churches, and exhort them to introspection. John used a distinctive narrative style,[9] almost an "anti-language" that challenged the world surrounding his readers.[10] This anti-language may also have diverted the scrutiny and enmity of outsiders.

A staging of Revelation can reclaim the Seer's originality and recapture his evangelistic aim. Such an effort has the potential to reveal the multi-dimensional facets of the vision and lets the audience experience firsthand its appeal to the five senses of smell, vision, sound, touch, even taste. Staging Revelation as drama also helps visualize the contrast John set between the affairs of God and humankind. The present article examines first how Revelation fit the first-century drama genre. Then, the text is used as a script for a production of the drama and imagines what the book may look like in performance, providing insights on the setting, the props, and the characters' movements and gestures.[11] No doubt, the staging proposed in this article is not sealed as the vision is. The staging, though, hopefully will help contemporary readers conceive of the book as a unified whole, as well as popularize its content.

8. Bowman believes that John purposed to answer some of his readers' questions: "Has history a meaning? A purpose? A goal? Is it 'getting anywhere'? Will good or evil eventually triumph? And in either case, why and how? Is God's hand discernible in the affairs of men? Is he actually directing the course of events? Is it perchance his purpose that history fulfills in the end?" Bowman, *The Drama of the Book of Revelation*, 10.

9. Solecisms or ungrammatical constructions, passive voice to indicate divine activity, the thickening of sentences and the lengthening of lists with the repetitive usage of "and," the introduction of objects or characters as if already familiar to the audience and before their description, the reverse of logical sequence, the alternation between what he hears and what he sees, embedded interludes or intercalation to slow down the narrative pace. See Resseguie, *The Revelation of John*, 47–54.

10. Maier, *Apocalypse Recalled*, 116. Also noted by Resseguie, *The Revelation of John*, 49.

11. The actors' facial expressions and vocal intonations are left to the director's discretion.

FIGURE 22. Hierapolis Theater. This view from the top of the theater at Hierapolis looking down to the stage illustrates the basic physical structures of the orchestra, *skēnē, proskēnē, paraskēnē,* and *parodos.* One even can see the remaining arches supporting underground passageways that accommodated special movements of actors and props unknown to the audience. These ancient theaters are still used today. Notice a contemporary acting troupe getting ready to practice their performance of an ancient Greek play (photograph by Gerald L. Stevens).

FIRST-CENTURY DRAMA

John conceived the cosmic stage with elements that were familiar to his readers. A large part of the life of the seven cities revolved around theaters that followed the standardized plan of the Greco-Roman stage. The orchestra, a circular space where the chorus sang and danced, separated the audience from the stage proper. The actors performed on a raised platform (the *proskēnion*) in front of the *skēnē,* a building that served as a background scene or a space for the actors. They used a theatrical device called the *mekanē* (machine) that could lower them onto the stage.[12] On either side of the stage building laid projecting wings, called *paraskēnia*

---

12. Bieber, *Greek and Roman Theater,* 77–78.

FIGURE 23. Theater of Marcellus in Rome. This exterior view of the famous Theater of Marcellus in Rome shows the partial remains of the typical three-story Roman construction. The Theater of Marcellus, initiated by Julius Caesar but completed by Augustus, was named for Augustus's nephew, the son of his sister Octavia, who was intended to be Augustus's heir. Whereas Greek theaters tended to be open-air constructions built into the natural slope of a hillside, Roman theaters could be independent buildings (photograph by Gerald L. Stevens).

("beside the *skēnē*").[13] The *parodos* (a space parallel to the *paraskēnia*) permitted the entrance and exit of both chorus and audience.[14]

The Roman stage was elevated. The *scaena* (background) was three stories tall and longer than the Greek *skēnē*. The action took place on the *pulpitum* that stood between the *scaena* and the *proscaena*. The *frons scaena*, or the *scaena*'s façade, usually included three to five doors. "The standard Roman play [took] great care to justify the entrances and exits of its characters,"[15] so the doors were active participants in the play; exits

13. Visit http://www.greatbuildings.com/buildings/Theater_at_Epidauros.html for a drawing showing the plan of the Epidauros theatre.

14. The chorus included about 12 to 15 men. They usually represented the citizenry. The chorus and all actors (as well as the audience) were generally male (*Greek Drama: From Ritual to Theater*, DVD).

15. Jacobus, *Bedford Introduction to Drama*, 191. See examples of *scaenae frons* on wall paintings from Pompeii in Bieber, *History of the Greek and Roman Theater*, 232–33.

and entrances made visible conflicts, alliances, and resolution.[16] Roman theater also used machinery that permitted actors to be moved through the air and make entrances from the heavens.

The first source of Roman plays was the Greek theater. Roman drama, however, faced many competitive forms of entertainment[17] and did not compare with Greek productions. "The Roman people preferred to laugh than to feel the pity and terror of tragic emotion."[18] Many dramas were written to be read or recited rather than played on stage; such was the case of Seneca's plays.[19] Reading a play is an experience that requires a high level of concentration because readers have to exercise mentally the functions of director, actors, and scene designers. Most of the Christians from the seven churches did not even have the privilege of reading the story. As pure listeners without visual clues to conceptualize John's complex vision, they had to base their understanding solely on verbal cues. This visual limitation explains why John used many parallelisms, solecisms, and repetitions to provide a framework for comprehension.[20]

The basic elements of Greco-Roman plays were plot, characters, themes, dialogues, movements, setting, and song-composition for Greek tragedies. Most "critics feel that character, plot, and theme are the most important elements of drama while setting, dialogue, music, and movement come next."[21] The Greek tragedy had developed psychological characters and a very intense plot. The story often was presented through a narrator's perspective. The narrator's point of view was revealed in the selection of events, the involvement of the characters, and comments and evaluations. The plot was the thread of events or actions that unified the beginning, middle section, and end.[22] "Plots generally involve

16. Brant, *Dialogue and Drama*, 27–30. See also Taplin, *Greek Tragedy*, 31.

17. Among these were sports events, gladiator shows, chariot races, competition in prose declamation, and more. See Suetonius, *Dom. 4.*

18. Jacobus, *Bedford Introduction to Drama*, 189. When they attended plays, they enjoyed farces, coarse humor, and what may have resembled musical comedies (Jacobus, *Bedford Introduction to Drama*, 8).

19. Boyle disagrees with this argument. Although no record exists of Seneca's plays being performed, Boyle remarks that they are still performable (*An Introduction to Roman Tragedy*, 192).

20. Of course, Christians have the benefit of the Holy Spirit as their primary interpreter.

21. Jacobus, *Bedford Introduction to Drama*, 22.

22. The tragedy encompassed three parts: the prologue established the conflict; the

conflicts having to do with actions, characters, points of view, world-views, values, norms, and so forth. The conflicts may be physical, mental, emotional, spiritual, or moral."[23] Between the sections, the chorus performed songs.[24]

The audience was expected to respond to this complex arrangement as if becoming part of the unfolding action. The objective was to let the public experience a catharsis, a purging or purifying of certain emotions.[25] "Readers or witnesses [were] energized by the movement of the characters in a play."[26] The plot and the setting also influenced the audience's emotional, intellectual, and spiritual reaction.[27]

REVELATION AS DRAMA

Revelation presents the characteristics of a drama plot: the story begins with an exposition of how the main characters—Jesus, John, and the seven churches—arrived at their present situation. The story uses suspense to build tension, develops a rising action, and moves to a climax. Eventually, the action proves satisfying to the audience. Revelation has more commonality with the structure of Greek tragedy than Roman comedy, although the book cannot be classified as a pure tragedy since the reversal of situation at the end of the book turns out to the benefit of the main characters. Nevertheless, the majority of the book tends toward tragic events.

The Characters

The characters of Revelation are complex. The audience comes to know them not so much by what they say[28] but by what they do, what they

---

agons (episodes or contests) established the dramatic relationships between the characters, and the exodus concluded the play. Jacobus, *Bedford Introduction to Drama*, 35.

23. Resseguie, *The Revelation of John*, 44.

24. Songs had four kinds: *parodos* (moving onto the stage), *stasima* (standing still), *strophē* (moving from right to left), and *antistrophē* (moving back to right). See Jacobus, *Bedford Introduction to Drama*, 35–36.

25. See "The history of the catharsis concept between 'purging' and 'purifying'" in Scheele, "Back from the grave," 203–5.

26. Jacobus, *Bedford Introduction to Drama*, 21.

27. *Greek Drama: From Ritual to Theater*, DVD video.

28. Most of the speeches of Revelation come from heavenly beings and have the characteristics of soliloquies.

wear, what other characters say about them, and what constitutes their appearance. The central character or protagonist is Jesus himself. The tragic figures who experience the three stages of development (purpose, passion, and perception) are the church members and the Christian martyrs. Surprisingly, these tragic figures rarely take central stage even though their presence is vital for carrying out God's purpose. In the Roman stage, the play was built not only on dialogues but also on the recitation of a narrator. This herald or interpreter of the theme would appear in the prologue.[29] In Revelation, the herald is John who is Jesus' mouthpiece. John's commentary brings new insights into the characters' motives and personality. The following catalog lists the characters in the order they appear in the book:[30]

- *Narrators or heralds:* John (Jn) the narrator, three church members, John the Seer (Se), an eagle

- *Heavenly court:* God, Jesus, seven lamps/spirits, twenty-four elders, four living creatures, seven angels in front of God, angels around the throne, angel Michael, other angels (twenty-eight specifically mentioned as A1 to A28)

- *God's people:* seven people representing the church (Ch),[31] two witnesses, twelve people representing the 144,000, the woman, the child

- *God's enemies:* the Dragon, two dark angels, the Sea-Beast, the Earth-Beast, the Prostitute, the Scarlet-Beast, Death and Hades

- *Negative characters:* four riders, a crowd of eighteen people representing humanity (C1), ten locusts, ten horsemen, the crowd of Rev 13 (C2), people groups of Rev 17 and 18 with kings, captains, and merchants (C3), ten kings, soldiers of Rev 19, end crowd (C4)

29. Bowman, "Revelation," IDB, 4:64.

30. If the number of actors is limited, some can perform two identical roles (two angels, twice crowd members, etc.).

31. God's people rarely speak in Revelation although they remain active witnesses. Rev 12:11 summarizes their activity throughout the play. See Blount, *Can I Get a Witness?* Blount also believes that the *martyrs* of Revelation engage in active witnessing and non-violent resistance, yet not sacrificial passivity (*Can I Get a Witness,* 39, 47).

The Theme and Plot

Resseguie claims that the masterplot of Revelation is "a quest of the people of God to find their way home, to the new promised land."[32] Even if the denouement of the book is the safe arrival of God's people in their promised land, they already know their way home. Their primary concern is the total destruction of Death and Hades. The Apocalypse reveals that conquering these two characters is part of God's purpose and will come through the church's willingness to suffer as a faithful witness.[33] Revelation responds to the martyrs' cry "When are you going to avenge us?" at the opening of the fifth seal in 6:10. The theme, therefore, is the victory of the Lamb and his followers.

Resseguie conceives the plot of Revelation in the U-shaped structure of a comedy, instead of the inverted U shape of a tragedy.[34] However, the Apocalypse resembles more a tragedy in a check-mark mold: a cascade of calamities falls on the ungodly until the climactic entrance of the victorious rider of Rev 19 reverses the direction of the play. Three elements could constitute the plot of Greek tragedy: (1) peripety was a reversal of fortune; (2) recognition was a shift from ignorance to awareness; and (3) pathos was a series of actions brought by destruction, suffering, or distress.[35] The book of Revelation is a complex action plot that combines all three.

The Setting

John used symbolic props taken both from the Jewish temple and pagan circles.[36] He also gave spiritual or symbolic meaning to topographical

32. Resseguie, *The Revelation of John*, 46. Masterplots involve stories of universal values, tackling questions such as the meaning of life, the question of origin, the quest for identity, etc.

33. See Raquel, "Blessed Are the Peacemakers," in the present volume.

34. Resseguie, *The Book of Revelation*, 45–46. For Resseguie, the bottom of the U is the cross. Blount writes, "The upward movement of the U is marked by the active resistance to Babylon, patient endurance, and holding fast to the testimony of Jesus (13:10; 14:12)" (*Can I Get a Witness?* 46). However, the theme of the cross and the faithful witness is already set in chapter 1 and present in all chapters of Revelation.

35. Brant, *Dialogue and Drama*, 46–63.

36. Bowman writes, "While all [the] stage props are taken bodily from the furnishings/paraphernalia of the Jewish temple (seven lampstands, ark of the covenant, altars, golden bowls full of incense, etc.) or else serve to give expression to the Christian ideology (Lamb, elders, content of the hymns, and the like) and to concepts shared by both

settings: the temple is the heavenly sanctuary where God dwells; the New Jerusalem is the ideal city, while Babylon is its satanic parody.[37] Some *loci*[38] have double meaning: the wilderness can be a sanctuary or the haunt of demons; the river can be either a life-sustaining force (flowing out of God's throne) or a threat to life (12:15–16). Many of the props such as clothing and accessories are markers of inner traits. "The color of garments and their condition, whether clean or soiled, are especially important. Being clothed or unclothed is symbolic of watchfulness or spiritual somnolence."[39] Some characters even wear names on their foreheads.

The Structure

Most scholars adopt a spiraling or a linear view of the Apocalypse's structure. Certainly John used repetitions of words, phrases, and imagery to help the hearers notice, give more details, or clarify a progression.[40] Yet, as Resseguie states, "A linear progression communicates the urgency and necessity of repentance in the strongest possible terms. It heightens the tension and angst of the reader/hearer until the climax is reached and the moment of decision can no longer be postponed."[41] A linear progression does not have to be purely sequential but also can display a telescopic arrangement. This configuration transpires when the seventh element of each cycle introduces the next cycle with added intensity.

Bowman conceives the structure of Revelation in a sevenfold pattern, with act 4, scene 4 being the epicenter of the play.[42] His outline is

church and synagogue (the four creatures representing all God's animate creation, the angels of the Presence and of God's wrath), at the same time, however, their very use as stage settings is suggestive of the Greco-Roman stage . . ." ("Revelation," IDB, 4:63).

37. For this paragraph, consult Resseguie, *The Revelation of John*, 32–38.

38. Plural of *locus*, a literary term to refer to a place given special, representative significance determined by specific conditions or activities in its own literary context.

39. Resseguie, *The Revelation of John*, 36.

40. Rhoads, *Reading Mark*, 74.

41. Resseguie, *The Revelation of John*, 57.

42. Merging the earlier book's outline with that of the later IDB article, the result is: Prologue, 1:1–8; Act 1: Vision of the church on earth, 1:9—3:22; Act 2: Vision of God in Heaven, God's purpose in history, 4:1—8:1; Act 3: Vision of the Seven Angels of the Presence, the church in tribulation, 8:2—11:18; Act 4: Vision of the Church Triumphant, the salvation of the church, 11:19—15:4; Act 5: Vision of the Seven Angels of God's Wrath, the world in agony, 15:5—16:21; Act 6: Vision of Babylon's Overthrow,

somewhat artificial, which seems to have forced odd choices.[43] For example, he considers Rev 11:19—15:4 as representative of the triumphant church. However, the church's first cry of victory arises only in Rev 19. The effort offered in this article tries to follow the natural flow of the narrative. As the story unfolds, the number of scenes increases within each act. This propels the story forward and sets a sense of urgency, a tsunami of events that climaxes with the victory of the Lamb and his followers.

REVELATION AS CONTEMPORARY PERFORMANCE

Staging the book of Revelation helps visualize the contrasts between the realm of God and the realm of Satan, that is, heaven versus earth, the woman and the child versus the Prostitute, the rider versus the Dragon, the throne of God versus the throne of Satan.[44] Justo L. González writes that Revelation is like "a drama that takes place on two levels. These two levels are interconnected."[45] John stood at the intersection of these two levels , a vantage point from which he could view the earthly world from heaven through privileged access to heavenly visions. How are these levels interrelated? Does what happens on earth also happen in heaven? Is what happens on earth a consequence of what happens in heaven (or vice-versa)? Or, does each earthly happening have its equivalent in heaven? A dramatic representation of Revelation leaves the viewer the freedom to make that decision. Regardless of one's interpretation, the immovability of God seated on the throne attests his absolute sovereignty.[46]

---

the judgment of the world, 17:1—20:3; Act 7: Vision of the Church in the Millennium, 20:4—22:5; Epilogue, 22:6–21 (*The Drama of the Book of Revelation*, 15–16; IDB 4:64–65; IDB gives just the outline, while *Drama* gives all the details).

43. His forced structure causes Bowman to create scenes with only 2 verses. He observes a strict parallelism of structure between the acts preceding and following his epicenter. Acts 3 and 5 elaborate the eschatological events narrated in 6:12—7:17; Act 3 portrays the church in the tribulation while Act 5 sets forth the effect of the same events on the secular world. Acts 4 and 6 also are complementary; Act 4 presents the *modus operandi* of God's salvation of his people during the tribulation, and Act 6 presents his judgment on the secular world opposed to his will. Act 7 presents the period of the first resurrection. Cf. Bowman, "Revelation," IDB, 4:68–70.

44. Resseguie writes, "Everything or nearly everything in John's world has its opposite, its double, a perversion of that which is good" (*The Revelation of John*, 43). The only world that shows balanced harmony is God's abode.

45. González, *Three Months with Revelation*, 54.

46. Resseguie considers the throne to be "the primary prop of Revelation" (*The Book of Revelation*, 40).

Staging the two levels of heaven and earth along with John's own unique vantage point produces a three-level drama: one upper level (Ul) for the heavenly realm, one middle level (Ml) where the Seer stands, and one lower level (Ll) for earthly events.[47] The present script fits the demand of an average university stage's size and shape.[48] A dark curtain first covers Ul. As the curtain opens, the illusion is given that heaven's door is opening. A veil covers the entrance of the heavenly tabernacle behind the throne. A screen on one side of the stage will lower and rise as needed. To allow for a faster change of setting, Ll can include three pivoting sets, similar to the Greek *eccyclema*.[49]

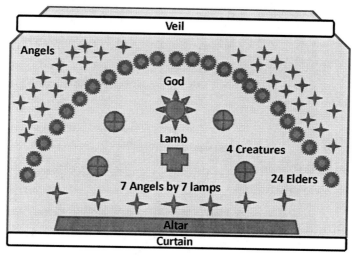

Upper Level

FIGURE 24. Diagram of Upper Level Stage. This diagram depicts an arrangement for the Upper Level Stage (diagram by Sylvie T. Raquel).

47. Ml is an extension of Ul. Heavenly events that happen in front of Ul's curtain will be performed on Ml.

48. If the troupe does not have access to such a setting, slight modifications can be made. Instead of the curtain, two mobile panels can be used and rolled up and down to meet the needs of the scene.

49. Latinized form of the Greek word, *ekkyklēma*, a rectangular or circular pivoting platform on the center of which was mounted a panel that served as background. See Bieber, *Greek and Roman Theater*, 76.

Lower Level

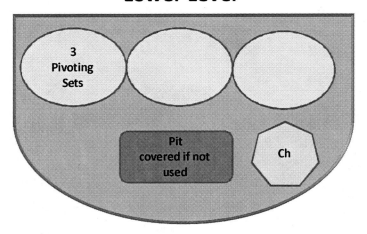

FIGURE 25. Diagram of Lower Level Stage. This diagram depicts an arrangement for the Lower Level Stage. The three sets are used for: the seven churches, the Temple door, the Dragon and the Beasts, the gates of the New Jerusalem, etc. (diagram by Sylvie T. Raquel).

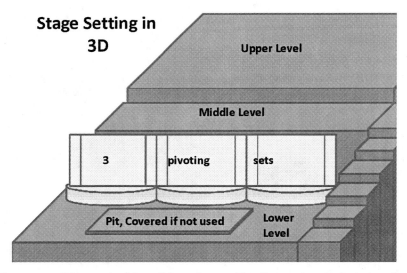

FIGURE 26. 3D Diagram of Overall Stage Setting. This diagram is a 3D depiction of the overall stage setting for general orientation to the Upper and Lower level stages (diagram by Sylvie T. Raquel).

To preserve the integrity of the message, the narrator reads the text word for word. Since dialogues and monologues are minimal in the book of Revelation, the strength of the play will rest on the actors' aptitude to "speak" through bodily language (gesture, facial expressions, posture, pace, etc). Directors can use modern visual techniques, as suggested below. Throughout the entire play, the spotlights will follow the appropriate actors.

Prologue (Rev 1:1–8)

On the far left side of the stage, Jn stands with the church members. He opens a codex and begins the narration.[50] The following phrases appear consecutively on the screen: "Jesus Christ, the faithful witness"—"loves us"—"has freed us"—"by his blood" (last words drip "blood")—"Look."

Act 1: The Seven Churches

Act 1 begins with blinking lights. Echo and reverb effects give majesty to God's voice. Seven lampstands, arranged in a circle on Ml, light up one by one at each church's appellation.

Scene 1 (1:9–20). The lights are on Jn until verse 12. Then, Jesus enters Ul through the curtain and stops in the midst of the lampstands. A zoom while filming video follows Jn's description on the screen.[51] Se stands on the side of Ml and falls on his knees.

Scene 2 (Rev 2–3).[52] As Jn reads each letter, the church's deeds are revealed on Ll. The director has three options: (1) illustrate the churches' commendations and rebukes on the screen; (2) have a representation on cardboards placed on Ll; and (3) have 2 actors per church act them out.[53] For choices 2 and 3, the spotlight should reveal the churches one at a time.

Act 2: A Vision of Heaven[54]

The lampstands are removed.

---

50. The church members can take turns reading the text. The use of suitable music will enhance the dramatic effects.

51. Use the same technique at each church's address. The visual repetitions will reinforce the unity of the vision.

52. Bowman counts seven scenes, one for each church (The Drama of the Book of Revelation, 21–39; cf. IDB 4:64). He follows the same pattern for the trumpets and the bowls.

53. For each rebuke, each actor can carry the corresponding prop: a smiling face for each commendation and a downcast face for each condemnation (with the word "repent" forming the mouth).

54. Bowman regards these two chapters as the prologue of Act 2 (The Drama of the

Scene 1 (4:1–6a). The spotlight is on "heaven's door." After Spirit speaks, the curtain opens and reveals the throne scene. Spotlights of different colors flash under the throne to reflect God's brilliance. Other lights emulate flashes of lightning. Drum rolls imitate the rumblings and peals of thunder.

Scene 2 (4:6b–11). The four creatures cover their faces with their wings until the reading of verse 8 when they unveil their identity and praise God. The 24 elders bow down and lay their crowns in front of the throne and praise God.

Scene 3 (Rev 5). God raises the scroll up. After A1's query, Se sobs until the elder speaks. The Lamb who was lying down rises up between the throne and the 4 creatures and takes the scroll. The creatures and elders fall flat on their faces. A play of lights represents the myriads of angels who begin their song. The scene ends with Jesus ready to open the seals.

Act 3 : The Seven Seals[55]

Scene 1 (6:1–8). Jn is still narrating. Each time the Lamb opens a seal, the lights turn off, and flashes of lightning strike downward. The horses appear one by one as the light touches Ll. Ch remains seated on the right side of Ll. Its members keep on praying and reading the Scriptures.

Scene 2 (6:9–17). The slain saints sit on Ml. Some members of Ch join them. New people replace them.[56] At the sixth seal, the lights turn off at the cadence of a rumbling sound. The screen goes down to allow the projection of the events that the sixth seal unleashes. The actors freeze in fear at the end of the scene and remain that way until the end of Act 3.

Scene 3 (7:1–8). A2 to A5 stand at the four corners of the Ll, arms lifted in a V form. A6 appears on Ml. At the enunciation of each tribe, a banner bearing that name unrolls toward Ll.

Book of Revelation, 42–47; cf. IDB 4:64). If God and the Lamb are the central characters of the story, the vision of the heavenly court can hardly be just an introduction. For this reason, they are treated in this essay as an entire act.

55. Bowman creates one scene per rider (*The Drama of the Book of Revelation*, 48–49; cf. IDB 4:64). However, keeping all the riders in the same scene helps the viewer to understand that they all work together as an integrated unit in one continuous movement through the first four seals.

56. Each member who dies is replaced, as a symbol of the enduring witness of God's people. Therefore, Ch's number remains seven throughout the play.

Scene 4 (7:9—8:1). From both sides of Ml, people from different ethnic backgrounds enter, socialize, and sit, rejoicing, in front of the throne. Angels bow down and sing. The scene ends in complete silence.

Act 4: The Seven Trumpets

Scene 1 (8:2–12). A7 approaches the altar with the golden censer. To illustrate the calamity that each trumpet's blow unravels, one can either use the projection of images or have C1 depict the events through body expression. By Rev 8: 11, three of them die.

Scene 2 (8:13—9:12). The eagle flies across the stage. A star comes down from the ceiling. When the star touches Ll, the floor opens up. Smoke envelops Ll while locusts erupt from the opening. By verse 10, the remaining C1, tortured by the scorpions, wail. Members of Ch look horrified but continue on testifying.

Scene 3 (9:13–21). A8 to A11 appear on Ll and one-third of C1 falls down. Horses and riders enter Ll. Another one-third of C1 dies. The last one-third acts mockingly.

Scene 4 (Rev 10). A12[57] steps down from Ul to Ll and interacts with Se. After the reading of verse 11, complete darkness falls on the stage.

Scene 5 (Rev 11). Se picks up a measuring rod from the floor. Spotlights light up Ll where the two witnesses are standing in front of the temple's door. As they prophesy, part of C2 dies. They fall as dead and come back to life. The crowd falls in terror. Rumbling and lightning simulate the earthquake. Complete darkness resides for the reading of verses 15–19. The seventh trumpet blows. At verse 19, Ul's veil opens and reveals the heavenly ark of the covenant.

Intermission

Act 5: Interlude

Scene 1 (12:1—13:1). The woman appears on the right side of Ml and the Dragon on the left side. The woman gives birth; an angel takes her baby and brings the child to God's throne. The woman moves to the left side of Ll and sits down. Michael and 6 angels fight against the Dragon and 2 dark angels. The latter are pushed to the Ll. During the reading of

---

57. He has many characteristics of the Son of Man described in chapter 1, so the question is raised whether this image is meant to be understood as a distinct angel or actually as the Son of Man figure of the opening vision in 1:9–20. He also is the only character besides God who wears a rainbow above his head.

Rev 12:10–12, all lights are on Ul. The Dragon tries to attack the woman who disappears. A river forms. Enraged, he turns around and attacks Ch, who are still praying and witnessing on the right side of Ll. He stops in the middle of Ll, between his throne and the river-sea.[58]

Scene 2 (13:2–10). The Sea-Beast appears and sits on the Dragon's throne, its hands raised toward heaven in a threatening attitude. C2 appears in front of the stage and worships the Sea-Beast and the Dragon. They all move toward Ch, beat them, and then return to their worship. Darkness persists during the reading of verses 9–10.

Scene 3 (13:11–18). The Earth-Beast appears and performs wonders. C2 sets up an image of the Sea-Beast on the side of the stage. They receive its number. Some Ch members try to buy food but refuse to worship the image and are pushed back in their corner; half of them die but some members of C2 join them. Darkness resides at the reading of verse 18.

Scene 4 (14:1–5). The lights are on Ml and Ul. Twelve people, counting those who died in the previous scene, represent the 144,000. Standing in front of the Lamb, they receive the name of God on their foreheads. Harps are playing.

Scene 5 (14:6–13). A12 to A14 appear on Ml. Each delivers a message to C2 and Ch.

Scene 6 (14:14—15:4). The Son of Man appears on Ul. A15 to A17 burst out from behind God's throne. When A16 swings his sickle over the earth, what has the appearance of a red fabric, representing the blood, unfolds on Ul. The victors of scene 4 stand besides the glassy sea and sing the song of the Lamb.

Act 6: The Seven Bowls

Scene 1 (15:5—16:11). A18 to A24 emerge on Ul. One of the four creatures gives each angel a large golden bowl. Smoke comes out of the temple. As each angel pours out his bowl from Ul, C2, the Beasts, and the Dragon respond accordingly.[59] After the fifth bowl, the stage is plunged into darkness. One can only hear the wailings of C2.

Scene 2 (16:12–16). The river-sea disappears. The three spirits-frogs gather the kings of the earth in the middle of Ll. The lights turn off.

---

58. His throne is placed right under God's throne.

59. For example, after the pouring of the first bowl, C2 acts as suffering pain because of the sores. After the second bowl, red lights flash under the river-sea because the waters turn into blood.

Scene 3 (16:17–21). Spotlights on Ul. A24 pours his bowl into the air. Loud noises of crashes, screams, rumblings of thunder, and rapid blinking of lights mimic the earthquake. C2 and the kings continue to curse God. On Ll, Ch is protected from the calamities and still praying.

Scene 4 (Rev 17). A24 shows Se the Prostitute. She goes to Ch, kills some of them, comes back with a cup full of their blood, and sits on the Scarlet-Beast. Hands and heads of people and kings pop out of under the stage as if the woman was sitting on them, submerging them. Ten kings come out of the beast's head and stand behind the woman.

Scene 5 (18:1–8). A25 speaks. C3 comes out from under the stage and performs according to the text. Some members of C3 join Ch. They all pray and the Prostitute catches on fire.

Scene 6 (18:9–24). The kings, terrified, curse the woman. In vain, people groups try to offer the items listed in the text. They weep, curse the city, and throw dust on their heads.

Scene 7 (18:21—19:10). A26 throws a large millstone where the Prostitute was sitting. C3 fall flat on their faces. All characters in heaven shout of joy and sing in a jubilant celebration. The twenty-four elders and the four creatures worship God. Se is forbidden to worship A26.

Act 7: Finale

Scene 1 (19:11–18). Ch is not on stage. The rider appears on the white horse on Ul with several horsemen behind him. Neon lights underscore his title. A bright light shines behind A27 when he proclaims his message.

Scene 2 (19:19–21). The Beast, the ten kings, the false prophet, and soldiers stamped with the mark of the Beast appear on Ll and try to climb on Ml. The rider and his army move forward and engage in battle on Ll. A lake of fire appears under Ll and swallows the Beast and the false prophet. A short-lived foul smell rises. All earthly characters fall as they come in contact with the rider's double-edged sword.

Scene 3 (20:1–10). A28 descends to Ll with a large key in one hand and a chain in the other. He enchains the Dragon and throws him into an opening on the side of Ll's floor. People dressed in white, representing Ch, enter Ll and gather around the rider. Satan comes out of the Abyss. He runs around Ll, gathering nations to destroy Christ and His people. C4 moves in a concentric circle toward them. Fire comes down from heaven and Satan and part of C4 fall into the lake of fire. Once more, a short-lived odor of sulfur mounts.

Scene 4 (20:11–15). On the veil behind the throne plays a short movie of rapidly advancing clouds. Angels are holding books. The Lamb is holding the Book of Life. C4 and Ch intermingle and move toward the throne. One by one, they stop in front of the throne. Books are consulted, including the Book of Life. Death and Hades are thrown in Satan's pit along with C4. Ch stays on Ml, rejoicing.

Scene 5 (21:1–11). A24 invites Se to move down to Ll. A glittery light fabric curtain on which the title "New Jerusalem" shines drops down to Ll. The throne of God, illuminated and visible by transparency, descends at the same time as the curtain.

Scene 6 (21:12–27). The curtain opens slowly and reveals the throne of God at the center of the Ll, with the Lamb at his side. A bright light behind the throne emanates God's glory. Three opened doors are visible in the background, each bearing the name of one Israelite tribe; toward the floor, are written the names of three apostles.[60] An array of lights reveals the city's brilliance and magnificence.

Scene 7 (22:1–5). A28 speaks. Se now stands at the front of the stage. The Lamb sits on the throne and Spirit stands behind the throne. The tree of life is planted over the river that runs in the middle of the stage.

Epilogue (Rev 22:6–21)

The lights are slowly dimming as the last characters speak. Jn finishes his reading and solemnly closes the book. Lights go out.

ACTIVITIES FOR REFLECTION

1. Individually or collectively, study one of the seven acts. Design the decor, costumes, and setting, using drawings, collages, diagrams, pictures, or other audio-visual means. Think of a musical accompaniment that would enhance the dramatic effects.

2. Use the projects suggested above to create stations. Present them to your institution.

3. Put on the play.

---

60. The boards that hold the names of the tribes and apostles flip three times until all names are disclosed.

12

Let the One Who Has Ears

Hearing What the Spirit Says to the Church Today!

STEPHEN N. HORN

INTRODUCTION

A SMALL GROUP DECIDES THAT their next study is going to be a verse-by-verse journey through the book of Revelation. Each person agrees to take a turn leading the rest in a discussion. The first weeks through the first chapter and letters to the churches go reasonably well, but then the group encounters numbers and bizarre images that surely must mean something. At least one of the members has read every installment in the *Left Behind* Series. Another has been exposed to a system of thought that has an explanation for every symbol including exactly the symbol that represents the United States of America. Another believes that all events in the Revelation occurred in the first century. Hopefully, at least one in the group recognizes the missing ingredient to their approach that has been the staple of every other study previously pursued. Or as pastor, professor, and author, Eugene Peterson asks, "What does this mean? How does this work in the community of believers in which I pastor?"[1] What is the present application of the book of Revelation? How does this book impact the discipleship of the present believer? What is the call

---

1. Peterson, *Reversed Thunder*, xiii.

of this book to life right now? Are not these the questions that usually dominate the struggle of interpreting Scripture?

Pursuing Life Applications

A revival of pursuing life applications in the book of Revelation is sorely needed in studying the book of Revelation.[2] The bulk of study and preaching in Revelation deals with the apocalyptic and end-time message seemingly ignoring modern day application. Several things are problematic with this approach. First, most serious followers of Christ believe that the goal of all Scripture is to point the reader to instruction.[3] Second, modern application is not ignored with other Scripture that has a prophetic nature. For example, with Old Testament prophetic material, even though the prophets wrote to a specific time and a specific prophecy, modern readers of this portion of Scripture still recognize contemporary application. Third, the historical nature of the original recipients mandate that modern readers seek the timeless truths to be taught to every generation. Modern readers understand that the Bible speaks specifically to those first recipients as well as to every following generation. Finally, Rev 1:3 sets the tone not just to be hearers of the prophecy of Revelation, but to be doers of the word.

Adopting an Approach

The mistake that some make in reading Revelation is to get caught up in the details of the powerful imagery and not read the book as a whole. If the reader is going to understand present-day life applications, the first requirement is to step back and consider the book as a whole. This approach allows the reader to see several recurring images, which then allows the reader to understand recurring themes. From these themes the reader is forced to deal with a contemporary impact.

Even in considering the book as a whole, readers must adopt some literary approach. Fee and Stuart in their helpful book, *How to Read the Bible for all its Worth: A Guide to Understanding the Bible*, suggests that Revelation is a drama. In this drama the author sets the characters and the stage in chapters 1–3. The worship scenes of chapters 4–5 also help

2. Actually, a case can be made that a revival of sorts is occurring if one considers more recent commentaries on the book of Revelation. Commentaries by Reddish in the Smyth and Helwys Series and Keener in the NIV Application Series both do this well.

3. 2 Tim 3:16–17.

set the stage for the drama to begin to unfold in chapters 6–7. Chapters 8–11 contain God's judgment. According to Fee and Stuart's proposal, chapter 12 is the theological key to the whole book. In dramatic fashion, Satan attempted to destroy Christ, but instead faced his own defeat. In chapters 13–14, John showed that for the church of his day Satan's revenge took the form of the Roman Empire with its emperors who were demanding the same allegiance as Christ. The crisis of the drama is resolved in chapters 15–16 with the pronouncement that the governments of the earth are doomed. The book concludes in chapters 17–22 by showing the final fate of the kingdoms of this world as compared to God's eternal kingdom. Fee and Stuart summarize the effect of the telling of this drama with the conclusion that every generation needs to rehear this message. Not to glean this message from the book of Revelation is to miss the entire story of the book.[4]

FOUR IMPORTANT TERMS TELLING THE STORY

Approaching Revelation as drama is helpful, as this effort puts due emphasis on seeing the lead actors and props as the keys to understanding the story's most important themes. John identified at least four important images with the use of repetitive terms throughout the Revelation. These four terms are: *pantokratōr* (Almighty), *nikaō* (overcome), *thronos* (throne), and *arnion* (lamb). Not only are these words repetitive in Revelation, but their importance to John's theology is further magnified by their usage in Revelation as compared to other New Testament books.[5]

---

4. Fee and Stuart, *How to Read the Bible*, 259–61. Also see Marshall, *New Testament Theology*, 549–66 for a similar proposal for a dramatic reading of Revelation. Both Stuart and Fee and Marshall conclude from a dramatic reading that the main theological themes emerge.

5. John used *pantokratōr* nine times, and the word is used otherwise in the New Testament only in 2 Cor 6:18. Of the twenty-eight times that *nikaō* appears in the New Testament, John used the word seventeen times. John employed *thronos* forty-seven times, and the word appears sixty-two times in the New Testament. Finally, of the thirty times that *arnion* occurs in the New Testament, John used the word twenty-nine times. The only example of *arnion* outside of Revelation is John 21:15. Here the word does not refer to Jesus. One occurrence, Rev 13:11, does not refer to Jesus either. The readers should note that another word, *amnos*, also usually is translated lamb. This word occurs four times in the New Testament: John 1:29, 36; Acts 8:32; and 1 Pet 1:19. As compared to other books, these four highlighted words have a high visibility and an important role in Revelation. All frequency statistics in this article were derived from the Kohlenberger, Goodrick, and Swanson concordance.

All four of these words have a theological importance in the book and therefore a practical implication for contemporary life. Two of the words, *pantokratōr* and *arnion*, have a theological significance in that they refer to God and Jesus, respectively. God is the only referent to *pantokratōr*, and *arnion* refers to Jesus in every case except Rev 13:11. John's use of *thronos* can be interpreted as theologically motivated because all but six of the examples refer to either God or Jesus' throne. The theological usage of *nikaō* is harder to detect, but can be verified by realizing that the one who overcomes usually is either Jesus or those who believe in him. Thus, *pantokratōr* theologically relates to God, *arnion* to Jesus, *thronos* to God and Jesus, and *nikaō* primarily to humanity's relationship to God. A brief look at each image can show how the main themes in Revelation's drama unfold. That is, each image helps to tell part of the story.

The Story in Pantokratōr

John used *pantokratōr* nine times in Revelation. Four times the word occurs in a hymn of the worship scenes. In all nine occurrences, the term is employed to refer to God. In all but two instances, Rev 16:14 and 19:15, the title is used in conjunction with *kyrios*. Four times, Rev 1:8, 4:8, 11:17, and 16:14, *pantokratōr* is used in conjunction with a variation of the characteristic saying, "the one who was, is, and is coming." Two times, Rev 16:14 and 19:15, John used the word in the context of the wrath of God. The common denominator in all of John's usages of *pantokratōr* is that the word is essentially a title for God. For John, *pantokratōr* is more than just synonymous with the name of God. The title is representative of everything that can be said about God. More than a mere title, *pantokratōr* is the last word about God.

FIGURE 27. Temple of Trajan at Pergamum. The beautiful Temple of Trajan crowns the very top of the acropolis at Pergamum. The ancient city of Pergamum, whose acropolis ruins lie next to the modern city of Bergama, Turkey, was honored to be one of the "temple wardens" of the emperor cult in Asia Minor, that is, a city invested with special rights to service the imperial cult, including the maintenance of an imperial temple (photograph by Gerald L. Stevens).

John's use of *pantokratōr* only in reference to God and as a title for him indicates that nothing else is like God. As Reddish comments, "The emphasis in this title is that God is the supreme ruler."[6] John used the word in such a way as to convey God's ultimate power and control in the affairs of the world. To the suffering world to which John originally wrote, being reminded of God's control serves as an important affirmation of who controls final destiny.[7]

6. Reddish, *Revelation*, 38.

7. Ibid., and Keener, *Revelation*, 75.

FIGURE 28. Trajan Inscription at Pergamum. This inscription records the honors paid by the ruling elite of Pergamum to the emperor Trajan as a part of the emperor cult in Asia Minor at the beautiful Temple of Trajan perched atop the Pergameme acropolis. The first word of the inscription is *autokratora*, usually translated "emperor," with the inference of independent strength of rule. John has countered this empire propaganda by declaring God *pantokratōr*, the one who rules by all strength (over any claimed power), or "Almighty" (photograph by Gerald L. Stevens).

The theological impact of *pantokratōr* is strong. The image highlights the theme of sovereignty in the book. In fact, *pantokratōr* best tells the story of God's sovereignty. John employed the image in a way that indicates that for him *pantokratōr* is the final and most important image of God. John cannot think of God as anything less than the Almighty. For the reader, in a world of chaos that is seemingly ruled by evil, John reminded them that God, not human powers, was sovereign.

The Story in Arnion

John used the word *arnion* twenty-nine times in Revelation, with only one occurrence (13:11) not referring to Jesus. All references to *arnion* are influenced by the first mention of this image in Rev 5:6. John saw the lamb standing and slaughtered. This imagery refers the reader back to Rev 1:5, which indicates that sins were released by Jesus' blood. The author intended to indicate that the slaughtered Lamb was Jesus. John's first vision of the Lamb also included seven horns and seven eyes, which he said were the seven spirits of God. The imagery of a slaughtered Lamb with seven horns and seven eyes portrays Jesus not only as the one sacrificed, but also a ruler.[8] John's vision of Christ as the Lamb is the most widely used description of Jesus in Revelation. The image of the lamb indicates Christ as both sacrifice and victor. As Smalley rightly points out, "The character of the Lamb throughout the Apocalypse (except at 13:11, which refers to the beast) is exalted. Christ in Revelation is the victorious Lamb, who overcomes the forces of evil and whose death removes sin. . . . He is ruler, in addition to Redeemer."[9]

The Story in Nikaō

John used *nikaō* seventeen times in Revelation. The word occurs most frequently in the seven letters and in the Judgment Cycle (6–19). Most frequently, John employed the word in the context of either the church or followers of God and Christ as the ones who overcome. In fact, the word is used in each of the seven letters as a call for the church in order for them to gain a reward. In addition to the seven letters, believers are also the subject of *nikaō* in Rev 12:11, 15:2, and 21:7. John also employed *nikaō* with Jesus being the subject in Rev 3:21, 5:5, and 17:14. Finally, John used *nikaō* to indicate the victories of the false Christ (6:2), the beast over the two witnesses (11:7), and the beast over the saints (13:7).

When considering the meaning of *nikaō*, the most difficult task is to understand the concept in relationship to the seven churches. In each letter the church is promised a reward if they overcome. The theological question is what does the church overcome? The context of the letters, as well as John's use of the word in reference to Jesus, the false Christ, and the beast, aids in interpreting the meaning of *nikaō* for the seven churches.

The story told with *nikaō* connected to Jesus, a false Christ, and the beast is a story of victory. The clearest examples of victory in association with the word are in 6:2, 11:7, 13:7, and 17:4. The literary context of each of these passages is war; thus, *nikaō* indicates victory as in war. John also used *nikaō* in allusions to Christ's victory in Rev 3:21 and 5:5. The

---

8. Aune, *Revelation 1–5*, 368.

9. Smalley, *The Revelation to John*, 132.

emphasis on victory is only implied in these passages, but another aspect of *nikaō* is insinuated. Both of these passages have a note of accomplishment. Jesus' overcoming in 3:21 affords him the position of sitting down on his father's throne. The indication of accomplishment in 5:5 is the result of Jesus' doing what no one else could do—opening the book and the seven seals. John's use of *nikaō* with Jesus, the false Christ, and the beast as subjects indicate both victory and accomplishment.

The contexts of the seven letters also aid in understanding the meaning of *nikaō*. First, the churches are under stress. Perseverance and endurance have a prominent place in these seven letters. The letters also indicate an eternal promise if the recipients do overcome. These rewards are all privileges that only God can give. These rewards are determined on the whole of one's life and are granted at death. Thus, the call to overcome implies the challenge to be faithful until death. The meaning of *nikaō* in Revelation is not a one-time victory, but a final and complete victory.[10]

The letter to Thyatira perhaps is the most helpful for grasping the sense of *nikaō*. First, in the letter to Thyatira, one can observe the relationship between overcoming and keeping the work of Christ. Second, another important factor is that the duration of service is until the end. The implication of Jesus' call to the people of the church at Thyatira is that to overcome is to keep the work of Christ for the rest of their lives. They are not listed among the overcomers if they do not keep the work of Christ. Because these letters are a unit,[11] the meaning of overcome is tied to the meaning of the word in the message to Thyatira. That is to say, overcoming implies keeping the work of Christ until death.

Thus, *nikaō*, as related to the followers of the Lamb throughout Revelation, carries connotations from the letter to Thyatira of keeping the work of Christ until death. In telling this kind of story in Revelation, *nikaō* should impact the way contemporary readers apply the book. The word indicates an important element of one's relationship to God. Because of Jesus' promise of eternal reward attached to the call to overcome, John has indicated the nature of a relationship with God, as well as benefits from that relationship. In Revelation, a relationship with God must be marked by overcoming, which indicates keeping the work of

10. The obvious exception is the victory of the false Christ and the beast. Their victories would be complete except that they are overturned by God.

11. See Aune, *Revelation 1–5*, 119–24; Beale, *The Book of Revelation*, 224–28; Smalley, *The Revelation to John*, 105; Reddish, *Revelation*, 51–52.

Christ until death regardless of pressure to compromise. However, the keeping of one's relationship is not merely contingent upon the individual. The crucial statement in Rev 12:11 indicates that believers overcome by the blood of the Lamb, as evidenced in their personal testimony until death. The power to overcome is, first of all, based on the Lamb's blood. Testimony and commitment until death are evidence of one who has overcome. As often suggested, the nature of the saints' belief in the blood of the Lamb is more than accepting his sacrifice; the shedding of their own blood may also be a possibility.[12] This reality of overcoming is the chief implication of a human's response to God in Revelation.

The Story in Thronos

If God the *Pantokratōr* and the Lamb are the major actors, and if overcoming is the major storyline for believers, then one could say that the throne is the major prop in that drama. The word translated "throne," *thronos*, is used sixty-two times in the New Testament and forty-seven times in Revelation. In thirty-six of the forty-seven instances, the word refers to God's throne. Others occupying thrones are Satan (2:13), the twenty-four elders (4:4; 11:16), the beast (13:2; 16:10), Jesus (3:21; 7:17), God and the Lamb jointly (22:1; 22:3), and followers of Jesus (20:4).[13] Studying the contexts of these passages helps the reader to draw important life applications from the book of Revelation.

In examining the context of *thronos* in relationship to God, two observations emerge. First, the continual use of "one sitting upon the throne" becomes a way of identifying God. John established the link with the elaborate description of the throne and the One on the throne in Rev 4. After the link is established, the phrase "one who sits on the throne" becomes a customary way of referring to God.[14] The second observation is that sometimes in Revelation, the throne stands for God.

12. Strand, "Overcomer," 252. See also Fee and Stuart, *How to Read the Bible*, 262, where they point out that "discipleship goes the way of the cross." Modern readers must read Revelation in the sense that following Christ is not freedom from suffering, but instead a discipleship in which suffering is characteristic. Keener remarks, "This passage emphasizes that our witness for Jesus is worth even our lives" (*Revelation*, 332).

13. The reference in 20:4 is ambiguous because of the indefinite third person plural verb. The rationale for understanding the subject to be followers of Jesus is based on the assumption that enemies of God would not be receiving thrones at this point in the narrative story line.

14. See 4:2, 9, 10; 5:1, 7, 13; 6:16; 7:10, 15; 19:4; and 21:5.

The clearest example is Rev 7:9, which indicates people standing before the throne and the Lamb. No mention of God's name is indicated, but the clear statement of this description is that the worship was intended to God and the Lamb.[15] Another example is Rev 14:3, which describes the singing before the throne, the four living creatures, and the elders.[16]

In addition to the observations about God's throne, references to Satan's throne in 2:13 and the beast's throne in 13:2 and 16:10 also aid in understanding the image of the throne. The church in Pergamum is told that they live where Satan's throne is, or where Satan dwells (2:13). Jesus' statement implies that they are living in a world under the control of Satan. The beast's throne first is mentioned in the context of his power and authority (13:2). The other allusion describes the destruction of the beast's throne (16:10). When the throne is destroyed, the kingdom becomes darkened. Thus, a literary relationship exists between the beast's throne and his kingdom. In Revelation, a throne represents having a kingdom or at least a right to reign in a kingdom.

Associated with the image of the throne in Revelation is the idea of reigning. God is the one who reigns in all things. His reign is prominent to the point that the mention of the throne image causes association with God. Jesus also reigns with God by virtue of his power to overcome (3:21). Satan is the one who has a partial reign in the world, but his reign is temporary and given to him by God. The twenty-four elders and other followers of Jesus are described as having thrones and enjoying reigning with God. Examining the contexts of John's use of *thronos* indicates a meaning of having authority to reign.

Two theological implications are confirmed by John's use of *thronos* as a key image in Revelation. First, the sovereignty of God is a key idea expressed by the image. In Revelation, the one on the throne indicates power and authority belonging to that person. The continual use of God being identified as the "one on the throne" suggests his supreme authority. Though the throne appears to be separated from the earth, by virtue of being on the throne, God is the one in control of things on the earth.[17]

15. Aune calls this a "circumlocution for the name of God" (*Revelation 1–5*, 467). However, the term circumlocution might be taken to mean that John was trying to *avoid* using God's name. To the contrary, the point being made here is that the importance of the word *thronos* is such that in some cases the image actually represents God himself.

16. In addition, cf. 8:3; 16:17; 19:5; 20:12; and 21:5.

17. Beale, *The Book of Revelation*, 320.

The other theological implication of the throne imagery is the relationship between God and the Lamb. Twice in the last chapter of the book, John referred to the singular throne of God and the Lamb. After all the references to *thronos* in Revelation, the final image is to only one throne that God and the Lamb share.

IMPLICATIONS FOR CONTEMPORARY DISCIPLESHIP

So, what do these images have to do with life application for today's believer in Jesus Christ? Though certainly much application can be drawn from the Revelation, the focus here is on two important discipleship themes that impact every generation.[18] The predominant use of God as *Pantokratōr*, Jesus as Lamb, the image of a throne, and the theme of overcoming signal God's sovereignty in the world and the disciple's need for endurance. The encouragement to overcome is dependent upon the disciple's recognition of God's sovereignty in the affairs of the world.

The theme of God's sovereignty is truly a theme that runs from beginning to end of the Revelation. The language of the first chapter is replete with overtures of God's sovereignty. The first description of God is the one "who is and who was and who is to come." He is further described as the "Alpha and Omega" and the "Almighty." (1:8) The general description of God as the Son of Man in 1:13–20 continues the idea of his splendor and absolute control for all of eternity. The sovereignty of God runs through the letters of chapters 2 and 3 by tying the description of Jesus back to the descriptions of chapter 1. The sovereignty of God in chapters 4 and 5 are central to the worship of the ages being described in these two chapters. In the Judgment Cycle that follows (6–19), the delineation of God's sovereignty continues. God is the one who is in control of the judgment. Judgment is his to give as well as his to postpone, as indicated by the dramatic interludes before the revelation of the seventh and concluding judgment in each cycle of the seals, trumpets, and bowls.

The application of God's sovereignty to the present-day believer are multiple. First, God's sovereignty speaks to the faith that should be typified by every person who seeks to follow the Lamb. As Fee and Stuart

---

18. See Keener, *Revelation* for a section by section approach to the book. In keeping with the series, Keener divides each textual section into three sections: "original meaning," "bridging the contexts," and "contemporary significance." Keener skillfully balances an engagement with both scholarly and practical works. Keener's commentary could assist those who lead in the study of Revelation.

note, "the church and state are on a collision course," and "initial victory will appear to belong to the state."[19] The true believer cannot lose faith in God's ultimate control. God is the one ultimately on the throne.

Recognition of this control on the part of the believer in Christ will impact both faith and allegiance. As Keener states boldly, "Revelation allows for no divided allegiance."[20] The call of God on one's life is to follow God instead of the world. This allegiance to God impacts every decision and every action, including, for example, a range that runs from what one purchases to how one votes. The believer will face multiple temptations to give in to the world's system, but radical discipleship means that the individual always acknowledges not only who sits on the eternal throne of the universe, but who sits on the throne of one's life.

Recognition of God's sovereignty also impacts worship. One cannot truly understand the absolute control of God and not be a passionate worshipper of God. If God is indeed in control, then he above all ought to be worshipped. The message of Revelation is that crisis is never the time to abandon worship. Rather, times of anguish ought to be the times that the person of faith embraces worship.[21] Worship of God has a way of putting into perspective "persecution, poverty, and plagues."[22]

God's sovereignty is also the theological premise that calls the believer to be an overcomer. Overcoming is not dependent upon the individual's will power and own ability, but upon God. Reddish points out the direct correlation between sovereignty and overcoming. "An unswerving belief in the sovereignty of God is what provides John with the resounding hope that sustains the Apocalypse."[23] The mark of the true believer in Christ is indicated by perseverance and overcoming. The continued good news of the Apocalypse is that overcoming has a great reward. As clearly emphasized in all seven of the letters of chapters 2–3, a destiny of eternal life for the ones who overcome is confirmed throughout the rest of Revelation.

Meanwhile, in a Revelation study back in the living room of someone's home, a college dorm room, or corner classroom in the local church, someone is debating the precise meaning of 666. For all the

19. Fee and Stuart, *How to Read the Bible*, 258.

20. Keener, *Revelation*, 366.

21. Reddish, *Revelation*, 44–45.

22. Keener, *Revelation*, 182.

23. Reddish, *Revelation*, 118.

energy expended, at the end of the day not much is gained by these exhausting discussions. Life is no better; faith is not really challenged. However, when focused on the idea of God, the Almighty, seated eternally upon the throne of the universe, life and faith could hold no greater meaning. Reddish gives the concluding hope of this scene. "All of creation has seen who sits on the heavenly throne. The occupier of the throne is not the Roman emperor or any other earthly ruler. The one who sits on the throne is God. For that reason, John is certain that ultimately everything will be alright—certainly not now, but one day."[24] Ah, one day! Until that day, the disciples of Jesus are called to endure, knowing that *the day* is coming.

QUESTIONS FOR REFLECTION

- Why do you think so many discussions on Revelation focus on end-time prophecy instead of present-day application?

- According to the Revelation, how do we reconcile the absolute control of God in the world with the apparent control that evil enjoys in the world?

- What are the contemporary implications of John's message of overcoming in our world, given that we do not live in such a time as the original recipients of the Revelation?

- Eugene Peterson suggests that Revelation be outlined as a series of last words. According to this assessment, what is the last word in Revelation on evil? What is the last word on the church?

- According to Rev 1:3, those who read, hear, and keep the words of Revelation receive a blessing. Is there a difference in reading, hearing, and keeping? What is the blessing?

- If you were asked to lead a Bible study on Revelation, what do you think would be a good starting point?

24. Ibid.

Bibliography

Accordance, Version 8.4. OakTree Software Specialists. Altamonte Springs, FL, 2009.

Aland, Barbara, Kurt Aland, Johannes Karavidopoulos, Carlo M. Martini, and Bruce M. Metzger, editors. *The Greek New Testament.* 4th rev. ed. Stuttgart: United Bible Societies, 1993.

Aland, Barbara, Kurt Aland, Johannes Karavidopoulos, Carlo M. Martini, and Bruce M. Metzger, eds. *Novum Testamentum Graece.* 27th ed. Stuttgart: German Bible Society, 1993.

Aland, Kurt, ed. *Kurzgefasste Liste der griechischen Handschriften des neuen Testaments.* 2nd ed. Arbeiten zur neutestamentlichen Textforschung 1. Berlin: de Gruyter, 1994.

Aland, Kurt and Barbara Aland. *The Text of the New Testament.* 2nd ed. Translated by Erroll F. Rhodes. Grand Rapids: Eerdmans, 1989.

Aristides, Aelius. *The Complete Works: Orations 1–16.* Leiden: Brill, 1997.

Athenagoras. *The Ante-Nicene Fathers.* Vol. 2. Edited by Alexander Roberts, James Donaldson, and A. Cleveland Coxe. 10 vols. New York: Christian Literature Company, 1885–1896. CD-ROM. Logos Research Systems Version 2.0, 1997.

Augustine. *The Nicene and Post-Nicene Fathers of the Christian Church.* Series 1. Vol. 1. Edited by Philip Schaff and Henry Wace. 14 vols. New York: Christian Literature Company, 1886–1889. CD-ROM. Logos Research Systems Version 2.0, 1997.

Aune, David E. *Revelation 1–5.* WBC 52A. Dallas: Word, 1997.

———. *Revelation 6–16.* WBC 52B. Nashville: Thomas Nelson, 1998.

———. *Revelation 17–22.* WBC 52C. Nashville: Thomas Nelson, 1998.

Barclay, John M. G. "Deviance and Apostasy: Some Applications of Deviance Theory to First-Century Judaism and Christianity." In *Modeling Early Christianity: Social-Scientific Studies of the New Testament,* edited by Philip F. Esler, 110–23. New York: Routledge, 1995.

Barr, David L. "The Lamb Who Looks Like a Dragon? Characterizing Jesus in John's Apocalypse." In *The Reality of Apocalypse: Rhetoric and Politics in the Book of Revelation,* edited by David L. Barr, 205–20. SBLSymS 39. Atlanta: Society of Biblical Literature, 2006.

———. "The Story John Told: Reading Revelation for Its Plot." In *Reading the Book of Revelation: A Resource for Students,* edited by David L. Barr, 11–24. Resources for Biblical Study, No. 44.. Atlanta: Society of Biblical Literature, 2003.

———. *Tales of the End: A Narrative Commentary on the Book of Revelation.* Storytellers Bible 1. Santa Rosa, CA: Polebridge, 1998.

————. "Towards an Ethical Reading of the Apocalypse: Reflections on John's Use of Power, Violence, and Misogyny." In *Society of Biblical Literature 1997 Seminar Papers* 358–73. Atlanta: Scholars, 1997.

Bauckham, Richard. *The Climax of Prophecy: Studies on the Book of Revelation.* Edinburgh: T. & T. Clark, 1993.

————. *The Theology of the Book of Revelation.* Cambridge: Cambridge University Press, 1993.

Beale, Gregory K. *The Book of Revelation: A Commentary on the Greek Text.* NIGTC. Grand Rapids: Eerdmans, 1999.

Beard, Mary. *The Parthenon.* Cambridge: Harvard University Press, 2002.

Beard, Mary, John A. North, and Simon R. F. Price. *Religions of Rome.* Vol. 1: *A History.* Cambridge: Cambridge University Press, 1998.

Beasley-Murray, George R. *Revelation.* NCBC. Grand Rapids: Eerdmans, 1981.

————. "Revelation." *New Bible Commentary: 21st Century Edition.* Edited by G. J. Wenham, et al. Downers Grove, IL: InterVarsity, 2004.

Bieber, Margarete. *The History of the Greek and Roman Theater.* Princeton: Princeton University Press, 1961.

BibleWorks, Version 7.0.012g. BibleWorks, LLC. Norfolk, VA, 2006.

Birdsall, J. Neville. "The Text of the Revelation of Saint John: A Review of Its Materials and Problems with Especial Reference to the Work of Josef Schmid." *Evangelical Quarterly* 33 (1961) 228–37.

Blount, Brian K. *Can I Get a Witness? Reading Revelation through African American Culture.* Louisville: Westminster John Knox, 2005.

Boring, M. Eugene. "The Theology of Revelation: 'The Lord our God the Almighty Reigns.'" *Interpretation* 40 (1986) 257–69.

Bouma-Prediger, Steven. *For the Beauty of the Earth: A Christian Vision for Creation Care.* Grand Rapids: Baker Academic, 2001.

Bowman, John Wick. *The Drama of the Book of Revelation.* Louisville: Westminster, 1955.

————. "Revelation, Book of." In vol. 4 of *The Interpreter's Dictionary of the Bible*, edited by George Arthur Buttrick, 58–71. New York: Abingdon, 1962.

Boxall, Ian. *The Revelation of Saint John.* BNTC. Peabody, MA: Hendrickson, 2006.

Boyer, Paul S. *When Time Shall Be No More: Prophecy Belief in Modern American Culture.* Cambridge: Harvard University Press, 1992.

Boyle, Anthony James. *An Introduction to Roman Tragedy.* New York: Routledge, 2006.

Brant, Jo-Ann A. *Dialogue and Drama: Elements of Greek Tragedy in the Fourth Gospel.* Peabody, MA: Hendrickson, 2004.

Bredin, Mark. *Jesus, Revolutionary of Peace: A Nonviolent Christology in the Book of Revelation.* Paternoster Biblical and Theological Monographs. Carlisle: Paternoster, 2003.

Brouskari, Maria. *The Monuments of the Acropolis.* 3rd ed. Athens: Ministry of Culture, Archaeological Receipts Fund, 2006.

Burge, Gary M., Lynn H. Cohick, and Gene L. Green. *The New Testament in Antiquity: A Survey of the New Testament within Its Cultural Context.* Grand Rapids: Zondervan, 2009.

Burkett, Delbert. *The Son of Man Debate: A History and Evaluation.* SNTSMS 107. Cambridge: University Press, 1999.

Burrell, Barbara. *Neokoroi: Greek Cities and Roman Emperors.* Cincinnati Classical Studies, New Series 9. Leiden: Brill, 2004.

Camp, John M. *The Archaeology of Athens.* New Haven: Yale University Press, 2001.

Casey, Maurice. *The Solution to the 'Son of Man' Problem*. New York: T. & T. Clark, 2009.

Cimak, Fatih. *Pergamum*. İstanbul: A Turizm Yayinlari, 2004.

Clement of Alexandria. *The Ante-Nicene Fathers*. Vol. 2. Edited by Alexander Roberts, James Donaldson, and A. Cleveland Coxe. 10 vols. New York: Christian Literature Company, 1885–1896. CD-ROM. Logos Research Systems Version 2.0, 1997.

Clement of Rome. *The Ante-Nicene Fathers*. Vol. 1. Edited by Alexander Roberts, James Donaldson, and A. Cleveland Coxe. 10 vols. New York: Christian Literature Company, 1885–1896. CD-ROM. Logos Research Systems Version 2.0, 1997.

Collingwood, R. G., and J. N. L. Myres. *Roman Britain and the English Settlements*. 2nd ed. The Oxford History of England. Oxford: Oxford University Press, 1937.

Collins, Adela Yarbro. *The Apocalypse*. New Testament Message. Collegeville, MN: Liturgical, 1990.

———. *Crisis and Catharsis: The Power of the Apocalypse*. Philadelphia: Westminster, 1984.

Collins, John J. *The Apocalyptic Imagination: An Introduction to Jewish Apocalyptic Literature*. The Biblical Resource Series. Grand Rapids: Eerdmans, 1998.

Cooper, Michael. "Necessity of Worldview Understanding for Sustainable Peace: A Case Study of United States Relations with Native Americans in the 18th–19th Centuries." *Sacred Tribes Journal* 4.2 (2009). http://www.sacredtribesjournal.org/images/Articles/Vol_4/Cooper_US_NA_Relations_final.pdf.

Delebecque, Édouard. *L' Apocalypse de Jean: Introduction, Traduction, Annotations*. Paris: Mame, 1992.

deSilva, David A. *Honor, Patronage, Kinship, and Purity: Unlocking New Testament Culture*. Downers Grove, IL: InterVarsity, 2000.

———. *Seeing Things John's Way: The Rhetoric of the Book of Revelation*. Louisville: Westminster John Knox, 2009.

Diobouniotis, Constantin, and Adolf Harnack, eds. *Der Scholien-Kommentar des Origenes zur Apokalypse Johannis*. Texte und Untersuchungen zur Geschichte der altchristlichen Literatur 38, 3. Leipzig: J. C. Hinrichs, 1911.

Douglas, Mary. *Purity and Danger: An Analysis of the Concepts of Pollution and Taboo*. New York: Routledge and Kegan Paul, 1966.

Duff, Paul B. *Who Rides the Beast? Prophetic Rivalry and the Rhetoric of Crisis in the Churches of the Apocalypse*. New York: Oxford University Press, 2001.

Elliott, Neil. *The Arrogance of Nations: Reading Romans in the Shadow of Empire*. Paul in Critical Contexts Series. Minneapolis: Fortress, 2008.

Eusebius. *The Nicene and Post-Nicene Fathers of the Christian Church*. Series 2. Vol. 1. Edited by Philip Schaff and Henry Wace. 14 vols. New York: Christian Literature Company, 1886–1889. CD-ROM. Logos Research Systems Version 2.0, 1997.

Fee, Gordon D., and Douglas Stuart. *How to Read the Bible for All Its Worth*. Grand Rapids: Zondervan, 2003.

Ferguson, Everett. *Backgrounds of Early Christianity*. 3rd ed. Grand Rapids: Eerdmans, 2003.

Fox, Robert Lane. *Pagans and Christians*. New York: HarperCollins, 1986.

Friesen, Steven J. "The Beast from the Land." *Reading the Book of Revelation: A Resource for Students*, edited by David L. Barr, 49–64. Resources for Biblical Study 44. Atlanta: Society of Biblical Literature, 2003.

———. *Imperial Cults and the Apocalypse of John: Reading Revelation in the Ruins*. New York; Oxford: Oxford University Press, 2001.

Gates, Charles. *Ancient Cities: The Archaeology of Urban Life in the Ancient Near East and Egypt, Greece, and Rome*. London: Routledge, 2003.

Geisel, Theodore Seuss. *The Lorax*. New York: Random House, 1971.

Gonis, N., J. Chapa, W. E. H. Cockle, and Dirk Obbink, editors. *The Oxyrhynchus Papyri*. Vol. 66. London: Egypt Exploration Society, 1999.

González, Justo L. *Three Months with Revelation*. Nashville: Abingdon, 2004.

Gregg, Steve, editor. *Revelation, Four Views: A Parallel Commentary*. Nashville: Thomas Nelson, 1997.

Greek Drama: From Ritual to Theater. DVD. Princeton: Films for the Humanities and Sciences, 2005.

Grenz, Stanley J. *The Millennial Maze: Sorting Out Evangelical Options*. Downers Grove, IL: InterVarsity, 1992.

Grizzle, Raymond E., Paul E. Rothrock, and Christopher B. Barrett. "Evangelicals and Environmentalism: Past, Present, and Future." *Trinity Journal* 18:1 (1998) 3–27.

Grudem, Wayne. *Bible Doctrine: Essential Teachings of the Christian Faith*. Edited by Jeff Purswell. Grand Rapids: Zondervan, 1999.

Hanson, Anthony T. *The Wrath of the Lamb*. London: S.P.C.K., 1957.

Hanson, Kenneth C. "Blood and Purity in Leviticus and Revelation." *Listening: Journal of Religion and Culture* 28 (1993) 215–30.

Hanson, K. C., and Douglas E. Oakman, *Palestine in the Time of Jesus: Social Structures and Social Conflicts*. Minneapolis: Augsburg Fortress, 1998.

Hays, Richard B. *The Moral Vision of the New Testament: Community, Cross, New Creation. A Contemporary Introduction to New Testament Ethics*. San Francisco: HarperSanFrancisco, 1996.

Herbert, A. S. *Historical Catalogue of Printed Editions of the English Bible 1525–1961*. Rev. and exp. ed. London: British and Foreign Bible Society, 1968.

Heemstra, Marius. "How Rome's Administration of the Fiscus Judaicus Accelerated the Parting of the Ways Between Judaism and Christianity: Rereading 1 Peter, Revelation, the Letter to the Hebrews, and the Gospel of John in Their Roman and Jewish Contexts." PhD diss., Rijksuniversiteit Groningen, 2009.

Heim, S. Mark. *Saved from Sacrifice: A Theology of the Cross*. Grand Rapids: Eerdmans, 2006.

Heller, Matthew. "Psychological Perspectives on Peace: An Evangelical Analysis." *Sacred Tribes Journal* 4.2 (Fall 2009). http://www.sacredtribesjournal.org/images/Articles/Vol_4/Heller_Psychological_Perspectives_final.pdf.

Hemer, Colin J. *The Letters to the Seven Churches of Asia in Their Local Setting*. JSNTSup 11. London: Sheffield Academic, 1986.

Herodotus. *The Persian Wars*. 2 vols. Translated by A. D. Godley. LCL. Cambridge: Harvard University Press, 1921–1925.

Hippocrates. *On the Sacred Disease*. In *The Law, The Oath of Hippocrates, and On the Sacred Disease*. Translated by Francis Adams. Gloucesterchire: Dodo, 2009.

Hobson, Sarah, and Jane Lubenenco, editors. *Revelation and the Environment AD 95–1995*. Hackensack, NJ: World Scientific, 1997.

The Holman Illustrated Study Bible: Holman Christian Standard Bible. Nashville: Holman Bible, 2006.

Holmes. Arthur F. *War and Christian Ethics: Classic and Contemporary Readings on the Morality of War*. 2nd ed. Grand Rapids: Baker Academic, 2005.

Holmes, Michael W. *The Apostolic Fathers: Greek Texts and English Translations*. Updated ed. Grand Rapids: Baker, 1999.

Hood, Renate Viveen. "The Parthians." *Baker Illustrated Bible Dictionary*. Edited by Temper Longman and Peter Enns. Grand Rapids: Baker Academic, forthcoming.

Hoskier, H. C. *Concerning the Text of the Apocalypse: Collations of All Existing Available Greek Documents with the Standard Text of Stephen's Third Edition Together with the Testimony of Versions, Commentaries and Fathers*. 2 Vols. London: Bernard Quaritch, 1929.

Humphrey, Edith M. "In Search of a Voice: Rhetoric Through Sight and Sound in Revelation 11:15–12:17." In *Vision and Persuasion: Rhetorical Dimensions of Apocalyptic Discourse*, edited by Greg Carey and L. Gregory Bloomquist, 141–60. St. Louis: Chalice, 1999.

———. "The Ladies and the Cities: Transformation and Apocalyptic Identity in 'Joseph and Aseneth', 4 Ezra, the Apocalypse and the Shepherd of Hermas." PhD diss., McGill University, 1991.

———. "A Tale of Two Cities and (At Least) Three Women." *Reading the Book of Revelation: A Resource for Students*, edited by David L. Barr 11–24. Resources for Biblical Study 44. Atlanta: Society of Biblical Literature, 2003.

Hylen, Susan E. "The Power and Problem of Revelation 18." *Pregnant Passion: Gender, Sex, and Violence in the Bible*, edited by Cheryl A. Kirk-Duggan, 205–20. Society of Biblical Literature Semeia Studies. Atlanta: Society of Biblical Literature, 2004.

Ignatius. *The Ante-Nicene Fathers*. Vol. 1. Edited by Alexander Roberts, James Donaldson, and A. Cleveland Coxe. 1885–1896. 10 vols. New York: Christian Literature Company, 1885–1896. CD-ROM. Logos Research Systems Version 2.0, 1997.

Ioulis. *On Keos*. In *Sylloge Inscriptionum Graecarum*, Vol. 3. Edited by Wilhelm Dittenberger. Leipzig: Hirzel, 1920.

Irenaeus. *The Ante-Nicene Fathers*. Vol. 2. Edited by Alexander Roberts, James Donaldson, and A. Cleveland Coxe. 1885–1896. 10 vols. New York: Christian Literature Company, 1885–1896. CD-ROM. Logos Research Systems Version 2.0, 1997.

Jacobus, Lee A. *The Bedford Introduction to Drama*. 6th ed. New York: Bedford/St. Martin's, 2009.

Järvinen, Arto. "The Son of Man and His Followers: A Q Portrait of Jesus." In *Characterization in the Gospels*, edited by David Rhoads and Kari Syreeni, 180–222. JSNTSup 184. Sheffield: Sheffield Academic, 1999.

Jones, B. W. *Suetonius: Domitian*. Bristol: Bristol Classic, 1996.

Josephus. *The Works of Flavius Josephus, Complete and Unabridged*. Updated edition. Translated by William Whiston. Peabody, MA: Hendrickson, 1987. CD-ROM. Accordance Bible Software. OakTree Software, Altamonte Springs, FL. Greek text, ver. 1.5, 2005. Based on 1890 Niese edition. English text, ver. 1.3, 2005.

———. Translated by H. St. J. Thackery et al. 10 vols. LCL. Cambridge: Harvard University Press, 1926–1965; reprint 1968.

Justin Martyr. *The Ante-Nicene Fathers*. Vol. 1. Edited by Alexander Roberts, James Donaldson, and A. Cleveland Coxe. 1885–1896. 10 vols. New York: Christian Literature Company, 1885–1896. CD-ROM. Logos Research Systems Version 2.0, 1997.

Kasher, Aryeh. *Jews, Idumaeans, and Ancient Arabs: Relations of the Jews in Eretz-Israel with the Nations of the Frontier and the Desert During the Hellenistic and Roman Era (332 BCE–70 CE)*. Texte und Studien zum antiken Judentum 18. Tübingen: Mohr/Siebeck, 1988.

Keener, Craig S. *Revelation*. The NIV Application Commentary. Grand Rapids: Zondervan, 2000.

Keillor, Steven J. *God's Judgments: Interpreting History and the Christian Faith*. Downers Grove: InterVarsity, 2007.

Kilpatrick, G. D. "Professor J. Schmid on the Greek Text of the Apocalypse." *Vigiliae Christianae* 13 (April 1959) 1–13.

Kim, Jean K. "Uncovering Her Wickedness: An Inter(con)textual Reading of Revelation 17 from a Postcolonial Feminist Perspective." JSNT 73 (1999) 61–81.

Klaus, Carl H., Miriam Gilbert, and Bradford S. Field Jr., editors. *Stages of Drama: Classical to Contemporary Theater*. 5th ed. Boston: Bedford/St. Martin's, 2003.

Klein, William, Craig Blomberg, and Robert Hubbard. *Introduction to Biblical Interpretation*. Rev. ed. Downers Grove: InterVarsity, 2004.

Klostermann, Erich, and Ernst Benz, editors. *Origenes: Matthäuserklärung*. Vol. 2: *Die lateinische Übersetzung der Commentariorum Series*. Griechischen christlichen Schriftsteller 38. Origenes Werke 11. Berlin: Akademie-Verlag, 1976.

Koester, Craig R. *Revelation and the End of All Things*. Grand Rapids: Eerdmans, 2001.

Koester, Helmut. *Introduction to the New Testament*. Vol. 1: *History, Culture, and Religion of the Hellenistic Age*. 2nd ed. New York: de Gruyter, 1995.

Kohlenberger, John R. III, Edward W. Goodrick, and James A. Swanson. *The Exhaustive Concordance to the Greek New Testament*. Grand Rapids: Zondervan, 1995.

Kraybill, J. Nelson. "Apocalypse Now." *Christianity Today*, Oct. 25, 1999. http://www.christianitytoday.com/ct/1999/october25/9tc030.html.

Ladd, George E. *A Commentary on the Revelation of John*. Grand Rapids: Eerdmans, 1978.

Logos Bible Software. Ver. 3. Logos Research Systems. Bellingham, WA, 2003.

Longenecker, Bruce W. *The Lost Letters of Pergamum: A Story from the New Testament World*, with extracts from Ben Witherington III. Grand Rapids: Baker Academic, 2003.

Maier, Harry O. *Apocalypse Recalled: The Book of Revelation after Christendom*. Minneapolis: Fortress, 2002.

Malina, Bruce J. *Christian Origins and Cultural Anthropology: Practical Models for Biblical Interpretation*. Atlanta: John Knox, 1986.

———. *The New Testament World: Insights from Cultural Anthropology*. Rev. ed. Louisville: Westminster John Knox, 1993.

———. *The New Testament World: Insights from Cultural Anthropology*. 3rd ed. Louisville: Westminster John Knox, 2001.

Malina, Bruce J., and John J. Pilch. *Social-Science Commentary on the Book of Revelation*. Minneapolis: Fortress, 2000.

Manns, Frédéric, "L'Évêque, ange de l' Église." *Ephemerides Liturgicae* 104.2–3 (1990), 176–81.

Marshall, I. Howard. *New Testament Theology: Many Witnesses, One Gospel*. Downers Grove, IL: InterVarsity, 2004.

McGrath, Alister E. *Christian Theology: An Introduction*. Oxford: Blackwell, 1994.

Melon, Michael P. *"Yet You Would Not Return to Me": Prophetically Speaking in an Age of Terror*. Longwood, FL: Xulon, 2004.

Metzger, Bruce M. *A Textual Commentary on the Greek New Testament: A Companion Volume to the United Bible Societies' Greek New Testament (Fourth Revised Edition)*. 2nd ed. Stuttgart: German Bible Society, 1994.

Michaels, J. Ramsey. *Revelation*. IVPNT. Downers Grove, IL: InterVarsity, 1997.

Moffatt, James. *The Revelation of St. John the Divine*. The Expositors Greek Testament. Grand Rapids: Eerdmans, 1990.

Morris, Leon. *The Book of Revelation: An Introduction and Commentary*. Tyndale Rev. ed. Grand Rapids: Eerdmans, 1987.

Mounce, Robert H. *The Book of Revelation*. NICNT. Grand Rapids: Eerdmans, 1977.

———. *The Book of Revelation*. Rev. ed. NICNT. Grand Rapids: Eerdmans, 1997.

Moxnes, Halvor. "Honor and Shame." In *The Social Sciences and New Testament Interpretation*, edited by Richard Rohrbaugh, 19–40. Peabody: Hendrickson, 1996.

Müller, Mogens. *The Expression 'Son of Man' and the Development of Christology: A History of Interpretation*. Copenhagen International Seminar. Edited by Thomas L. Thompson. London: Equinox, 2008.

Murphy, Frederick J. *Fallen Is Babylon: The Revelation to John*. The New Testament in Context. Edited by Howard Clark Kee and J. Andrew Overman. Harrisburg, PA: Trinity, 1998.

Newport, John P. *The Lion and the Lamb*. Nashville: Broadman, 1986.

Neyrey, Jerome H. "The Idea and the System of Purity." In *The Social Sciences and New Testament Interpretation*, edited by Richard Rohrbaugh, 80–106. Peabody, MA: Hendrickson, 1996.

Niles, D. T. *As Seeing the Invisible*. London: SCM, 1962.

O'Rourke, John J. "The Hymns of the Apocalypse." *The Catholic Biblical Quarterly* 30 (1968) 399–409.

Oden, Thomas C. *The Rebirth of Orthodoxy: Signs of New Life in Christianity*. San Francisco: HarperSanFrancisco, 2003.

Origen. *The Ante-Nicene Fathers*. Vol. 4. Edited by Alexander Roberts, James Donaldson, and A. Cleveland Coxe. 1885–1896. 10 vols. New York: Christian Literature Company, 1885–1896. CD-ROM. Logos Research Systems Version 2.0, 1997.

———. *Commentary on the Gospel of Matthew*. In vol. 9 of *The Ante-Nicene Fathers*. Edited by Alexander Roberts, James Donaldson, and A. Cleveland Coxe. 1885–1896. 10 vols. Repr. Grand Rapids: Eerdmans, 1988.

Osborne, Grant R. *Revelation*. Baker Exegetical Commentary on the New Testament. Grand Rapids: Baker Academic, 2002.

Parker, David C. "A New Oxyrhynchus Papyrus of Revelation: P115 (P. Oxy. 4499)." *New Testament Studies* 46 (2000) 159–74.

Parker, Robert. *Miasma: Pollution and Purification in Early Greek Religion*. Oxford: Clarendon, 1983.

Perriman, Andrew. *The Coming of the Son of Man: New Testament Eschatology for an Emerging Church*. Milton Keynes, UK: Paternoster, 2005.

Peterson, Eugene H. *Reversed Thunder: The Revelation of John and the Praying Imagination*. San Francisco: Harper & Row, 1988.

Petronius. Translated by W. H. D. Rouse and E. H. Warmington. LCL. Cambridge: Harvard University Press, 1913; updated by Michael Heseltine, 1987.

Pippin, Tina. *Death and Desire: The Rhetoric of Gender in the Apocalypse of John*. Literary Currents in Biblical Interpretation. Louisville: Westminster John Knox, 1992.

Plevnik, Joseph. "Honor/Shame." In *Handbook of Biblical Social Values*, edited by John J. Pilch and Bruce J. Malina, 106–115. Peabody, MA: Hendrickson, 1998.

Pliny the Younger. Translated by Betty Radice. 2 vols. LCL. Cambridge: Harvard University Press, 1969.

Plutarch. Translated by Bernadotte Perrin et al. 28 vols. LCL. Cambridge: Harvard University Press, 1914–1969.

Price, S. R. F. *Rituals and Power: The Roman Imperial Cult in Asia Minor*. Cambridge: Cambridge University Press, 1984.

Prigent, P. *Apocalypse et Liturgie*. Cahiers Théologiques 52. Paris: Delachaux et Niestle, 1964.

Raquel, Sylvie. "Perspectives on a Biblical Theology of Peace." *Sacred Tribes Journal* 4.2 (Fall 2009). http://www.sacredtribesjournal.org/images/Articles/Vol_4/Raquel_Theology_Peace_final.pdf.

Reddish, Mitchell G. *Revelation*. SHBC. Macon, GA: Smyth & Helwys, 2001.

————, editor. *Apocalyptic Literature: A Reader*. Peabody, MA: Hendrickson, 1995.

Regev, Eyal. "Moral impurity and the temple in early Christianity in light of ancient Greek practice and Qumran ideology." Harvard Theological Review. 97 (2004) 383–411.

Resseguie, James L. *The Revelation of John: A Narrative Commentary*. Grand Rapids: Baker Academic, 2009.

Rhoads, David M. *Reading Mark, Engaging the Gospel*. Minneapolis: Fortress, 2004.

Richardson, Peter. *Herod: King of the Jews and Friend of the Romans*. Studies on Personalities of the New Testament. Columbia: University of South Carolina Press, 1996.

Rossing, Barabara R. *The Choice Between Two Cities: Whore, Bride, and Empire in the Apocalypse*. Harvard Theological Studies. Harrisburg, PA: Trinity, 1999.

Routley, Erik. *Christian Hymns Observed: When in Our Music God Is Glorified*. Princeton: Prestige, 1982.

Scheele, Brigitte. "Back from the Grave: Reinstating the Catharsis Concept in the Psychology of Reception." In *The Psychology and Sociology of Literature: In Honor of Elrud Ibsch*, edited by Dick Schram and Gerard Steen, 201–24. Utrecht Publications in General and Comparative Literature 35. Amsterdam: J. Benjamins, 2001.

Schillebeeckx, Edward. *The Church: The Human Story of God*. London: SCM, 1990.

Schmid, Josef. *Studien zur Geschichte des griechischen Apokalypse-Textes*. 2 Vols. Munich: Karl Zink, 1955–56.

Schüssler Fiorenza, Elisabeth. "Babylon the Great: A Rhetorical-Political Reading of Revelation 17–18." In *The Reality of Apocalypse: Rhetoric and Politics in the Book of Revelation*, Edited by David L. Barr, 243–69. SBLSymS 39. Atlanta: Society of Biblical Literature, 2006.

————. *The Book of Revelation: Justice and Judgment*. 2nd ed. Minneapolis: Fortress, 1998.

Scrivener, Frederick H. A. *A Plain Introduction to the Criticism of the New Testament: For the Use of Biblical Students*. 4th ed. 2 vols. Edited by Edward Miller. London: George Bell & Sons, 1894.

Smalley, Stephen S. *The Revelation to John: A Commentary on the Greek Text of the Apocalypse*. Downers Grove, IL: InterVarsity, 2005.

Stowers, Stanley K. "On the Comparison of Blood in Greek and Israelite Ritual." In *Hesed Ve-Emet: Studies in Honor of Ernest S. Frerichs*, edited by Jodi Magness and Seymour Gitin 179–96. Brown Judaic Studies 320. Atlanta: Scholars, 1998.

Strand, Kenneth. "'Overcomer': A Study in the Macrodynamic of Theme Development in the Book of Revelation." *Andrews University Seminary Studies* 28 (1990) 237–54.

Suetonius. *The Lives of the Caesars*. Translated by J. C. Rolfe. 2 vols. LCL. Cambridge: Harvard University Press, 1914; reprint 1965.

Tacitus. Translated by M. Hutton et al. 5 vols. LCL. Cambridge: Harvard University Press, 1914–1937.

Talbert, Charles H. *The Apocalypse: A Reading of the Revelation of John*. Louisville: Westminster John Knox, 1994.

Taplin, Oliver. *Greek Tragedy in Action*. Berkeley: University of California Press, 1978.

Tertullian. *The Ante-Nicene Fathers.* Vol. 3. Edited by Alexander Roberts, James Donaldson, and A. Cleveland Coxe. 1885–1896. 10 vols. New York: Christian Literature Company, 1885–1896. CD-ROM. Logos Research Systems Version 2.0, 1997.

Thompson, Leonard L. *The Book of Revelation: Apocalypse and Empire.* New York: Oxford University Press, 1990.

———. *The Book of Revelation.* Abingdon New Testament Commentaries. Nashville: Abingdon, 1998.

Tödt, Heinz Eduard. *The Son of Man in the Synoptic Tradition.* NTL. London: SCM, 1965.

Troeltsch, Ernst. *The Christian Faith.* Fortress Texts in Modern Theology. Minneapolis: Fortress, 1991.

Virgil. Translated by H. Rushton Fairclough. 2 vols. LCL. Cambridge: Harvard University Press, 1916.

Wainwright, Arthur W. *Mysterious Apocalypse: Interpreting the Book of Revelation.* Nashville: Abingdon, 1993.

Walhout, Edwin. *Revelation Down to Earth: Making Sense of the Apocalypse of John.* Grand Rapids: Eerdmans, 2000.

Wenham, G. J., J. A. Mortyer, D. A. Carson, and R. T. France. *New Bible Commentary: 21st Century Edition.* Rev ed. Downers Grove, IL: InterVarsity, 1994.

White, Leland J. "Grid and Group in Matthew's Community: The Righteousness/Honor Code in the Sermon on the Mount." *Semeia* 35 (1986) 61–90.

Wiersbe, Warren W. *The Bible Exposition Commentary.* Wheaton, IL: Victor, 1989.

Williams, Clifford. "A Philosopher's Reflections on Peacemaking and the Just War Theory." *Sacred Tribes Journal* 4.2 (Fall 2009). http://www.sacredtribesjournal.org/images/Articles/Vol_4/Williams_Peacemaking_final.pdf.

Witherington III, Ben. *Revelation.* NCBC. New York: Cambridge University Press, 2003.

Wittmer, Michael E. *Heaven Is a Place on Earth: Why Everything You Do Matters to God.* Grand Rapids: Zondervan, 2004.

Wright, N. T. *Surprised by Hope: Rethinking Heaven, the Resurrection, and the Mission of the Church.* New York: HarperCollins, 2008.

Yamauchi, Edwin M. *New Testament Cities in Western Asia Minor: Light from Archaeology on Cities of Paul and the Seven Churches of Revelation.* Grand Rapids: Baker, 1980. Reprint, Eugene, OR: Wipf & Stock, 2003.

Zanker, Paul. *The Power of Images in the Age of Augustus.* Translated by Alan Shapiro. Jerome Lectures. 16th ser. Ann Arbor: University of Michigan Press, 1990.

Scripture Index

Ancient Documents Index

Modern Authors Index

Subject Index